Logics of American Foreign Policy

Theories of America's World Role

Patrick Callahan

DePaul University

PEARSON
Longman

New York   Boston   San Francisco
London   Toronto   Sydney   Tokyo   Singapore   Madrid
Mexico City   Munich   Paris   Cape Town   Hong Kong   Montreal

Vice President and Publisher: Priscilla McGeehon
Executive Editor: Eric Stano
Senior Marketing Manager: Megan Galvin-Fak
Production Manager: Denise Phillip
Project Coordination, Text Design, and Electronic Page Makeup: WestWords, Inc.
Cover Designer/Manager: John Callahan
Cover Photo: Courtesy of Getty Images, Inc.
Manufacturing Manager: Dennis J. Para
Printer and Binder: Phoenix Color Book Technology Park
Cover Printer: Phoenix Color Corporation

Library of Congress Cataloging-in-Publication Data
Callahan, Patrick.
    Logics of American foreign policy : theories of America's world role / Patrick Callahan.
        p. cm.
    Includes bibliographical references.
    ISBN 0-321-08848-4
      1. United States—Foreign relations—Philosophy. I. Title.

JZ1480.C35 2003
327.73'001—dc22   2003058838

Please visit our website at http://www.ablongman.com

ISBN 0-321-08848-4

1 2 3 4 5 6 7 8 9 10—PHH—06 05 04 03

Contents

Preface

Some years ago, I'm pretty sure while Ronald Reagan was president, I was visiting with my friend Jim McGregor. We had been graduate students together at Ohio State. Jim worked for the United States Information Agency. We were taking one of our traditional long walks during which we discussed many things. Quite predictably, we ended up discussing, that is, disagreeing about, some new foreign policy adventure of the administration. After disputing each others' pragmatic arguments, Jim made a point that impressed me profoundly. He defended what the United States was doing because "that's what great powers do." The U.S. is a great power. That role carries with it certain obligations. Those obligations direct the day-to-day behavior of the country. That's what I heard Jim say.

That conversation was the seed that gave birth to this book, though only after a long and leisurely gestation. In teaching U.S. foreign policy, I had always emphasized a cognitive approach to foreign policy analysis, emphasizing how foreign policy actors' worldviews decisively influence how they respond to particular situations. The cognitive approach has three virtues. First, it encourages students to see the coherence, if not necessarily the wisdom, of each administration's foreign policy. Second, by showing how foreign policy flows from ideas about how best to promote legitimate values, including the national interest, it counters some of the cynicism that is too prevalent among contemporary students. Third, it encourages students to formulate or reconsider their own beliefs about the nature of the world and what would be an appropriate foreign policy for the United States. I began to incorporate ideas about how the theories of international relations that policy makers hold in their heads are related to their conceptions of the U.S. world role. That developed into a series of lectures that, for several years, I inflicted on my students. Eventually I transcribed those lectures into a lengthy essay called, remarkably, "Logics of American Foreign Policy," which I required the students to read, thereby sparing them the pain of having it lectured at them. That essay eventually became this book.

This book identifies six logics of U.S. foreign policy. A logic is a conception of an appropriate U.S. world role or foreign policy strategy, based on a conception of the power of the United States, its national interests, and its moral obligations. Those conceptions in turn reflect different theories of international relations. The six logics are:

- Hegemonism, which prescribes that the United States, as the world's dominant power, provide the world with leadership, in order to stabilize the international political system and regulate the international economic system;

- Realism, which prescribes that the United States act to preserve the world's balance of power by preventing the emergence of a dominant power;
- Isolationism, which prescribes that the United States avoid entangling commitments abroad that would harm its economy, society, and governmental system at home;
- Liberalism, which prescribes that the United States promote liberty abroad through the expansion of free markets, democracy, human rights, and national self-determination;
- Liberal internationalism, which prescribes that the United States join with other countries in collaborative undertakings to address a large and diverse agenda of common global problems;
- Radical anti-imperialism, which prescribes that the United States cease its program of preserving and expanding an exploitative and destructive empire.

The book also sketches how these logics have influenced U.S. foreign policy, or debates about policy, since the founding of the republic, and, through three case studies, shows how they shape debates about contemporary issues.

ACKNOWLEDGMENTS

I have many people and institutions to thank for this book. I'll begin with DePaul University, whose generous support made this book possible. Some important support was tangible: a summer research grant from the College of Liberal Arts and Sciences and a University Research Council paid leave of absence for one academic quarter gave me time to write Chapters 4–7. Thank you to the University Research Council, the LAS scholarship committee, Dean Michael Mezey, and Rose Spalding, my department chair, for their support.

The University also provided me with essential intangible support without which this project would never have gotten started: An academic environment where both teaching and scholarship are valued, including scholarship that derives from and directly supports one's teaching. Perhaps most important was the intangible support of colleagues in the Department of Political Science, who proved that one could be a dedicated teacher and a productive scholar. Without their examples I probably would never have had the nerve to undertake this project. Thank you.

Thank you to my able and energetic undergraduate research assistants, Cristina Franzoni and Jason Coronel. Cristina tracked down the information on the Kosovo debate in Chapter 9 and Jason pulled together, among other things, the public opinion polling data and much of the material on reactions to the terrorist attacks of September 11—the information base of the argument in Chapter 10. Thank you to the university for providing me with that form of tangible support, too.

Thanks, also, to the several people who read all or parts of the book in draft form. To Mike Alvarez, Mike Budde, and Mike McIntyre, all of DePaul University, for reading and critiquing the draft of the chapter on radical anti-imperialism. To John Mearsheimer of the University of Chicago for his comments on the

chapter on realism. To Meredith Sarkees, of St. Mary's College, and Endy Ze-
menides, who read the whole manuscript and offered many helpful constructive
criticisms. To my good buddy Bill Goodman, who eagerly pored over several
drafts, ferreting out misspelled words and other mechanical problems and calling
my attention to the places where my impulse to seem intellectual led to in-
scrutable phrasing and construction and who on occasion did voluntary service
as a research assistant.

I would especially like to thank my daughters Kathleen Callahan and Mary
Beth Schaefer and son-in-law Matt Schaefer, who read the manuscript with the eyes
of intelligent young people without deep backgrounds in political science, foreign
policy or diplomatic history, that is, the people for whom I wrote the book.

Thanks to Melissa Butler of Wabash College, Peter Forster of Pennsylvania State
University, Greg Granger of Northwestern State University, Forest Grieves of the
University of Montana, Patrick J. Haney of Miami University, Waltraud Q. Morales
of the University of Central Florida, Jeffrey L. Prewitt of Brewton-Parker College,
George H. Questor of the University of Maryland, David Reilly of Niagara University,
Kanishkan Sathasivam of Salem State College, Lewis W. Snider of Claremont Graduate University, Joseph E. Thompson of Villanova University, Kenneth W. Thompson
of the University of Virginia, and Bruce Unger of Randolph-Macon College, who read
the manuscript at the behest of my editor, Eric Stano, and who offered much needed
guidance and encouragement. Thanks, too, to Eric, who gave me vital encouragement
at moments of despair.

Thanks to Joanne Callahan, who did not read the manuscript but who did keep
me grounded and sane.

Finally, thank you to Jim McGregor, who died on December 31, 2000, struck
down too young by non-Hodgkins lymphoma. While working full-time in the foreign affairs bureaucracy, Jim managed to sustain an active career of research and
publication in political science. His discipline and dedication eclipsed mine. Indeed, his dedication was an inspiration for me and his discipline a goad. Jim frequently proposed joint research and writing projects, but they never got off the
ground, primarily due to the ballast I provided. Then he was gone. Though we
never wrote a book together, this book would never have been written had it not
been for him. I am honored to dedicate it to his memory.

CHAPTER 1

Introduction

In May 2000, Washington braced for a mythic political battle. The Clinton administration unleashed its full effort to get Congress to approve legislation making China's normal trading relationship permanent. Previously, China's normal trading status was subject to annual review and renewal. Corporations and business interests not normally friendly to the policies of Democrats were backing the administration. The administration organized a spectacular display of bipartisan support at which former President Carter joined Republican former Presidents Ford and Bush and Secretaries of State Kissinger and Baker to endorse permanent normal trade relations (PNTR) status for China. Opposing the change was an odd collection of progressive Democrats and conservative Republicans backed by labor, environmental, human rights, and anticommunist groups.

The press covered the clash extensively. Much of the reporting concerned politics: the politics of coalition building as the administration sought votes through persuasion, pressure, and political payoffs; the politics of the presidential election, as the decision would affect the fortunes of candidates Bush and Gore; the politics of Clinton's presidency, his ability to lead in the twilight of his term in office.

The emphasis on politics tended, unfortunately, to obscure one important fact: At its core, the debate about trade with China was a debate about the substance of policy. It was as if someone who attended the Super Bowl had written an essay describing the weather, the stadium, the food, the uniforms, the fans, the commercials, and the halftime extravaganza, noting only rarely and in passing that a football game happened. Everything mentioned would have been true and part of the Super Bowl experience but the overall portrayal would have missed the point.

The substantive debate over PNTR reflected disagreements about the consequences of granting China that status. The editors of the conservative periodical *National Review* endorsed it for its economic benefits: Increasing trade would be good for the businesses that would export to China and for the workers they employ.[1] Cutting tariffs, which are taxes paid by purchasers of imported goods, would benefit consumers.

1

National Review's position reflected less a judgment about trade with China in particular than a general commitment to a policy of free trade. "Free trade was once a populist, and popular issue. Let it be so again."[2]

Among those opposing PNTR was Arthur Waldron of the American Enterprise Institute, a conservative think tank. Testifying before the Senate Foreign Relations Committee, he warned that changing China's trading status would pose military dangers. China's policies had become increasingly militarized, he observed, and its aggression flows from its repressive politics; it uses foreign conflict "to divert popular attention by waving the flag."[3] "Over the past 12 months," he continued, "the threat of war from Beijing has become almost routine." Rewarding China with PNTR while it threatens its neighbors would send the wrong signal. It would "convince the Chinese that we depend so much on their market and are so eager to invest in their country that we will sacrifice our security interests in order to do so" and this "miscalculation" could "push them over the edge into military action" (173).

Others opposed PNTR simply because China's internal repression was abhorrent. One was Lori Wallach, director of the public lobby group Global Trade Watch. Testifying before a Senate committee, she observed that "[g]reater trade links and economic liberalization with China have not resulted in improvement in China's human rights conduct nor promoted the growth of democracy in China" (177). Rather, the Chinese state has "brutally repressed the most basic freedoms Congress pledges to defend" (181). Granting China permanent normal trade relations would deprive the United States of the leverage it could have if it made annual renewal contingent on improvements in China's human rights conditions.

Supporters of PNTR shared the goal of promoting human rights in China. One, Secretary of Commerce William Daley, testified: "As a world leader we have an obligation to foster further reform in China" (170). Indeed, he argued, expanding trade would be the most effective way to promote political reform in China. Trade would increase Internet use in China, for instance, and "unfettered access to outside influences and ideas through satellites and the Internet . . . cannot help but promote greater economic and political reform in China" (176).

Not only would expanded trade stimulate liberalization within China, claimed Daley, it also would check the aggressive tendencies so worrisome to Dr. Waldron. "Encouraging China to join the rules-based world trading system gives it a greater stake in the stability and prosperity of its regional neighbors and the rest of the world. It will create a better, more stable, safer world" (170).

HIDDEN ASSUMPTIONS AND POLICY ARGUMENTS

Each of those arguments rests on implicit assumptions. Some concern how the world works. The *National Review's* analysis assumes that free trade enriches the nations that practice it, that is, that the gains for those it benefits outweigh the losses for those who are harmed by international competition. Dr. Waldron's argument rests on three assumptions. First, it assumes that dictatorships are more aggressive than are democracies. Second, it assumes that the United States has and will continue to have sufficient power to deter China from attacking its neighbors. Third, it assumes that Chinese policy makers draw inferences about U.S. military-strategic behavior from its economic policies. Ms. Wallach's argument assumes that the potential to sever trade relations gives the United States sufficient leverage to induce the Chinese to stop or reduce their violations of human rights. Like Dr. Waldron, she assumes that the United States has or could have the power to shape China's behavior. Finally, Secretary Daley assumes that economic interdependence makes countries more peaceful.

Identifying the assumptions on which those arguments rest in no way implies that either the assumptions or the arguments are wrong. All arguments rest on assumptions. Some assumptions are true; all are subject to dispute. The assumptions themselves rest on other assumptions. To illustrate that point, consider Secretary Daley's assumption that economic interdependence yields peace. Among the assumptions necessary to support that assumption are:

- either trade is equally beneficial for all parties or nations are unconcerned about their share of the benefits of trade;
- economic gains do not endanger a nation's other values, such as its power or independence;
- policy makers perceive a trade-off between conflict and prosperity such that any disturbance of the peace risks a serious constricting of international trade;
- policy makers are motivated by externally oriented national interests rather than internal political interests;
- policy makers are rational.

If any of those assumptions are wrong, a nation could become more interdependent economically without becoming more peaceful.

The arguments over PNTR rest as well on a second kind of assumption. They make assumptions about the purposes of the United States. Consider, for instance, the claim that the United States should follow a policy of free trade because free trade makes its producers and consumers more prosperous; it assumes that the purpose of foreign policy should be to make the United States more prosperous. While it seems obvious, on its face, that U.S. foreign policy should have that purpose, it is not. What if free trade, by making the United States more economically interdependent, also eroded its political and cultural independence? What if free trade, while making the United States more prosperous, also made the poor countries of the world poorer?

The argument that PNTR would make China more belligerent also rests on assumptions about U.S. foreign policy purposes. It assumes that the United States should seek to prevent Chinese aggression against its neighbors. To most people, that assumption would seem plausible, peace being better than war. But several questions could be posed. Why should the United States take on that task? Should it do so as a matter of national interest? If so, how would Chinese aggression against its neighbors degrade the national interests of the United States? What would be the costs and risks of containing China? Why would the harm caused by Chinese aggression outweigh the costs and risks of containing China? Perhaps the task of containing China depends less on interests than on morality: Because aggression is wrong, it ought to be prevented. But if that is so, why should the responsibility be borne by the United States?

Finally, arguments about the impact on human rights also rest on assumed purposes. They assume that the United States ought to base its foreign relations on how other countries treat their citizens. But why should that be so? Is it a matter of U.S. national interests, reflecting a causal link between a state's treatment of its citizens and its treatment of other nations? Or is it a matter of ethics, reflecting a moral obligation to promote respect for human rights in other countries?

The substantive debate about granting China PNTR, in summary, operated at three levels. It worked, first, at the level of particular claims about the consequences of the policy: whether it would increase or decrease American prosperity, strengthen human rights in China or abandon the Chinese people, and make China a more peaceful country or a more dangerous foe. It operated, second, at the level of assumptions about the condition of the world and about the cause-effect relationships that determine how the world works. And it operated, third, at the level of assumptions about the appropriate international role of the United States, the purposes it ought to pursue. The clash over trade policy with China, then, represented deeper clashes over different interpretations of the nature of the world and the American role in it. Those clashes of interpretation are foundational to all important debates over foreign policy.

THE TASK OF THIS BOOK

This book introduces those fundamental debates, using the foreign policy logic as its organizing concept. A foreign policy logic is a stripped down ideology or worldview consisting of a limited number of mutually supporting ideas about (1) the country's basic foreign policy purposes or strategy, (2) the content of its national interests, (3) the nature and amount of its power, and (4) the substance and importance of its ethical obligations. Each of the six logics presented in this book incorporates a model of international relations—that is, an understanding of the nature of the world and how it works—which informs its interpretation of national interests, power, and ethical obligations and the prescription of basic strategy. The next section of this chapter provides a more extensive exposition of the concept of a foreign policy logic.

The book's core chapters describe the six most important foreign policy logics competing to define U.S. foreign policy. Each has deep historical roots. Each incorporates a theory of international relations formulated no more recently than 150 years ago. Each influenced debates about and the content of U.S. foreign policy during most of the twentieth century; two were influential throughout the nineteenth century as well. There is every reason to suppose that they will continue to provide the foundation for debates and decisions about the international role of the United States.

Understanding these logics should serve three purposes. First, it should allow a deeper understanding of debates over specific foreign policy questions. It should help identify and critically evaluate the assumptions that support policy arguments. Second, it should allow foreign policy arguments to be placed in a context of broader issues of U.S. purpose and of the historical development of foreign policy thinking. Third, and most important, it should encourage and provide the raw material for thinking through one's own views about what role the United States should play in the world. A study of foreign policy logics, then, should make one a better observer of U.S. foreign relations and should make American citizens better agents in setting the direction of their country's foreign policy.

This chapter undertakes two preliminary tasks. It develops the concept of a foreign policy logic and considers how it can be employed in thinking about foreign policy and then briefly previews the six logics.

THE NATURE OF FOREIGN POLICY LOGICS

Every foreign policy logic has four key elements: a prescription of a basic foreign policy strategy or world role, an analysis of U.S. national interests, an interpretation of U.S. power, and a perspective on morality.

Foreign Policy Strategy

A foreign policy logic prescribes a world role or basic foreign policy strategy, which can be described along a number of dimensions, including:

- Level of engagement: Should the United States be actively involved in international affairs? What, if any, limits are there to the international commitments it should undertake?
- Priorities: What should be its most important goal or goals?
- Geographic scope: Should engagement be fully *globalist,* or should it focus on key nations or geographic regions?
- Unilateralism-multilateralism and leadership: How should the United States collaborate with other countries? Should it follow a policy of *unilateralism* in which it acts on its own, or should it follow a policy of *multilateralism* in working with others? If the United States follows a multilateralist path, should it play a leadership role? If so, of what sort and how? What should be its relationship to international institutions such as the UN?
- Militarization: To what extent and in what ways does foreign policy depend on military might?
- Interventionism: Should foreign policy be *interventionist,* seeking to shape or transform the domestic structures and processes of other countries, or should it be *noninterventionist?*

- Globalization: How should the United States relate economically with the outside world? Should it expand its commercial relations or contract them? Should it promote the world's adoption of the capitalist model of economics based on principles of free trade and investment, or should it subject international economic relations to political regulation in order to promote political or moral goals?

National Interests

The second element of a foreign policy logic is the enumeration of interests based on an interpretation of the nature of world politics. Among the questions that inform the interpretation of national interest are:

- Is conflict the essence of world politics or do common interests dictate substantial cooperation among countries? Are war and rumors of war and balances of power the basic stuff of world politics? Or are other problems as important as war?
- What conditions mitigate and what conditions amplify the threat of war?
- Are international events tightly linked so that an event in one place reverberates throughout the world? Or, instead, are international systems decomposable into largely self-contained geographic regions and issue areas that can be dealt with separately from the rest?
- Is world politics fundamentally what states do to each other, or are internal developments within countries part of the agenda of international affairs? Who are the key actors in international affairs? Are they states? If so, are they all states, or only the major powers? Or are international organizations and private groups such as corporations and nongovernmental actors important players on the world stage?
- To what extent is prosperity the crucial value to be advanced by international economic relations? How is American prosperity related to global prosperity?

Power

The third element is the assessment of power. In an often quoted essay, Walter Lippmann, the most prominent American political journalist of the twentieth century, offered what he called "the fundamental principle of foreign policy," which is that commitments and power have to be brought into balance. A statesman "must bring his ends and means into balance. If he does not, he will follow a course that leads to disaster."[4] As with U.S. interests, perceptions of U.S. power are bound up with views about the nature of the world. Key questions are:

- What is power? Is it the resources a state can bring to bear, or is it the state's actual influence or control over events in its environment?
- To what extent is power dependent on military might?
- What factors other than material resources determine levels of power?
- How much power does the United States need? How much does it have?
- How does America's international role enhance or degrade its power?

Morality

The role of morality in foreign policy has been a persistent issue of political analysis since Thucydides wrote the first international relations book, *The Peloponnesian War*, 2400 years ago. The element of morality raises two sets of questions: First, what role ought morality play in international affairs; second, what are the substantive international obligations of the United States?

Interrelationships Among Elements

Those four elements shape each other. Logics, like all belief systems, tend toward internal consistency. Their coherence is not, however, based on a hierarchical ordering of ideas. In a purely rational world, the first element, the prescribed role or strategy, would be derived from the others; once U.S. interests, power, and ethical obligations and constraints had been determined, the foreign policy strategy would follow logically. In the actual world, humans are not purely rational. Quite often, we unconsciously adjust our perceptions in order to preserve our core beliefs while keeping them consistent with the full set of our ideas. Thus, for example, someone who believes that either a country's national interests or moral obligations require a costly commitment will be under inner pressure also to believe that its power is sufficient for the commitment.

THE PLAN OF THE BOOK

Chapters 2–7 present the most important logics used in contemporary debates over American foreign policy. Although these logics inform today's disputes, they all have lineages that trace back several decades.[5]

The first three are members of a broader realist tradition that emphasizes the pursuit of national interest, constrained by power. They represent different points along a continuum of perceived U.S. power. At one end is the *logic of hegemonism*, which sees the United States as having overwhelming power and correlatively expansive conceptions of its international role, national interests, and ethical obligations. Hegemonism emphasizes the practical and moral imperatives for the United States to be the world's leader. In effect, it prescribes the role of benevolent imperial power. Hegemonism has been the predominant logic since World War II; that is why it is presented first, in Chapter 2.

Chapter 3 presents the *logic of realism*. It holds that the United States is strong enough to maintain a stable balance of power and thus to prevent the disaster of general international warfare caused by power imbalances. The United States is not powerful enough to pursue a more exalted purpose abroad, though; efforts to do so would fail and, worse, would sabotage its ability to maintain the balance. The foreign policy role of the United States, then, is to muster sufficient power, especially military power, and prevent others from mustering too much, so that it can preserve international equilibrium.

At the far end of the continuum of the realist tradition is a logic that sees the United States as having quite limited power. It is strong enough to be secure from traditional military threats to its national security. It is not strong enough, however, to bring about real reforms of international affairs. Moreover, attempting to do so would cause grievous harm to itself. Therefore, its involvement in the world must be most limited. This *logic of isolationism* is the oldest of the foreign policy logics. For roughly the first century of the country's existence, its leaders prescribed that it separate itself from the rest of the world, especially politically and militarily, in order to protect itself from foreign dangers. Nowadays, few people call themselves isolationists. Nevertheless, important elements of the worldview and value judgments that underlay isolationism continue to resonate in modern America. It is described in Chapter 4.

Chapters 5 and 6 present two logics that many experts treat as one, often referring to it as Wilsonianism, after its most famous proponent, President Woodrow Wilson. This book treats them as separate logics because of a single but important contradiction between them. One, presented in Chapter 5, is the *logic of liberalism*. Unlike hegemonism and realism, both of which place some emphasis on conflict and military power, liberalism focuses on international cooperation. Its defining element is the national interest and moral obligation to increase human liberty through political democracy and economic freedom. Promoting liberty was at the core of the political thought of the nation's founders and emerged as a central goal of American diplomacy when Wilson articulated his vision for a peaceful international order following World War I.

The other element of Wilsonianism, here called the *logic of liberal internationalism*, is the subject of Chapter 6. Liberal internationalism prescribes conforming foreign policy to the conditions of complex international interdependence. Liberal internationalism is easily conflated with liberalism. In addition to having similar names, both are part of the idealist tradition of international affairs; both emphasize cooperation among nations; both address consequences of interdependence; both seek to promote human rights. Many people use both logics in advocating public policies. Nevertheless, they are distinguishable logics. They differ in their assumptions about power, in the range of international interdependence with which they deal, and in their diagnoses of American national interests. Some of the diplomatic tools used in pursuit of the logic of liberalism, moreover, contradict aspects of the liberal internationalist policy.

Chapter 7 presents a logic that shares hegemonism's perception of the United States as exercising predominant power. It diverges from realist tradition by rejecting the national interest as the primary consideration for evaluating and making foreign policy. It focuses instead on the consequences of U.S. policy on other countries and especially on the poor and weak of the world. It finds those consequences to be deeply harmful. The United States, according to this logic, is fundamentally a predatory, bellicose, imperialist country, and will be unless and until revolutionary change liberates it from its capitalist economy. Until then, primarily on moral grounds, the logic stands in opposition to the undertakings of the U.S. government, not so much to protect the United States from the world as to protect the world from the United States. It is therefore is called the *logic of radical anti-imperialism*.

Chapter 8 briefly provides a comparative analysis of the six logics along a number of important dimensions. Comparative analysis brings the similarities and the dissimilarities of the logics into focus and highlights the points at which different logics converge to support similar qualities of U.S. foreign policy. The logics are abstract theoretical constructs. Brief illustrations of their use in actual policy debates are scattered throughout their presentations. To provide a more thorough and systematic demonstration of their empirical use, Chapter 9 presents case studies of how the logics are reflected in debates about two recent U.S. foreign policies: The 2000 decision about PNTR for China and the 1999 military intervention in Kosovo.

The last chapter looks to the future. In the near term, the significance of the competition among foreign policy logics wanes if the United States operates under a foreign policy consensus, as it did during the first decades of the Cold War. According to one common view, the terrorist attacks of September 11, 2001, may have created a new foreign policy consensus. Chapter 10 examines that idea. In looking at the foreign policy actions of Congress, the patterns in public opinion, and the points of view expressed by elite shapers of opinions during the first months after the attack, it finds that the competing logics still hold sway and that a new foreign policy consensus has not emerged.

A WORD ABOUT METHOD

Each chapter presenting a logic has three main parts, each written in a different voice. The first presents the logic's views on foreign policy strategy, national interests, power, and morality. The views are distilled from scholarly publications and contemporary political debates about U.S. foreign policy. They are, moreover, generalizations; no one individual or group completely adheres to any single logic. Each logic, instead, represents a general line of reasoning that individuals and groups subscribe to and use to a greater or lesser degree. The voice used in presenting each logic is that of an adherent. Its views are stated in the strongest possible light, sometimes in the spirit of devil's advocacy. On occasion that has meant inventing arguments to elaborate the rationale for particular logics, to put into words ideas that must be assumed if the logic is to make sense.

Each chapter then analyzes the role that its logic has played in U.S. diplomatic history. Here, the voice shifts to that of the objective observer. The reader will find that several instances are covered in more than one chapter. That is because the several logics operate simultaneously in American political culture and even in the minds of particular individuals. Important undertakings, then, typically result from the convergence of two or more logics supporting the same policy but for different reasons.

The third part raises questions for further discussion. Here, I have tried to place myself in the role of the instructor, leading readers to think about the logics critically and creatively.

Within the limits of my scruples, intelligence, and capacity for diligence, I have avoided doing one thing in this book. I have not said which of the logics is true or the most true, that is, which one I believe. I hope, moreover, that I have hidden my views on their comparative worth. During this book's development, several readers perceived bias but disagreed about which logics I was favoring and which ones I was treating unfairly. I take some comfort in that. I hope that the presentation inspires the reader to form his or her judgment through his or her observation of U.S. foreign policy seen through the lenses of the logics of American foreign policy.

ENDNOTES

1. William F. Buckley, Jr., "On the Right: More Trade With China?" *National Review*, December 31, 1999.
2. "After the Deal" *National Review*, June 19, 2000, 16.
3. The testimony of Arthur Waldron, and that of Lori Wallach and Commerce Secretary William Daley (discussed later) is reprinted in "Pro & Con: Should Congress Grant Permanent Normal Trade Relations to the People's Republic of China?" *Congressional Digest*, June-July 2000. Quoted passage is on page 171.
4. Walter Lippmann, *U.S. Foreign Policy: Shield of the Republic*, (Boston: Little, Brown and Company, 1943), 9–10.
5. Alternative interpretations about how to classify competing U.S. worldviews are presented in: Cecil V. Crabb, Jr., *Policy-makers and Critics: Conflicting Theories of American Foreign Policy*, (New York: Praeger Publishers, 1976); Stanley J. Michalak, Jr., *Competing Conceptions of American Foreign Policy: Worldviews in Conflict*, (New York: HarperCollins Publishers, 1992); Richard N. Haass, *The Reluctant Sheriff: The United States After the Cold War*, (New York: Council on Foreign Relations Books, 1997): 52–68; Richard N. Haass, "Five Not-So-Easy Pieces: The Debates on American Foreign Policy," *Brookings Review* Vol. 18, No. 2 (Spring 2000): 38–40; Stephen M. Walt, "International Relations: One World, Many Theories," *Foreign Policy* 110 (Spring 1998): 29–46; Barry R. Posen and Andrew L. Ross, "Competing Visions for U.S. Grand Strategy," *International Security* 21 (Winter 1996–1997):5–53; Charles William Maynes, "Contending Schools," *The National Interest* No. 63 (Spring, 2001): 49–58; Norman Podhoretz, "Strange Bedfellows: A Guide to the New Foreign-Policy Debates," *Commentary* (December 1999): 19–32.

CHAPTER 2

The Logic of Hegemonism

On March 27, 2002, a young Palestinian set off a bomb that killed himself and 22 Jews attending a Passover Seder. Enraged, Israeli Prime Minister Ariel Sharon ordered a dramatic escalation of efforts to crush the Palestinian uprising in the occupied territories. Israeli forces invaded key Palestinian towns. Although outgunned, the Palestinians resisted; casualties were many. Israeli forces also invaded the headquarters of Palestinian leader Yassir Arafat, isolating him and several of his closest associates in a single room. The world waited to see whether Israeli forces would storm Arafat's last outpost, killing him in the process.

With the escalating violence came calls for the United States to stop the fighting. University of Chicago historian Rashid Khalidi, for one, wrote that the United States is "the only power capable of imposing a settlement." Why should the United States take on such a large and risky project? Professor Rashidi's reason was both pragmatic and principled: "The stability of the entire Middle East is in danger" because of "the failure of the U.S. to accept its responsibilities as the world's sole superpower."[1] In calling for an imposed peace, he was invoking the logic of hegemonism.

INTRODUCTION

Overview

This chapter presents the logic of hegemonism by developing the following points:

- Hegemonism calls upon the United States, as the world's most powerful country, to provide the world with the leadership necessary for the effective functioning of vital international systems and to maintain its power dominance for that end;
- the effective functioning of international systems is essential to the national interests of the United States;
- the United States has sufficient power to provide the international system with leadership: Its resources dominate contemporary international relations;

its influence is augmented by other countries' willingness for the United States to be the leader; and its position of primacy can be sustained through a prudent national foreign policy strategy;

- leadership must serve the common good, both for pragmatic reasons and because it is morally obligatory;
- since the late 1940s, hegemonism has been the dominant foreign policy logic.

Hegemonism Defined

The word hegemonism comes from "hegemony," which *Webster's Seventh New Collegiate Dictionary* defines as "preponderant influence or authority, especially of one nation over another." The logic of hegemonism calls for the United States to exercise such influence or authority so as to provide the leadership needed for the effective functioning of the international political and economic system. The logic holds that hegemony is a good thing. Effective exercise of hegemonic power would provide the world community with a stable order, a *Pax Americana*, that is prerequisite for all other good things.

Because predominant influence or authority is a necessary condition for effective leadership, hegemonism requires the United States to maintain and prolong its primacy. Indeed, according to power transition theory, the most dangerous condition for world politics would come if a challenger were to erode U.S. primacy.[2] Prolonging primacy requires that allies be followers who stay in line with U.S. policy and avoid destabilizing initiatives. Ideally, leadership elicits multilateral efforts so as to spread the costs of regulating international systems. If necessary, however, a leader must act alone.

Not all calls for the United States to play a leadership role reflect the logic of hegemonism. Hegemonism promotes a specific kind of leadership, namely, that which is required to ensure the effective functioning of international systems. The logic of hegemonism rests on two premises. First, American well-being requires establishing and maintaining effective international systems in both the political and economic realms. Second, U.S. leadership is "the drivewheel"[3] of such systems; to the extent that American leadership fails, international systems become disordered. Together, these premises define virtually unlimited national interests and prescribe almost limitless engagement and commitment.

U.S. NATIONAL INTERESTS

The well-being of the United States depends on the effective functioning of international systems in both political and economic realms.

International Political System

Any political system must provide order and thus security for its members. An effective international political system minimizes international instability, that is, armed conflicts between states and acts of terror directed across national borders. It also must minimize any internal instability (for example, revolutions, civil wars, genocides) that might spawn international instability.

Instability is dangerous because it spreads, like an epidemic or a wildfire. "The sickness of the world is also our sickness," declared a famous essay calling upon the United States to enter World War II and thus assume its role as world leader.[4] Sixty years later, Secretary of State Madeleine Albright used the health metaphor to justify military intervention in Kosovo: "[T]he great lesson of this century is that when aggression and brutality go unopposed, like a cancer, they spread."[5]

Instability tends to spread for four reasons. One, instability creates an incentive for others to intervene due to the disruption of social systems. For example, violent conflict causes the mobilization of labor into the armed forces, the flight of other labor away from the zone of turmoil, and the placing of the economy on a wartime footing. These in turn create scarcities and ignite inflation that harm trading partners. Violence also forces people to seek refuge in neighboring countries, sometimes exacerbating their own serious internal conflicts. Two, ethnic, racial, religious, linguistic, cultural, or historical ties will tend to draw countries to intervene in support of those who are like them. Three, violent conflict disturbs regional balances of power. Regional powers may be tempted to meddle in order to enhance their status or influence at their rivals' expense or to preempt their rivals' intervention. Four, successful aggression encourages aggression. It emboldens the aggressors and others who learn that aggression can be successful.

International instability also harms U.S. interests by impeding the solution of other pressing international problems. Conflict devours resources and dissipates the cooperative impulses necessary to organize global problem solving. Stability is the first prerequisite for human progress.

Because instability tends to grow, harms American interests, and pulls it into others' conflicts, the United States is destined to be the world's police officer. Hence it must insure that it is respected. Those who would destabilize international relations must anticipate that the United States will block them and, therefore, be deterred. Unless the United States successfully deters aggression, it will be dragged into an exhausting series of law-enforcement actions. Successful deterrence, however, is self-reinforcing, as is its breakdown. Therefore, when instability erupts, the United States must demonstrate that it will act like a great power, lest it lose credibility, and see challenges to the *status quo* proliferate.

International Economic System

The United States also has vital interests in the effective functioning of the international economic system. American prosperity and domestic tranquility require continual economic growth. With growth, politics involves struggles over how to distribute increases in the nation's wealth. Without growth, economics and politics become zero-sum games: Any gain for one party means a loss for others. Difficult conflicts over the distribution of the nation's wealth become intractable battles over its redistribution. Racial, class, generational, and regional cleavages deepen and widen; ugly, possibly violent confrontations could follow.

To grow, the United States needs international commerce. A self-sufficient United States could not sustain its present abundance. The U.S. economy needs, first of all, markets for the production of its farms, factories, and service industries. Such markets cannot exist unless other countries have the wealth to purchase American goods. Therefore, a growing American economy necessitates a growing world economy.

Ideally, given that the U.S. economy is basically capitalist, the world economy would be open, that is, characterized by free trade.* An open world economy, however, is not enough. Removing trade barriers will not increase American exports if other countries lack the money to pay for them. In technical terms, the international economic system must have adequate *liquidity*. It therefore must have mechanisms for funneling financial resources to states to enable them to continue to import when their export earnings and accumulated savings are insufficient. Such resource flows could be in the form of loans, credits, or outright grants. Depending on the financial condition of the recipient, loans and credits might have to be concessional, that is, at low interest rates and with a long time for repayment. In extreme cases, loans might have to be written off, canceling the obligation to repay.

The need for liquidity may require short-term deviations from free trade. To pay for what it imports, countries must earn money; one important way is to sell goods and services, that is, export. Capacity to export depends on the strength of the economy, but the strength of the economy depends on the volume of exports. National economies can get stuck in a vicious circle in which the inability to export feeds economic stagnation, which further weakens its export sector. All the while, moreover, the national economy is removed from the world economy, for the country cannot pay to import. To break the circle, countries with strong economies would have to bend the rules of international economics in order to foster an artificial increase in the exports of the weaker economy. More specifically, states with strong economies would have to lower tariffs and other trade barriers while allowing those with weak economies to subsidize exports and impede imports via tariffs, import quotas, and other barriers. They would have to direct such programs primarily toward countries with large potential markets that eventually could add substantially to the size of the global market.

Other situations may require other deviations from open market economics. For instance, maintaining effective international systems requires accumulating and using political power. That may mean imposing economic sanctions when that is the most cost effective way to exert influence. In all cases, however, deviations from the principles of the market are short-term expedients intended to bolster the international economic system or the international political system on which it is founded.

U.S. Leadership

Leadership by the United States is essential for the effective functioning of international systems. Three points establish that fact. First, leadership is necessary. International systems will not spontaneously make the adjustments needed for effectiveness.

---

*This premise is shared by the logic of liberalism (Chapter 5).

Second, no other nation or group of nations can provide leadership. Third, international institutions cannot provide collective leadership. If leadership is required and no one else can provide it, then the United States is "bound to lead."[6]

The Necessity for Leadership

Leadership is necessary.[7] The benefits of effective international systems are long-term and diffuse. Moreover, the benefits are collective, or public, goods: All members of the system share in its workings whether or not they contribute proportionally to its upkeep. Therefore, all states are tempted to be free-riders, that is, to reap the gains while letting others pay the costs. Left to their own, states would go their own way and the collective action necessary for effective systems would disappear. Action by the system's leaders is required to break this logic of collective inaction. They must provide individual states with separate and distinct incentives for acting collectively—promises of benefits they can gain only if they cooperate or threats of punishments if they fail to cooperate. Alternatively, the system's leaders can act on their own to provide the collective goods, doing so because they calculate that the benefits to be gained by action, or the costs of inaction to be avoided, would outweigh the costs of acting on their own. Such a cost-benefit calculus reflects the realization that they can make the system function effectively acting on their own, that their stakes in the system are so great they would stand to lose much if it failed, and that their power is so great they can do so at costs that, relative to their stakes, are relatively low. Clearly, states that have the resources realistically to see themselves that way, and act accordingly, are leaders.

The United States Is the Only Country That Can Provide Leadership

In the present and foreseeable world, the United States is the only actor able to provide such leadership. No other country can match its resources. Japan and a few other countries have economic clout but no military strength. Russia has nuclear weapons, but its economy is a shambles and its military is in disarray. India has a huge population and territory but it is too poor to have real power except in its immediate region. Japan, Russia, India, Brazil, Indonesia, and a handful of other countries could play a leadership role in their regions, but could not replace the United States as the world's leader.

Although China has certain attributes necessary to become a global leader, it too seems ill suited for that role. It has a huge population, large and increasingly modern armed forces, and a dynamic economy. But China's deficiencies are severe: Its political structures are weak and its rapid economic growth has ignited serious social problems that could distract it from playing a leadership role.

Nor is Europe likely to regain its place in the global pecking order. Germany is an economic power, but lacks the military muscle and political will to be a leader. France and England—despite their nuclear weapons and seats on the UN Security Council—are secondary powers. A unified Europe would have sufficient resources to play a leadership role, but European political unification is not an imminent prospect. The conflict over whether to back the invasion of Iraq in 2003 glaringly revealed Europe's internal divisions. Even if the European Union were to acquire sovereignty over its constituent member states, it would have to solve many internal difficulties, which could make it too inward looking to play the role of leader. Moreover, the unification of Europe itself may require American hegemony to tamp down Europe's latent internal rivalries.[8]

International Institutions Cannot Provide Leadership

The responsibility and burden of leadership cannot be delegated to international institutions such as the UN, either. The United States might use international institutions in organizing collective action. They provide the appearance of multilateralism and thus increase the policy's legitimacy. Multilateral action also allows more equitable burden sharing, thus reducing the costs to the United States. International institutions, therefore, can complement but not replace American leadership. Without it, international institutions would be unable to make and implement decisions. "For better or for worse," concluded one international economics expert, "it is now up to the United States, as it has been since World War II, to help shape the future of [the International Monetary Fund and the World Trade Organization] and arguably the course of the global economy."[9]

Indeed, to rely on international institutions would be disastrous. Other countries may not really want international institutions to provide multilateral leadership, because that would require them to stop being free-riders and to pay the costs of foreign affairs. They want the appearance of participation in global problem solving but not its substance. Moreover, in the absence of genuine multipolarity, "multilateralism, if rigorously pursued, guarantees failure in meeting international crises."[10] Because multilateral institutions can never replace American leadership, they can never be allowed to constrain the United States, either. The United States can never allow inaction or opposition by international organizations to prevent it from taking necessary action. It must act unilaterally if necessary or organize "coalitions of the willing" on an issue-by-issue basis.

U.S. POWER

The power of the United States defies easy comprehension; it is history's first global superpower. "The United States possesses unprecedented—and unequaled—strength and influence in the world," begins the Bush administration's national security strategy statement.[11] America's power rests on pillars of economic strength, military might, and cultural attractiveness, is amplified by a favorable international environment, and can be augmented by implementing appropriate national strategies.

Economic Dominance

The economic power of the United States is impressive. In 2001, its GDP (gross domestic product; the dollar value of the total production of an economy) dwarfed that of all other countries. At $10.2 trillion, it was greater than the next three largest economies combined. Overall, it produces nearly one-quarter of the world's goods and services.[12] Its economic power is reflected, too, in the flow of goods, services, and money among countries. Its exports amount to 12 percent of the total of world exports and its imports amount to 19 percent.[13] In the period 1997–2001, it sold $44.8 billion in major conventional weapons systems in the global market, 45 percent of the world's total. Its sales almost equaled the sales totals of the seven next largest suppliers combined.[14] In 2000, the United States accounted for 45 percent of (private) direct foreign investment in the world and its official development assistance or foreign aid amounts to about one-fifth of the world's total.[15]

The United States also exercises tremendous influence on the decisions of critical international economic organizations, such as the World Bank and the International Monetary Fund; one critic calls the IMF "basically an institutional surrogate of the United States government. . . . a covert arm of the U.S. Treasury . . ."[16]

The strength and size of the U.S. economy generates power in several ways. First, it provides a lever for direct influence. Fearing being cut off from the U.S. market or the flow of its resources, or anticipating rewards, other countries have incentives to comply with U.S. wishes. Second, few if any international economic problems can be solved without U.S. cooperation. That gives it a veto power over ideas it does not like, which in turn spawns diplomatic leverage. Most importantly, though, it provides the resources for other levers of power, most importantly, military forces.

Military Prowess

The military power of the United States is staggering. Its armed forces are not the world's largest; at 1.4 million, it has considerably fewer persons under arms than does China (2.5 million) and only somewhat more than Russia (1 million), India (1.3 million) and North Korea (1 million).[17] Rather, its military dominance rests in the technological superiority of its armed forces. With the so-called "revolution in military affairs," its lead in such critical technologies as stealth, remote sensing, and precision guidance has opened a new era in which U.S. forces will be able to achieve decisive victories in short time at minimal loss of American lives.[18] The successful bombing campaign in Kosovo in 1999, the defeat of Taliban and Al Qaeda in Afghanistan in 2001–2002, and the victory in Iraq in 2003 displayed U.S. military prowess.

Technological dominance is founded on huge investments in military capabilities; every year, U.S. defense spending exceeds that of the next five countries combined. It accounts for one-third of the military expenditures of the world; its military expenditures are more than the rest of NATO combined, more than three times the highest estimate of Russian military expenditures, and more than four times those of China; at more than $27 billion, it spends more on intelligence than the total military budgets of all but five other nations.[19] It is the only country in the world able to mount and sustain large-scale combat operations far from its homeland. It is the only country that is able to use military forces virtually anywhere in the world; it has forces deployed at over 800 installations in more than 70 countries around the world, including 61 major bases in 19 countries.[20]

Total Resource Base

Despite concerns about overcommitment or "imperial overstretch"[21] eroding its power base, the United States could substantially increase its investments in foreign affairs. The burden of foreign policy is much less now than it was just a few decades ago. For instance, in 1995 the military was only half the size it had been in 1967. Defense expenditures in constant dollars (that is, having removed the distorting effect of inflation) are substantially below what they were during the Vietnam War and the 1980s and somewhat below their level in the years before Vietnam. More importantly, defense now accounts for less than 20 percent of the federal government's total budget, compared to over 50 percent in 1960. Its share of the national economy (less than 4 percent of GNP) is much less now than in every year until the 1970s. The same pattern holds for other instruments of policy. The country spends less on diplomatic representation, on foreign assistance, and on other crucial tools than it had in the 1950s and 1960s. Therefore, it could expand its efforts without dragging down economic performance.

Moreover, American economic power is not declining. During the three decades from the 1950s to the 1980s, it experienced a relative decline compared to the economies of Japan and Western Europe, but that should not cause alarm. In the postwar years the U.S. share of the world economy was artificially inflated by the wartime devastation of the other major nations. As Japan and Western Europe regained economic vitality, the U.S. share automatically declined. Now that the Europeans and Japanese have completed their postwar recovery, the relative decline of the United States is gradually ending, leaving it the world's dominant economy.

Cultural Influence

American influence rests also on its cultural dominance or "soft power."[22] Politically, the United States is an admired model in the eyes of the world. Its economy and to a lesser extent its social conditions also elicit respect from others. American popular culture has a global reach and a strong, if diffuse, effect. Together these make other countries more responsive to requests from the United States. They also make American arguments more persuasive than if other countries saw the world through diametrically different lenses. Effective persuasion renders coercion unnecessary.

Congenial International Environment

The ability of the United States to accomplish ambitious goals is enhanced by the congenial international environment of the twenty-first century. Most of the other major powers are generally friendly to the United States, which facilitates the building of coalitions and partnerships. With the collapse of the Soviet Union and the transformation of Russia, the United States faces no powerful adversary. International terrorism represents a serious problem: It can inflict catastrophic damage, is spread over a large number of countries, and will take time and resources to defeat. It poses a lesser challenge, though, than did the Cold War, because terrorists are backed by weak states, not superpower rivals.

Shrewd National Strategy

The ability of the United States to set and accomplish ambitious goals goes beyond its actual endowment of power in a friendly environment. An effective national strategy can, in effect, multiply its resources by preventing costly challenges and by mobilizing other powers' resources to augment those of the United States. Its main elements would be deterrence, asymmetrical response, recruitment of collaborators, and a diplomacy of reassurance.

Deterrence

For certain objectives, the United States could implement a policy of deterrence. Under deterrence, the United States would communicate, by threats or warnings, its desire that another country not do something. If deterrence works, threats would not have to be carried out and resources would not have to be expended. Effective deterrence thus prevents challenges at little cost. The first President Bush clearly understood that idea. Asked whether the U.S. victory in the 1991 Persian Gulf War signaled a "new era now of using U.S. military forces around the world," he answered: "No, I think because of what's happened we won't have to use U.S. forces around the world. I think when we say something that's objectively correct—like don't take over a neighbor or you're going to bear some responsibility—people are going to listen."[23] Very clearly, his son is following the same tack. His labeling of Iraq, Iran, and North Korea as an "axis of evil" bluntly warned those states to desist any support for international terrorism.

Asymmetrical Response

Deterrence could be backed by a strategy of asymmetrical response.[24] Asymmetrical response involves, one, choosing actions that draw on one's strengths and exploit the opponent's weaknesses and, two, strategically overreacting rather than tailoring a response proportional to the nature and degree of the provocation. A credible threat to overreact should intimidate opponents from attempting trial-and-error tests of the *status quo* or small-scale but cumulatively substantial incremental efforts to alter it. Simply stated, the risks of provoking an overreaction could not be justified by any expected gains from small-scale aggression. And when challenges come, responding according to one's strengths would minimize the cost of carrying out the threat. The overwhelming application of military force in Afghanistan signaled such an asymmetrical strategy. So did the March 2002 report that the United States would develop nuclear weapons to be used in certain combat contingencies.

Recruiting Collaborators

A third element of a prudent hegemonic strategy would be to enlist partners in *ad hoc* coalitions, much as a sheriff organizes a posse to round up outlaws,[25] or to "deputize" client states to act as its proxy in confronting sources of localized instability. The organization of a "coalition of the willing" for the 2003 war against Iraq and seeking contributions of other countries for the postwar reconstructions of Iraq and Afghanistan exemplify this tactic.

Diplomacy of Reassurance

Finally, an effective strategy must diminish the risk of counter-hegemonic balancing, that is, other states joining together to check American hegemony. An imbalance of power does not necessarily provoke counter-balancing behavior. States balance not against power but against threats;[26] they balance against imbalanced power if and only if the imbalance portends a threat. American diplomacy, therefore, must reassure other strong countries that its power does not endanger them. Such a policy of reassurance must have two key characteristics. First, it must avoid promoting narrow self-interests. If the United States can show that it will sacrifice its narrow interests for the sake of common interests, then its predominance will be reassuring rather than threatening and others therefore will not be moved to balance against it. Second, when possible, it must act multilaterally rather than unilaterally.[27] A multilateral policy, which gives others a check on what the hegemon does, also is reassuring to them.

MORALITY

More than pragmatic considerations of self-interest justify the United States taking on the mantle of global leadership. Effectively functioning international systems are good things. Some level of stability is a necessary precondition for all other forms of human progress. Wars and civil disorder not only slaughter people in large numbers, but they also open the door to widespread abuses of human rights; for instance, war universally leads to the abuse of women through rampant forced prostitution and rape. War and civil disorder impoverish societies through the destruction of productive capacity and the shifting of investment into arms. War and civil disorder also breed tyrannical rule. Certainly, the philosopher Thomas Hobbes was only mildly exaggerating when he wrote that the condition of humankind in a state of war is "solitary, poor, nasty, brutish, and short."[28] Preventing the horrors of widespread instability, then, is intrinsically good and gives hegemony a moral quality. One writer contends that "making the system work [is] the highest morality because the alternative [is] chaos."[29] "[T]he benevolent hegemony exercised by the United States" writes another, "is good for a vast portion of the world's population."[30]

Indeed, providing global leadership is more than an optional exercise in altruism; it is a duty. President George Bush expressed this dramatically in his 1989 inaugural address. As his "first act as President," he petitioned God: "Make us strong to do Your work, willing to heed and hear Your will, and write on our hearts these words: 'Use power to help people.' For we are given power not to advance our own purposes, nor to make a great show in the world, nor a name. There is but one just use of power, and it is to serve people."

American power carries a moral burden. The United States "has an obligation commensurate with its capacity to nudge a fallen, but not hopeless, world toward greater peace."[31] The United States can provide the world with leadership, therefore it ought to; the United States can prevent disasters, therefore it ought to. Because the United States can stop bad things from happening, if it fails to act and evil triumphs, then it has permitted the evil and is morally culpable.*

HEGEMONISM AND U.S. DIPLOMATIC HISTORY

Hegemonism became a significant theme in U.S. foreign policy thinking during the twentieth century and has been the predominant logic since roughly 1950.

Before 1900, the United States could not be a global hegemon. At its founding, it was too weak and too focused on domestic matters to wield influence abroad. By the end of its first century, it had become one of the world's powers, marked by its victory in the Spanish-American War (1898) and acquisition of an empire in the Caribbean and in Asia. As early as 1900, some intellectuals predicted it would become the world's leading power.[32] Still, it was only one of several major powers, hardly the dominant nation.

World War I (1914–1918) raised its status temporarily and led some to a new self-perception: "At last America had found her new role in world affairs: she was to remake the world."[33] Its joining the war in 1917 affected both how the war was fought and how it was ended. President Wilson's vision of peace, articulated especially in his Fourteen Points, profoundly shaped the negotiation of the Armistice and the peace settlement. Nevertheless, Wilson was unable to dominate the Paris Peace Conference, which wrote the Treaty of Versailles. Nor did the Covenant of the League of Nations ascribe to the United States any special role or responsibility. The United States was and would continue to be an ordinary major power.

The decade of the 1930s was the midwife of hegemonic logic. The Great Depression and the outbreak of World War II (1939–1945) seemed to prove the dangers of instability and the need for effective international systems. Henry Luce's famous essay "The American Century" captured the idea:

> In the field of national policy, the fundamental trouble with Americans has been, and is, that whereas their nation became in the twentieth century the most powerful and most vital nation in the world, nevertheless, Americans were unable to accommodate themselves spiritually and practically to that fact. Hence they have

---

*Indeed, some proponents of hegemonism argue that the obligation goes beyond merely preventing evils from happening and includes the affirmative promotion of freedom and other good things. Those views generally represent a hybrid of the logics of hegemonism and liberalism.

failed to play their part as a world power—a failure which has had disastrous consequences for themselves and all mankind. And the cure is this: to accept wholeheartedly our duty and our opportunity as the most powerful and vital nation in the world and in consequence to exert upon the world the full impact of our influence for such purposes as we see fit and by such means as we see fit.[34]

The United States did enter the war in 1941, but its thinking about the postwar international system only partly reflected the logic of hegemonism. President Franklin Roosevelt sought to establish effective international political and economic systems, with the United Nations providing a system of collective security and the Bretton Woods system—the International Monetary Fund and the World Bank—providing effective international economic regulation. On the other hand, he did not presume that the United States would act as the world's leader. Rather, he saw it sharing leadership with Britain and the Soviet Union.

Roosevelt's expectations for shared leadership did not long survive the end of the war. Even before 1945, the Soviet Union's imposition of a communist government in Poland created friction with the United States and Britain. By 1947 the USSR clearly was an adversary rather than a partner. The same years also saw Britain, impoverished by the war, abdicate its leadership role. The United States stood alone atop the international pyramid. It alone, of the major powers, did not suffer the war's destruction on its territory. Its economy accounted for one-third of the world's production. It alone could deploy troops thousands of miles from its shores. It alone had the atomic bomb.

Hegemonic logic influenced containment, the basic U.S. foreign policy during the Cold War.* Containment sought to prevent the spread of communism beyond the territory it already dominated by the late 1940s. The Truman administration (1945–1953) established it and subsequent administrations, until the collapse of communism in Europe in 1989, continued it. They differed somewhat in the ways they pursued containment but never abandoned its basic goal.[35]

At its birth, containment derived more from a realist balance of power logic than from a hegemonic logic in that it aimed primarily to prevent the Soviet Union from becoming powerful enough to threaten U.S. national security. Nevertheless, hegemonic logic influenced containment's design in three important ways. First, the United States sought to maintain not equivalence but a preponderance of power.[36] Second, it set out to bind Western Europe and Japan to itself, both as necessary for preponderance over the Soviet Union and to prevent Germany and Japan from once again disrupting international order. Containing the allies, in other words, was integral to containing the USSR. Third, hegemonic logic guided the evolution of containment from being focused on the few regions where potential power was concentrated into a global program. The stability of otherwise peripheral

---

*As discussed in Chapters 3 and 5, containment also reflected logics of realism and liberalism, specifically in its pragmatic objective of maintaining the global balance of power and its ideological objective of stopping the spread of a social system opposed to capitalist democracy. The convergence of the logics of hegemonism, realism, and liberalism in support of one basic foreign policy strategy provided much of that policy's dominance during the Cold War.

regions (Africa, much of Asia) became important because of the beliefs that their disorder could threaten the economic vitality of Europe and Japan and that successful communist revolutions would cause more revolutions (the domino theory) and erode the credibility of the U.S. commitment to contain communism.

The United States also took on the leadership role in the international economic system. Through the Marshall Plan, it gave billions of dollars of aid to its allies in Europe and Asia in order to jump-start their stalled economies and thus the world economy. In order to uplift the economies of the other industrialized powers and thus to revitalize the world economy, it also opened the U.S. market to imports without reciprocal openness to its exports. These policies not only had economic rationales, but also supported containment: If Europe and Asia were prosperous, they would be less susceptible to communist takeover by revolution or election.

Through containment, hegemonic logic continued to dominate U.S. foreign policy during the Cold War. Its provided the rationale for two major wars (Korea and Vietnam), a series of military interventions (for example, Lebanon in 1958, the Dominican Republic in 1965, Grenada in 1982), several covert operations, and numerous political interventions throughout the world. Until the late 1960s, this assertive foreign policy was sustained by broad public and elite support based on a so-called Cold War consensus whose content reflected hegemonic logic. After the 1960s and the war in Vietnam, the Cold War consensus disintegrated.[37] The administrations of the 1970s therefore conceived of foreign policies based on logics other than hegemonism.

In the late 1970s, the Cold War intensified and the logic of hegemonism regained its preeminence. The Reagan administration (1981–1989) adopted a foreign policy based on a hybrid of two logics: hegemonism and liberalism, which advocates the spread of democracy and free market economies. Its diplomacy aimed to topple communist governments, including that of the Soviet Union, and replace them with democratic capitalist ones to achieve victory in the struggle with communism.

In 1989, peaceful revolutions toppled communist governments in eastern and central Europe and the Warsaw Pact ended. In 1991, the Soviet Union itself dissolved and Russia began a process of transition to democratic government. The United States occupied a position of unchallenged global dominance, its one challenger having left the field of competition and then disappeared. The international system had gone from being roughly bipolar (meaning two centers of power) to being unipolar. There was only one center of power: the United States. This had two opposing effects. On the one hand, the main barrier to U.S. world domination had disappeared, and along with it went much of the risk of seeking to stabilize the world. That served to reinforce hegemonism. On the other hand, for many people, the implosion of communism and Soviet power also seemed to lessen the dangers posed by instability, which tended to weaken the plausibility of hegemonism.

Nevertheless, at key junctures in their foreign policies—in the Persian Gulf, in Bosnia, in Kosovo—the administrations of George Bush (1989–1993) and Bill Clinton (1993–2001) adopted foreign policies justified by the rhetoric of hegemonism. The Bush administration articulated a concept of a New World Order, in which international institutions like the UN, behind American leadership, would finally establish and enforce the rule of law in international affairs. The Department of Defense in 1992 adopted a Defense Planning Guidance statement under which the United States "will retain the pre-eminent responsibility for addressing selectively those wrongs which threaten not only our interests, but those of our allies and friends, or which could seriously unsettle international relations."[38] The emphasis on responsibility, for attending to collective interests, for preventing instability, and the underlying goal of retaining primacy all reflected hegemonic logic.

The logic of hegemonism suffused the foreign policy rhetoric of Bill Clinton's administration. The United States, in an often repeated phrase, was "the indispensable nation." National Security Advisor Sandy Berger stated that "America has arrived at a moment when our strength and prosperity are unparalleled."[39] That perceived predominance was paired with a perceived need to act and to lead. The *Washington Post's* State Department correspondent characterized the thinking of Secretary of State Albright as "action is better than inaction, . . . great powers have an obligation to intervene against evil, and . . . the unique history of the United States gives this country the moral standing to weigh in on the side of good in almost any global trouble spot."[40] The justification for action was more than just moral, though. The United States intervenes abroad, Mr. Berger said, because "big wars that harm our interests almost always start as small wars that the world does not care enough to do something about;" thus the United States has intervened ". . . both to help others and to protect ourselves from the consequences of unchecked conflict and violence." The president himself articulated the broadest leadership function. "The train of globalization cannot be reversed. But it has more than one possible destination. If we want America to stay on the right track, if we want other people to be on that track and have the chance to enjoy peace and prosperity, we have no choice but to try to lead the train."[41]

The logic of hegemonism powerfully influences the thinking of the George W. Bush administration. Vice President Dick Cheney, Secretary of Defense Donald Rumsfeld, and Deputy Secretary of Defense Paul Wolfowitz were members of the Project for a New American Century, whose stated principles hold that the United States "cannot safely avoid the responsibilities of global leadership. . . . America has a vital role in maintaining peace and security in Europe, Asia, and the Middle East. If we shirk our responsibilities, we invite challenges to our fundamental interests. . . . The history of this century should have taught us to embrace the cause of American leadership."[42] September 11 amplified its importance.

After the terrorist attacks, the administration promoted a distinctive conception of the U.S. role: For its own benefit and for the good of the world, it would lead in the global struggle for freedom. "Steadfast in our purpose," the president concluded his 2002 State of the Union Address, "we now press on. We have known freedom's price. We have shown freedom's power. And in this great conflict, my fellow Americans, we will see freedom's victory."[43] He defined America's fundamental objective as preventing "the terrorists and [bad] regimes . . . from threatening the United States and the world." It would do this by promoting "a balance of power that favors freedom."

The wording of these passages reflects hegemonism in several ways. First, the threat is not just to the United States but to the world; the United States has, in other words, a global role. The goal of tamping down and defeating terrorism, moreover, is the contemporary equivalent of hegemonism's traditional purpose: establishing and maintaining a functioning international political system that keeps order and limits instability. The administration referred to the system as a balance of power, but that phrasing could be misleading. It did not mean an equilibrium or rough equality of two or more major powers. It meant, instead, the United States leading an overwhelming coalition of like-minded states (25-8). Leading a coalition is necessary because "[w]e have finite political, economic, and military resources" (9). Nevertheless, two key provisions demonstrate the assumption that the United States will be the preeminent nation. American military forces will be strong enough not only "to discourage aggression or any form of coercion against the United States, our allies, and our friends," but also "to dissuade potential adversaries from pursuing a military build-up in hopes of surpassing, or equaling, the power of the United States" (30). Second, if action by a coalition is not forthcoming, "we will be prepared to act apart when our interests and unique responsibilities require" (31).

The logic of hegemonism also prescribes playing a leadership role, as a matter of responsibility and moral obligation. "In a single instant, we realize that this will be a decisive decade in the history of liberty, that we've been called to a unique role in human events," the president told the nation in his State of the Union Address. "History has called America and our allies to action, and it is our responsibility and our privilege to fight freedom's fight." He especially emphasized the theme of moral obligation, which is so constitutive of hegemonism. "Building this just peace is America's opportunity, and America's duty," he instructed the class of 2002 West Point graduates. Moral obligation inheres not only in the notion of duty, but also in the quality of the external challenge. "We are in a conflict between good and evil, and America will call evil by its name. By confronting evil and lawless regimes, we do not create a problem, we reveal a problem. And we will lead the world in opposing it."*

CONCLUSION

The logic of hegemonism calls for the United States to provide leadership for the international political and economic systems. The United States is more secure when the international political system fosters order and stability and it is more prosperous when the international economic system fosters growth. The United States must provide leadership because international systems will break down without it and no other actor can provide it. Indeed, providing world leadership is a

---

*Defining the problem as confronting and defeating evil could be interpreted as suggesting a mission consistent with hegemonism, but the context of the speech shows that the enemy is terrorism and tyranny, which are evil, not evil in general. Still, portraying it as a struggle against evil terrorism universalizes the problem, keeping it from being a matter of U.S. national interests, narrowly construed.

moral obligation. Fulfilling the role of hegemonic leader potentially could bring the world into a new era of peace and cooperation.

Hegemonism has been the most prominent U.S. foreign policy logic since it became a superpower during World War II. The end of the Cold War and the war on terrorism have sealed and enhanced its predominant status. Whether the United States can, should, or will play the hegemonic role is open to a number of questions. One, of course, is whether there are any alternatives. We turn now to the examination of the other logics.

DISCUSSION QUESTIONS

1. If power is understood as material resources, the United States undoubtedly is the world's predominant power. Is the United States predominant if power is understood as political influence or control? If not, what factors would account for a gap between its influence or control and its resource endowment? If there is a gap, would it negate the capacity and need for the United States to provide the world with leadership?

2. Other states have three basic options for dealing with U.S. predominance: They can follow its leadership and collaborate in its undertakings; they can oppose it in order to balance against its predominance; or they can become free-riders, neither helping nor opposing it but taking advantage of the benefits of its leadership while letting the United States bear all the costs. Which of those options will the other major powers be likely to adopt?

3. Would the United States, under the logic of hegemonism, be able to balance its commitments and its resources or would it be likely to undertake commitments that would overextend its resources?

4. Leadership entails sacrificing short-term self-interests for the long-term common interest. How likely is it that the United States would be able to make that trade-off consistently?

5. In what ways would a foreign policy based on the logic of hegemonism be morally appropriate and in what ways would it be morally objectionable?

6. Over the long run, will a foreign policy based on the logic of hegemonism be viable in the U.S. political arena? What aspects of the logic are likely to make hegemonism attractive to the American people and what aspects are likely to produce opposition?

ENDNOTES

1. Rashid Khalidi, "Basic Truths from Both Sides of the Conflict," *The Chicago Tribune*, April 3, 2001.

2. A.F.K. Organski and Jacek Kugler, *The War Ledger* (Chicago: University of Chicago Press, 1981); Geoffrey Blainey, *The Causes of War*, 3rd ed. (New York: Free Press, 1988), 108–119.

3. Robert Kagan, "The Benevolent Empire," *Foreign Policy* 111 (Summer 1998): 24.

4. Henry Luce, "The American Century," *Life*, February 17, 1941, reprinted in *Society* 31, No. 5 (July/August, 1994): 4.

5. Madeleine Albright, *Commencement Address at Georgetown University, School of Foreign Service* (online), Washington D.C.: U.S. State Department, May 29, 1999. Accessed June 26, 2003. Available at: http://secretary.state.gov/www/statements/1999/990529.html.

6. Joseph S. Nye, Jr., *Bound To Lead: The Changing Nature of American Power* (New York: Basic Books, 1991).

7. The argument in this paragraph draws heavily on the ideas in Mancur Olson, *The Logic of Collective Action: Public Goods and the Theory of Groups* (Cambridge, MA: Harvard University Press, 1965).

8. Kagan, "Benevolent Empire," 31; John J. Mearsheimer, "Why We Will Soon Miss the Cold War," *The Atlantic Monthly*, Vol. 266, No. 2 (August 1990): 35–50.

9. Robert Litan, "The 'Globalization' Challenge: The U.S. Role in Shaping World Trade and Investment," *Brookings Review*, Vol. 18, No. 2 (Spring 2000), 36.

10. Kagan, "Benevolent Empire," 33.

11. *The National Security Strategy of the United States of America*, September 2002, 1.

12. International Monetary Fund, *International Monetary Statistics 2002*, Vol. 55 (August 2002): 912. The calculation uses the CIA's estimate of world GDP for 2000.

13. IMF, *International Financial Statistics*, Vol. 55 (November 2002), 64–65.

14. Stockholm International Peace Research Institute, *Volume of Transfers of Major Conventional Weapons.* (online) Accessed August 26, 2002. Available at: http://first.sipri.org/index.php?/page=step2.

15. IMF, *International Financial Statistics*, Vol. 55 (August 2002): 220, 364, 384, 476, 488, 902, 910.

16. Chalmers Johnson, *Blowback: The Costs and Consequences of American Empire* (New York: Owl Books/Henry Holt and Company, 2001), 5, 210.

17. International Institute for Strategic Studies, *The Military Balance 2000–01* (London: Oxford University Press, 2000).

18. John Orme, "The Utility of Force in a World of Scarcity," *International Security* 22, No. 3, (Winter 1997/1998), 138–167.

19. Robert L. Borosage, "Money Talks: The Implications of U.S. Budget Priorities," *Global Focus: U.S. Foreign Policy at the Turn of the Millennium*, ed. Martha Honey and Tom Barry (New York: St. Martin's Press, 2000), 4, 12.

20. Ibid., 11; Johnson, *Blowback*, 4.

21. Paul Kennedy, *The Rise and Fall of Great Powers* (New York: Random House, 1987).

22. Nye, *Bound To Lead*, 29–35, 190–195. The cultural bases of hegemony are also emphasized in Zbigniew Brzezinksi, *The Grand Chessboard: American Primacy and Its Geostrategic Imperatives* (New York: HarperCollins Publishers, Basic Books, 1997), Chapter 1.

23. Robert W. Tucker and David C. Hendrickson, *The Imperial Temptation* (New York: Council on Foreign Relations, 1992), 153.

24. The concept of asymmetrical response is developed in John Lewis Gaddis, *Strategies of Containment: A Critical Appraisal of Postwar American National Security Policy* (New York: Oxford University Press, 1982), 147–153.

25. Richard N. Haass, *The Reluctant Sheriff: The United States After the Cold War* (New York: Council on Foreign Relations Books, 1997).

26. Stephen M. Walt, *The Origin of Alliances* (Ithica, NY: Cornell University Press, 1987).

27. G. John Ikenberry, "Getting Hegemony Right" *The National Interest* (Spring 2001): 17–24; Richard N. Haass, "Five Not-So-Easy Pieces: The Debates on American Foreign Policy," *Brookings Review* Vol. 18, No. 2 (Spring): 38–40.

28. Thomas Hobbes, *Leviathan, or the Matter, Forme and Power of a Commonwealth, Ecclesiasticall and Civil*, ed. Michael Oakeshott (Oxford: Basil Blackwell, n.d.), 82.

29. Robert D. Kaplan, *Warrior Politics: Why Leadership Requires a Pagan Ethos* (New York: Random House, 2002), 139.

30. Kagan, "Benevolent Empire," 26.

31. Ernest W. Lefever, *America's Imperial Burden: Is the Past Prologue?* (Boulder, CO: Westview Press, 1999), x.

32. Thomas J. McCormick, *America's Half-Century: United States Foreign Policy in the Cold War and After*, 2nd ed. (Baltimore: The Johns Hopkins University Press, 1995), 17–21.

33. David Fromkin, *In the Time of the Americans* (New York: Alfred A. Knopf, 1995), 121.

34. Luce, "The American Century," 8.

35. Gaddis, *Strategies of Containment*.

36. Melvyn P. Leffler, *A Preponderance of Power: National Security, the Truman Administration, and the Cold War* (Stanford, CA: Stanford University Press, 1992).

37. Ole R. Holsti, "The Three-Headed Eagle: The United States and System Change," *International Studies Quarterly*, Vol. 23, No. 3 (September 1979) 339–359; Ole R. Holsti and James N. Rosenau, *American Leadership in World Affairs: Vietnam and the Breakdown of Consensus)* (Boston: Allen & Unwin, 1984); Michael Mandelbaum and William Schneider, "The New Internationalism: Public Opinion and American Foreign Policy," in *Eagle Entangled U.S. Foreign Policy in a Complex World*, ed. Kenneth A. Oye, Donald Rothchild, and Robert J. Lieber (New York: Longman, 1979); Eugene Wittkopf, *Faces of Internationalism: Public Opinion and American Foreign Policy*, (Durham, NC: Duke University Press, 1990).

38. Quoted in Barry R. Posen and Andrew L. Ross, "Competing Visions for U.S. Grand Strategy," *International Security* 21, No. 3 (Winter 1996–1997), 34.

39. Sandy R. Berger, *American Leadership in the 21st Century: Remarks at the National Press Club* (online), Washington, D.C.: U.S. State Department, January 6, 2000. Accessed April 17, 2001. Available at: www.state.gov/www/policy_remarks/2000/000106_berger.htm.

40. Thomas W. Lippman, *Madeleine Albright and the New American Diplomacy*, (Boulder, CO: Westview Press, 2000), 90.

41. President William Clinton, "Remarks at the University of Nebraska at Kearney," *Weekly Compilation of Presidential Documents*, Vol 30, No. 49 (December 11, 2000): 3030.

42. Project for a New American Century, *Statement of Principles* (online). Accessed June 6, 2003. Available at http://www.newamericancentury.org/statementofprinciples.htm.

43. President George W. Bush, "Address Before a Joint Session of the Congress on the State of the Union, January 29, 2002," *Weekly Compilation of Presidental Documents*, February 1, 2002; President George W. Bush, "Commencement Address at the United States Military Academy in West Point, New York, June 1, 2002," *Weekly Compilation of Presidential Documents*, June 7, 2002. Office of the President, *National Security Strategy of the United States*, September 2003. Unless otherwise indicated, citations are to the *National Security Strategy*.

3

The Logic of Realism

On July 19, 2000, Representative Floyd Spence opened hearings of the House Armed Services Committee on the "Military Capabilities of the People's Republic of China." He warned of China's "impressive" military buildup, which "will likely have a significant impact on America's ability to defend its vital interests in East Asia. . . ."[1] Expert witnesses then analyzed the growing Chinese military threat. Their testimony painted a grim picture: China's growing power threatens vital U.S. interests; China may assert its power, leading to eventual military clash or war with the United States; even if China does not now intend to commit aggression, the United States must act as if it will, because assuming otherwise could lead to disaster; prudence requires increasing U.S. military strength and fortifying anti-China alliances to deny China any predominance in power. That portrayal of the challenge facing the United States and the appropriate strategy flows directly from the logic of realism.

INTRODUCTION

Overview

This chapter presents the logic of realism. In doing so, it develops the following main points:

- Because there is no effective world government, international relations is inherently a competition for the power necessary to guarantee national security;
- military power is the essence of national power;
- therefore, foreign policy must attend first and foremost to maintaining the balance of power by increasing the country's military power and preventing adversaries from gaining power;

- balancing power involves the use of three classes of strategies: internal balancing, external balancing, and reassurance; the logic of realism splits into two schools, called militant realism and diplomatic realism, over the value of reassurance strategies;
- the United States has no national interests beyond maintaining the global balance of power;
- the United States has sufficient power to maintain the balance of power but its power is limited and therefore must be focused on that purpose only;
- the United States has no moral obligations to the rest of the world because morality has no place in international relations;
- American foreign policy behavior has been substantially consistent with the logic of realism but only a few administrations have used that logic to explain or justify their policies.

As with the logic of hegemonism, the logic of realism seeks stability in the international system. Its commitment to stability is more limited, however. It seeks, at best, to prevent major war and is indifferent to wars or other forms of instability that do not threaten to disrupt the balance of power. Indeed, under some circumstances, realism encourages certain kinds of war. Unlike hegemonism, moreover, realism does not seek stability as a primary end. Stability may result from realist diplomacy but is not its immediate intention. The immediate goal of realist logic is to protect the country's security by whatever means necessary. If that is achieved, other good things are possible; failing that, all goes down the drain.

Realism is the oldest and the dominant approach to the interpretation and practice of world politics. As a body of thought, it subsumes several distinct theories and schools. All varieties of realism, nevertheless, share certain core assumptions. The differences represent variations on a common theme. The variations are significant though. They prescribe quite different strategies for dealing with rivals. More precisely, they determine whether the response to a challenger would be primarily and essentially conflictual or would include significant cooperative initiatives. The next section of this chapter presents the common core of realism and briefly introduces the most important division within the realist community.

REALIST THEORY OF INTERNATIONAL POLITICS

In the logic of realism, national interests are determined by the structure of world politics. Its most basic characteristic is its anarchy: There is no world government to exercise control over states or other parties to world politics. International institutions—the United Nations and other international organizations, international law, and international morality—are creations of the most powerful states to serve their interests and have little power independent of those states. They can be effective instruments for powerful states when it suits their purposes. By design, however, they cannot constrain powerful states.

States are the most important entities in world politics because they exercise more power than any other class of actors. States do so because, more than others, they organize power: They mobilize populations into large militaries; they tax economies and thus pool substantial financial resources to be applied to political purposes; they control the flow of commerce across national boundaries and thus can manipulate foreign trade to reward or punish others; they police territory and thus can sponsor or suppress terrorist operations. That states wield the most power in international affairs is embodied in the principle of sovereignty: States are independent of higher authority; they are not obliged under law or morality to do what any other entity tells them to do.

States pursue national interests. Their primary interest is security: States seek first to insure that they will survive, keep their territory and independence, and be safe from attack. Because the international system is anarchic, states bear responsibility for making themselves secure and then promoting other national interests. The international political system is a self-help system. Self-help depends on power.

Although power is a complex phenomenon, it ultimately depends on military strength.[2] War is the final resort in conflicts that cannot be resolved by other means. To be able to defeat another country in war is to be able to impose one's will. Indeed, a powerful state usually will not have to wage war to impose its will: It can intimidate others into conceding. No matter what its other capabilities, a state that lacks military power is weak and vulnerable. Military power is integral to all power and essential to all other instruments of foreign policy. One U.S. diplomat put it colorfully: "Diplomacy without the threat of force is like baseball without a bat."[3]

Military strength, in turn, depends primarily on the size and productivity of a nation's economy. Large, rich states can muster large, well-equipped militaries; small or poor states cannot.

Power is relative. War is decided by the relative strength of the opposed militaries. Similarly, economic capacity is relative. Whether a country's economy is large enough and productive enough depends on the size and productivity of the economies of other countries.

A country's policies affect its power. Some policies increase power by causing resources to increase faster than do those of other countries; other policies decrease power by allowing resources to grow more slowly than do those of other countries; still other policies cause an absolute decrease in power by squandering it on foolish undertakings.

International politics is fundamentally conflictual. States compete for inherently scarce resources and values. Territory is limited; any territory gained by one state must be lost to at least one other. Control over territory means control over the resources of that territory, so to some extent wealth is limited. Status (honor, prestige) is limited; for one state to gain higher status, others must be relegated to a lower one. Most importantly, though, power and security are limited. Power is limited because if one state gains power, it is better able to compel others and to resist their efforts to compel. Hence for any state to gain power, others must lose power proportionally. Security is limited because, in a self-help system, security depends on having sufficient power to protect oneself. But the power to protect oneself also enables one to endanger others. Hence, for any state to become more secure, others must become less secure; for any state to be absolutely secure, all others must be absolutely insecure.

International relations is, predictably, an arena of chronic conflict in which "peace and harmony are not the natural order of things but temporary oases in a perilous world where stability could be preserved only by vigilant effort."[4] Hence states must be power-seeking entities. Were a state to cease to be power-seeking, one of two consequences would follow. Either it would be gobbled up by its neighbors, in which case it would cease to exist, or it would experience a series of failures to protect its interests, leading to its learning to seek power. The structure of the system, in other words, socializes states to be power-seeking. The consequence is a tragic paradox: Even states that would prefer not to be aggressors are driven by the defensive motive of self-preservation in an anarchic international system to be aggressive. Not to do so is "foolish behavior" that "invariably has negative consequences." States, "if they want to survive," must expand their power while weakening their potential adversaries.[5]

Schools of Thought Within Realism

States cannot be constantly in conflict with every other state. To avoid squandering their power, they must choose their struggles selectively. They must conserve their resources for coping with the state or states that pose the most immediate or the most serious danger to their security. In addition, states often find it convenient or necessary to enlist others against a common foe. In those instances, the existential conflict of interest must be put aside while they pursue their temporary shared interest.

States, therefore, must decide which states pose threats requiring a response. The great divide among realists concerns exactly that judgment. Does every predominance, or move toward predominance, represent a threat to the other states in the international system?

One school of realism, here called *militant realism*, holds that it does. These realists argue that states cannot assume that a rising state will not use its power for aggression. One cannot know with certainty what another state's motives are. Even if one could, motives could change. So if a state has a useable superiority of power, one must assume that it might use its power, and, given the gravity of the stakes, one must act on the assumption that it will. Indeed, according to the theory, any powerful state likely will use its power to augment its power, aggressively, if necessary. No matter how powerful and secure a state might be now, it cannot be certain that another state will not rise to challenge its power position in the future. Therefore, to ensure its power and security in the future, it must increase its power in the present.

The other school of realist thought, here called *diplomatic realism*, contends that there can be slippage between the distribution of power and the perception of threat. First of all, some forms of power are better suited to self-defense than to offense. If the increase in power is predominantly and clearly of the defensive variety, it ought not to endanger the security of other states and thus ought not to create a threat. Moreover, in assessing threats, states consider other states' inclination to use their power. States that adhere to an aggressive ideology or that have unsatisfied grievances ("revisionist states") become dangerous when they gain power, which invariably would have offensive potential. States that are satisfied with their place in the international scheme of things ("status quo states"), on the other hand, would be unlikely to use their power offensively. Revisionist states are threatening, while status quo states are not. States can enhance their security, then, by converting revisionist states into status quo states.

Militant realism assumes that the essential condition of international relations is bipolarity: the division of the world's states into two camps, one headed by the challenger state, the other by the leading state of those who feel threatened by the challenger. The enmity between the challenger state and the challenged states is fixed; they are enemies. Relations are zero-sum; whatever benefits one harms the other equally; no common interests are possible. Diplomatic realism assumes that the essential condition of international relations is multipolarity. Under multipolarity, relationships are fluid. States that are antagonistic today may join forces tomorrow against a third party. Because one might need to join tomorrow with today's adversary, the relationship is not zero-sum; one would not benefit by utterly destroying one's adversary; common interests exist. Because the adversary might need one as an ally in the future, its enmity is variable and its motives open to adjustment.

U.S. NATIONAL INTERESTS

The United States has interests similar to those of any other great power. First and foremost, it must enhance its security. Therefore, second, it must maximize its power, both by taking advantage of opportunities to increase its power and by eschewing its wasteful use. Third, it must prevent any other country from gaining a position of dominance. Fourth, in pursuit of the second and third interest, it must prevent other powers from controlling the resources essential to military power or the economic production necessary for military power. "Geopolitically," writes Henry Kissinger, "America is an island off the shores of the large landmass of Eurasia, whose resources and population far exceed those of the United States. The domination by a single power of either of Eurasia's two principal spheres—Europe or Asia—remains a good definition of strategic danger. . . . For such a grouping would have the capacity to outstrip America economically and, in the end, militarily."[6] The ability to shape events is the ability to augment one's power and to avoid any incremental loss of power. To lose that ability is to endanger the security of the country, eventually if not immediately.

Were another state to control most of the world's power resources, the United States would be gravely endangered. Its actual conquest would be an extreme and unlikely outcome. The likely danger would be the loss of national autonomy as the militarily superior adversary could threaten to use force against the United States and thus achieve political domination through intimidation. Alternatively, a political struggle could end in war, which also would mean a real loss of security, especially if the United States lost.

Nor can the United States rely on the oceans or nuclear weapons to safeguard the homeland. The idea that the oceans assure security rests on three assumptions: that the threat to be prevented is an attack on the U.S. mainland, that the attack would be an amphibious assault from an extracontinental power, and that the United States is able to deploy sufficient naval and coastal defense forces to make such an attack infeasible. Those assumptions are unduly optimistic. Four scenarios illustrate why the oceans provide no guarantee of military security. First, a challenger could pose a threat to Hawaii by providing moral and material support for indigenous groups seeking independence. Second, Canada or Mexico could fall to conquest or domination by or enter into an alliance with a country seeking global hegemony, thereby becoming a base for invasion of the U.S. homeland.[7] Third, the oil reserves of the Persian Gulf could be denied to the United States, sending it into a prolonged period of economic decline, weakening its armed forces to a dangerous level. Fourth, China continues its spectacular economic growth for several decades, making it the world's largest economy and giving it military and political hegemony in Asia. It then engages the United States in an arms race, which harms the American economy more than it harms China's. Incrementally and continuously, the power gap widens until the United States also is forced to accept Chinese dominance or be blackmailed by threats of military action.

Nuclear weapons can assure security no more than can the oceans. "[G]reat powers still compete for security even under the nuclear shadow, sometimes intensely, and war between them remains a real possibility."[8] That is so for four reasons. First, nuclear weapons, by themselves, have no military significance. They must first be coupled with delivery vehicles, such as ballistic missiles or manned bombers, which are able to penetrate an enemy's defenses. In the past, no defense has existed against ballistic missile attack, so nuclear weapons seemed to be ultimate weapons. That, however, was a function of current technological evolution, not a fact of nature. The history of warfare has been a constant competition between offensive and defensive technologies and tactics, without any final outcome. Nuclear weapons have not ended that history. Revolutions in computing and sensing technologies could make effective defenses against ballistic missiles possible. Whether any country could deploy a fully effective defense against ballistic missiles or other nuclear weapons delivery vehicles would depend on several factors, including the relative level of technological development of the offensive and defensive forces, the diversity of the offensive arsenal, and the numbers of offensive and defensive weapons. Ultimately, an offensive/defensive nuclear arms race would be decided by the relative economic capabilities of the parties.

Second, in the extreme, relative nuclear strength matters. If a nuclear war were to be waged, a process of attrition would ensue. Each side's striking capability would dwindle as its forces were used to strike the enemy and were destroyed by the enemy's strikes. In the end, one party would be thoroughly disarmed while the other retained some reserve forces. The latter would have military victory and could use its military superiority to dictate the terms of peace, that is, surrender, to the loser.

Third, relative nuclear strength matters politically. To be stronger than one's adversary means that one will gain deference from the adversary and from third parties. Military inferiority, including nuclear inferiority, is a recipe for political inferiority.

Fourth, even if American nuclear forces were sufficient to deter nuclear attack on the United States, they would not be usable for nonnuclear situations. Indeed, a stable deterrence relationship would seem to make nonnuclear military aggression safe because the victims of the aggression could not escalate the fighting to the nuclear level without guaranteeing their own destruction. Nonnuclear challenges require the capacity for nonnuclear response.

It does not matter if these scenarios of danger despite the oceans and nuclear weapons are unlikely. It is sufficient that they are possible. That they could happen requires American policymakers to direct policy to their prevention, within the demands of other national interests and the constraints of U.S. power.

U.S. POWER

The United States has sufficient power to attain its basic national interests but cannot fulfill the responsibilities implied by the logic of hegemonism and should not try. Despite its tremendous resources, the United States is no more than an ordinary great power. Henry Kissinger puts the point well: "The end of the Cold War has created what some observers have called a "unipolar" or "one-superpower" world. But the United States is actually in no better position to dictate the global agenda unilaterally than it was at the beginning of the Cold War. America is more preponderant than it was ten years ago, yet, ironically, power has also become more diffuse. Thus, America's ability to employ it to shape the rest of the world has actually decreased. . . . America will be the greatest and most powerful nation, but a nation with peers; the *primus inter pares* but nonetheless a nation like others."[9]

Limits to U.S. Power

Five reasons dictate a modest view of U.S. power. The first two build upon a distinction between potential power and actualized power. (Potential power is the resource base that can be employed to support foreign policy; actualized power is the actual level of influence or control a nation exercises.) They identify forces that cause a slippage between potential power and actualized power: hindrances to the conversion of power into influence or control and the impact of domestic political forces in the United States. The remaining three indicate that U.S. superiority in power resources is not likely to continue because of the emergence of competitors and adversaries abroad, dynamics of balancing behavior in a unipolar international system, and the consequences of imperial overstretch.

Impediments to Converting Potential Power into Control

U.S. influence over international affairs is limited, first, by difficulties in transforming power into political control.[10] The process is complex and tricky. It is affected, among other matters, by the willingness of the United States to use its resources to get its way, by the willingness of the other party to go along with U.S. wishes or to bear the costs of resistance, and by the other party's perception of U.S. willingness to carry out its threats and promises, that is, the *credibility* of those threats and promises. Charles William Maynes certainly is correct that "the United States is perhaps now the only country in the world that can, to a very significant measure, get its way internationally if it is absolutely determined to bend others to its will. What is required is a sufficient commitment of political, economic and military resources."[11] In reality, though, the United States generally will not be "absolutely determined" and therefore will not commit sufficient resources. In many instances, an *asymmetry of interests* (the issues at stake being relatively unimportant for the United States but of vital importance to the other party) will produce an *asymmetry of will*, with the United States being less willing to use its resources than the other party is to resist. In just those instances, the credibility of U.S. policy will be low, too. Under those circumstances of low credibility and an adverse asymmetry of will, the United States very likely will not prevail in a struggle, despite superior resources.

Situations in which an asymmetry of will benefiting the other party more than compensates for an asymmetry of resources in favor of the United States are fairly common. They can occur whenever the United State pursues interests that are less than vital or are long-term (while the consequences for the adversary are immediate) or the United States is distracted by several simultaneous important commitments (while the problem is the adversary's overriding concern).[12]

Domestic Political Resistance

Internal political forces limit the actual American sway over international affairs despite its predominance in resources. Scholars and practitioners have often noted how domestic politics and public opinion weaken foreign policy.[13] Domestic political influences cut in both directions, of course, sometimes impelling the United States into imprudent action. Here, though, the critical consideration is that they sometimes constrain foreign policy makers from action. Former Defense Secretary James Schlesinger's diagnosis is apt. The public is more hesitant about an activist foreign policy than are many elites and "in the American democracy policies that are unsupportable by the public simply are unsustainable;" consequently, policy makers must exercise a "rigorous selectivity."[14] Two academic experts concur: "[S]hort of a compelling argument about an extant threat, the people of the United States are unlikely to want to invest much money or many lives either in global police duties . . . or in trying to cow others into accepting U.S. hegemony. . ."[15]

Domestic divisions also breed the gap between potential and actualized power. Except in rare conditions of severe international crisis, the early stages of war, or a popular war, Americans are not unified about foreign affairs. In almost all situations, they disagree over the goals of policy or the means for pursuing goals. Divisions are to be found across branches of government, across departments of the executive bureaucracy, among regions, between elites and masses, among adherents of different logics, and across ethnic and racial differences. Such divisions contribute to asymmetries of will. They also cause the United States to speak with many voices, thereby confusing allies and opponents about what the country wants and what it is willing to do. Promises and threats become less believable, especially to those with whom the United States is locked in conflict, whose own interests would be compromised were the United States to have its way, and who therefore are psychologically motivated to believe indications that the United States will give way. As American credibility erodes, so does its real political influence.

New Challengers

American primacy is a dwindling commodity. Other powers will emerge to challenge its predominance. One source of future challenges will be the dynamics of economic development. The law of uneven development dictates that the United States will not stay alone atop the global distribution of economic production. It occupies its pinnacle largely due to fortuitous circumstance: The United States is much larger than other advanced industrialized states and is much more industrialized than other large countries. That condition cannot continue indefinitely. As technology, knowledge, and modern organization diffuse to China and India, they will overtake the United States. Hence, "China and the United States are destined to be adversaries as China's power grows."[16]

The other source of future challenges is less certain but must be considered. New global cleavages may emerge, providing for a coalescence of new opposition forces. After the collapse of state socialism in East Europe and the fragmentation and demoralization of the Third World, international relations became highly atomized. Grand, global issues were replaced by hundreds of particular bilateral and subregional conflicts. That condition tempers the natural inclination to join together to challenge the United States. That state of world politics, however, is historically anomalous. New lines of cleavage are likely, though no one can predict what they will be. One famous essay, for instance, forecast that the fault lines of world politics will lie along the boundaries of cultural groupings, with the resulting "clash of civilizations" pitting Western liberal democratic capitalism against, among others, Islamic, East Asian, and Eastern Orthodox civilizations.[17]

Counter-hegemonic Balancing

U.S. primacy will call forth opposition from other powerful states to counterbalance its power. "As nature abhors a vacuum, so international politics abhors unbalanced power."[18] Proponents of hegemonism may argue that the United States can make its preponderance tolerable by acting to promote common interests rather than narrow U.S. interests, but they are wrong. Even if the United States were to orient its foreign policy toward some common good, other states would remain anxious. "Concentrated power invites distrust because it is so easily misused" (29). Just as the United States cannot count on the good intentions of others, so others cannot count on the good intentions of the United States. But hegemonism is wrong on another count. The very primacy of the United States will lead it to act in ways that alienate and scare others. Even "with benign intent, the United States has behaved and, until its power is brought into balance, will continue to behave in ways that sometimes frighten others" because "constancy of threat produces constancy of policy; absence of threat permits policy to become capricious. When few if any vital interests are endangered, a country's policy becomes sporadic and self-willed" (28, 29).

Overcommitment

The final reason why U.S. primacy will dwindle is suggested in this comment. "[F]or a nation as militarily powerful as the United States," writes a leading realist scholar, "the temptation to do too much is more serious than the temptation to do too little. The greatest nemesis of an imperial power—and the United States is an imperial power—is overreach."[19] The problem is the trade-off between expenditures to meet current commitments and investments for long-term preparedness. Assuming that the public is unwilling to fund such expenditures by decreasing current consumption—that is, they choose both guns and butter, at least in the short run—the revenues for current commitments inevitably are taken from the pool of resources available for investment for future growth. This accelerates that long-term loss of status and can be arrested only by shucking off commitments. Paradoxically, though, terminating commitments erodes influence in the short-term as other states, seeing U.S. strategic retrenchment, have less incentive to give much weight to its diplomatic initiatives. Therefore, one way or the other, U.S. influence has dwindled and will continue to dwindle. "Hegemony is always impermanent. . . ."[20]

Implications of Limitations on Power

Being the sole superpower poses the greatest danger to long-term security. It fosters dangerous attitudes of arrogance and complacency which in turn lead to imprudent diplomacy. Although the United States cannot script its future, it can shape it. That it will cease to be number one is written in the book of destiny; when it loses dominance, how far it falls, and how dangerous is the power transition, are not. The United States can shape a new balance of power that will provide for its security. Its present dominance gives it the leverage to control its destiny, if it uses the opportunity wisely.

Using power wisely requires awareness that it is variable and limited. Expending power prodigally squanders it. Alternatively, power can be invested wisely so that its use yields an increase in power. Expensive commitments undertaken in pursuit of some moralistic whim or sentimental attachment or to meet expectations of the superpower's role erode the nation's base of power and therefore are to be avoided. Moreover, they are likely to intensify the sense of threat of other major powers, thereby accelerating the process of balancing. "Any attempt . . . to assert hegemony is bound to fail as it will stimulate resistance, something that will make the costs of acting in the world greater and the benefits smaller."[21]

Conversely, undertakings that enhance American prestige, increase its economic vitality, attract powerful allies, or weaken adversary alliances make the United States more powerful and are to be encouraged. If, however, the United States believes that it is invincible, it will scorn such wisdom, thereby laying the foundation for future security threats.[22]

Nevertheless, no matter how prudently the United States uses its power, its decline from primacy is inevitable. As Paul Kennedy aptly puts it, "it is wise to recall Voltaire's question: 'If Rome and Carthage fell, which power is then immortal?' And his answer was 'None.'"[23]

Strategies of Realist Balancing[24]

To summarize, despite the protection of the oceans and the existence of nuclear weapons, the United States is not absolutely secure. Its vital national interests require it to increase its power while preventing any other state from acquiring sufficient power to dominate Europe, East Asia, or the Persian Gulf. In other words, it must follow what is called a *balance of power policy*. Over the millennia, realism's practitioners and theoreticians have developed myriad strategies for a balance of power policy, which can be grouped into three categories: internal balancing, external balancing, and reassurance.

Internal Balancing

Internal balancing refers to means of increasing the state's power resources. It can be done in four ways. First, develop the resource base of the country by fostering economic growth, so as to attain economic self-sufficiency, especially in key power resources, and to strengthen the armed forces. Second, to conserve resources, focus foreign policy on those regions that control the key resources that determine the global balance of power: Europe, East Asia, and the Persian Gulf. Mexico and Canada are important, too, for their geographic proximity. All other parts of the world are essentially irrelevant and should receive as little attention as possible. Third, design international economic policy to generate relative, not absolute, gains. Trade policy must seek not primarily to make the United States more prosperous but to increase its productivity and prosperity more than that of other parties. Fourth, use military force when it would enhance the nation's prestige, that is, its reputation for being willing to fight wars. Prestige is crucial to the credibility of threats and promises and hence to its ability to influence others through military coercion.

External Balancing

External balancing seeks to alter the distribution of power abroad. First, manipulate the system of interstate alliances. Alliances should be formed against any state that challenges the United States, including states seeking regional hegemony. The goal is to keep the U.S. coalition at least as strong as its rival's. Alliance partners therefore must be chosen *solely* for their contribution to the balance of power; the United States must ally itself with any nation whose power would make a necessary contribution to counterbalancing the power of the challenger state. Any other consideration—such as emotional ties or the attractiveness of their domestic political systems—must be excluded. If necessary to preserve the balance of power, the United States must ally itself with and strengthen the most odious of dictators. Nor can the United States allow prior conflicts to block the formation of balancing alliances. It must be willing to form alliances with former enemies. "An enemy of my enemy is my friend," says the proverbial wisdom.

Second, tolerate spheres of influence. Realism tends to accept spheres of influence in any case because strong states inevitably dominate their weak neighbors. The need to be able to partner up with other states reinforces that tolerance. Seeking to eradicate spheres of influence merely alienates potential allies while multiplying potential adversaries.

Third, weaken adversary states. Doing this may be extremely costly and risky, so it is undertaken only in an exceptional circumstance: when the other state is deemed to pose a threat to the United States, either because it is gaining a dangerous level of predominance or because it combines hostile intentions with substantial power. Several tactics can be used to weaken another state, including:

- Prying away its allies, thus weakening the power of its coalition.
- Weakening its hold on its sphere of influence, thus reducing its control over valuable resources, if countries were plied from the sphere of influence, or lessening its resources for application elsewhere by causing it to allocate its resources to bolstering its sphere of influence.
- Curtailing trade unless it was certain that it increased one's own economic strength more than it increased that of the adversary. Economic sanctions would be applied to weaken the adversary's economy and therefore its power potential.
- Executing covert or paramilitary operations to remove a hostile government and install one friendly to the United States.
- Waging preventive war while the adversary still is relatively weak, in order to defeat it and weaken it permanently.
- Fighting any war necessary to prevent developments that would threaten the equilibrium.

External balancing by coalition formation is most appropriate in multipolar international systems. Such systems are composed of several major powers, all at roughly the same level of power. Movement of a major power into or out of a coalition greatly affects the capabilities of the coalition. Bipolar systems, in which two countries dominate world politics, on the other hand, lead to an emphasis on internal balancing by directly weakening the opponent. In a bipolar setting, none of the other countries is crucial to the security of either of the superpowers. Adding or subtracting countries from the coalition or sphere of a superpower does little to enhance or degrade its security.

Reassurance

As under the logic of hegemonism, a state adopts strategies of reassurance in order to prevent other states from balancing against it. Strategies of reassurance seek to convince other states that one's own power does not threaten them. They would be appropriate only if it is uncertain whether another country will use its power to harm one's own interests. A strategy of reassurance could include the following tactics:

- Acceptance of another power's sphere of influence.
- A policy of détente. At a minimum, détente means entering into serious negotiations with another power. The willingness to negotiate implies that the powers have some shared interests, not just conflicting ones. It also suggests a willingness to compromise, which means accommodating the interests of the other party. Successful negotiations mean resolution of certain conflicts among the parties and can lead to the creation of a pattern of cooperation.
- A policy of appeasement, in extreme cases, in which the legitimate demands of a revisionist power are accepted in order to convert it into a status quo power.
- The deliberate and intentional abandonment of seeking unilateral gains at the expense of others.

Adherents of realist logic often vigorously disagree with each other about general strategy and specific policies. Those debates reflect the divergences between the militant and diplomatic schools of realism. They reflect the contradictory directives of the strategies of reassurance, which are more likely to be favored by adherents of diplomatic realism, and most of the strategies of internal and external balancing. As Kenneth Waltz noted many years ago, "There is in international politics no simple rule to prescribe just how belligerent, or how peaceful, any given state should strive to appear in order to maximize its chances of living at peace with neighboring states. One cannot say in the abstract that for peace a country must arm, or disarm, or compromise, or stand firm."[25] The choice of a line of policy depends on judgments about the distribution of power and the intentions of other states. Disagreements among realists about those judgments cannot be resolved by the logic of realism.

MORALITY

Moral norms should not be applied to international affairs.[26] International anarchy denies that ethical, moral, and legal principles—beyond the basic principles of international law, such as diplomatic immunity, which are necessary for the conduct of diplomacy—have any place in world politics. International politics is a realm of amorality in which the only legitimate national goal is the promotion of the national interest. Nevertheless, realism is not amoral. Rather, it develops the counterintuitive position that allowing moral and legal norms to trump national interest leads to immoral outcomes.

International anarchy means that there is little international morality or international law. International community is weak, so states feel relatively little obligation to sacrifice their interests for the well-being of others. Nor are there strong institutions to make and enforce international law. What appear to be international morality and law have no objective basis but instead are creations of world politics, shaped by the distribution of power. By and large, they are creations of the powerful states to reflect and promote their principles and interests. When the powerful states seem to comply with international morality and law, it is because it serves their interests. When compliance no longer serves their interests, they follow their interests. When weak states seem to comply with international law and morality, it is because they are accommodating the interests and power of the powerful states. Talk about morality is mere hypocrisy.

The weakness of international morality and law is self-reinforcing. International morality and law are weak because, when push comes to shove, states pursue their interests. States have no choice but to do so. A state that abided by moral norms and law without the assurance that every other state would do so would leave itself vulnerable to a shift of power in favor of the less scrupulous states. But because international institutions are weak, there is no effective agency to enforce international morality and law. Therefore, no state can assume that other states will comply with law and morality when it would conflict with their interests. Therefore, no state can afford to allow law and morality to override the dictates of its national interests. States pursue their interests at the expense of law and morality, which insures that international morality, international law, and international institutions remain weak.

Consequently, actions that under conventional morality would be considered improper sometimes are necessary and therefore acceptable in foreign policy. War is permissible if necessary to protect national security. Covert operations to overthrow hostile governments or purchase influence may be the only means to prevent a shift of power to one's enemies or to induce a favorable shift of power. Alliances with odious dictators are permissible because they control their country's power.

Nevertheless, following the logic of realism in the design of foreign policy actually will be morally superior to following a policy that is self-consciously moral. That is so for three reasons.

First, foreign policy makers have an overriding moral obligation to the national community. As office holders, they are constrained by their roles. They must comply with the demands of the office rather than use the office as a platform from which to pursue their personal visions of right and wrong. The foreign policy official is morally bound to protect the nation and has no authority to endanger national security, sacrifice national interests, or forego an opportunity to augment national power.[27] Thus leaders are placed in a dilemma: They "may have to choose between behaving *immorally* in international politics in order to preserve the state, on the one hand, and, on the other, abandoning their *moral* obligation to ensure their state's survival in order to follow preferred ways of acting in international politics."[28]

Second, a foreign policy based on moral principles is likely to produce outcomes whose consequences are quite immoral. Anarchy renders morality problematic. Morality can guide behavior within a political community because there is a common conception of what constitutes morality, because the effective operation of the norm of reciprocity provides some assurance that moral action by one party will elicit moral action by others, and because the state is able to enforce laws that embody the common morality. None of those conditions apply to international affairs. A foreign policy driven by morality, therefore, would lead the United States into needless and otherwise avoidable conflicts with other states whose moral code diverges from its own.

Prohibitions on the use of force and war are especially pernicious. Consider, for instance, Henry Kissinger's indictment of Woodrow Wilson's rhetorical commitment to collective security as implying that "it was henceforth America's duty to oppose aggression *everywhere*. . . . Even at his most exuberant, [The realist Theodore] Roosevelt would never have dreamt of so sweeping a sentiment portending global interventionism. But, then, he was the warrior-statesman; Wilson was the prophet-priest. Statesmen, even warriors, focus on the world in which they live; to prophets, the 'real' world is the one they want to bring into being."[29]

Worse, letting morality dictate policy changes the nature of conflict in morally unacceptable ways. George Kennan warns of the dangers of moralism. By creating "indignation" against the other party, which is viewed as guilty of wrongful action, "the legalistic approach to world affairs . . . makes violence more enduring, more terrible, and more destructive to political stability than did the older motives of national interest. A war fought in the name of high moral principle finds no early end short of some form of total domination."[30]

Third, whereas following morality leads to the expansion and intensification of violence, following the dictates of the national interest leads, paradoxically, to relative peace. The reasoning is portrayed well in Henry Kissinger's approving description of the thinking of his realist boss, Richard Nixon:

> If the major powers, including the United States, pursued their self-interests rationally and predictably, . . . an equilibrium would emerge from the clash of competing interests. . . . Nixon counted on a balance of power to produce stability, and considered a strong America essential to the global equilibrium. . . .
> "I think it will be a safer world and a better world if we have a strong, healthy United States, Europe, Soviet Union, China, Japan, each balancing the other, not playing one against the other, an even balance."[31]

REALISM IN U.S. DIPLOMATIC HISTORY

For most of its history, U.S. foreign policy substantially conformed to realist prescriptions while being described, explained, and justified on nonrealist grounds. Especially in its first century, the United States claimed to reject the balance of power as part of its renunciation of the old, corrupt European ways. The only presidents to openly base their foreign policies primarily on the logic of realism were Theodore Roosevelt (1901–1909), Richard Nixon (1969–1974), and, before September 11, George W. Bush.

Although George Washington is remembered for having set the country on an isolationist path, his presidency undertook three important initiatives derived from realist logic. First, it established good diplomatic relations with England and avoided favoritism toward France. This was essential if the United States were to avoid being drawn into a disastrous war on the side of France against the much more powerful England. Second, it created a national bank to promote commerce, commerce being necessary if the United States were to become strong enough to withstand pressure from Great Britain. Third, it promoted foreign trade. Foreign trade, like the national bank, was necessary to nurture an economy strong enough to sustain national independence.

For the rest of the nineteenth century, the two most important foreign policies were consistent with the logic of realism. The first was territorial expansion, substantially through wars and threats of war; the American empire was wrought "by negotiation and pillage."[32] Territorial expansion served the realist purpose of increasing the nation's strength. The second was the Monroe Doctrine. It declared that the country would not tolerate any effort by a European power to acquire territory in the Americas. In effect, it identified the Western Hemisphere as a U.S. sphere of influence, a classically realist ploy. Combined with territorial expansion, it removed European power from the continent, thereby reducing the threat it could pose.

Protecting national security was never the only purpose of territorial expansion, however. In all instances, promoting and protecting commerce was a main concern. Expansion also was a ploy in the struggles between the slave states and the nonslave states over the destiny of the country. Finally, Americans rationalized expansion on religious grounds (Manifest Destiny).

After completing continental expansion, the United States entered a phase of imperialism that culminated at the turn of the century in the Spanish-American War and with the acquisition of Hawaii, the Philippines, Puerto Rico, and the Panama Canal Zone. Proponents justified imperialism on the realist grounds that the United States had to increase its power in order to keep up with the increasing strength of the other major powers. They expected war. Another major initiative of these years was the "Open Door" policy. That policy rejected the spheres of influence that the other powers were creating for themselves by carving up China; it sought the realist purpose of weakening rivals.

Theodore Roosevelt became president at the end of the imperialist phase (1901–1909) and brought realist notions to office. As Assistant Secretary of the Navy, he had overseen the development of a navy capable of projecting power around the globe. As president, he continued to increase U.S. military strength. The development of the Panama Canal was instrumental to that purpose. His willingness to use armed force is seen in his famous proverb, "Speak softly and carry a big stick." He also mediated settlements of conflicts between Russia and Japan and between Germany against France and England. In both instances, he sought to reinforce the equilibrium of power so that no state could dominate Asia or Europe and thus be in a position to threaten U.S. interests.[33]

Although imperialism, the Open Door, and Roosevelt's diplomacy promoted realist purposes, they also served economic, ideological, and emotional ends unrelated to or inconsistent with realism. The U.S. economy suffered from overproduction for which, elites believed, the only solution was to expand foreign markets. The Open Door would open markets for U.S. exports; the empire would support the Open Door.[34] For Roosevelt, acting as a great power also had an ideological dimension quite contrary to realism. He adhered to a moral conception that he called righteousness, which called upon nations, as a matter of duty and honor, to use their power to uphold a higher morality, and to do so unilaterally if necessary. It was the

Wild West's code of chivalry, which Roosevelt greatly admired, projected into the realm of international relations.[35] Finally, the exercise of power would bring "moral improvement." It would do for the nation what the "strenuous life" would do for individuals: Ward off the decay that otherwise comes from the sedate and comfortable life made possible by material plenty.[36]

The embrace of the logic of realism did not last long. Woodrow Wilson (1913–1921) shifted the dominant foreign ideology away from realism; the United States rejected the balance of power and embraced collective security, international institutions and international law, disarmament, and a vigorous advocacy of democratic government and national self-determination of peoples.

Nevertheless, aspects of U.S. foreign policy behavior continued to conform to realist considerations. This was especially so just before and during the world wars. For instance, during World War II, the United States gave priority to defeating Germany, rather than Japan, because Nazi Germany represented the greater threat. It also allied itself with Stalin's Soviet Union, a nation completely offensive to American moral sensibilities, on the grounds that defeating Germany required working with whoever had power to achieve that end. President Franklin D. Roosevelt (1933–1945), recognizing that the major powers were the key to peace, designed a postwar system that was "largely a power-level arrangement in which the big three accepted, tacitly or explicitly, the new realities of power as the basis for postwar spheres of influence, and these spheres as the key to world order."[37]

During the Cold War, too, the core policy—containment—in large part but not wholly reflected the logic of realism. The containment policy sought first and foremost to prevent the Soviet Union from augmenting its power by acquiring control over western Europe. Toward that end, it used such external balancing strategies as forming alliances with the Europeans [NATO] and deploying large numbers of troops there, creating West Germany to be a member of the alliance, and using economic aid and foreign trade to strengthen its allies' economies. Because the system was essentially bipolar, though, the most important realist policy revolved around internal balancing. The United States increased its military power far beyond the levels it had previously maintained in peacetime. It sought to keep superiority in nuclear weapons. Finally, containment carried an element of reassurance. As a defensive strategy, it assured the Soviet Union that the United States would not act to topple the Soviet sphere of influence in eastern Europe.

Richard Nixon (1969–1974) was the first president since Theodore Roosevelt to conceive and justify a foreign policy on realist grounds. His national security advisor, Henry Kissinger, a Harvard political scientist, articulated the theoretical foundation of the administration's foreign policy, a policy that continued under Gerald Ford's presidency (1974–1977). Nixon's administration designed a new strategy for containing the Soviet Union. Two differences were most important. First, it engaged the USSR diplomatically in a policy of détente. Détente accepted that the superpower relationship fundamentally was and would remain competitive. Nevertheless, it sought grounds for cooperation within the overall competitive relationship. Both parties could benefit from trading nonstrategic goods, keeping conflicts in the Third World from escalating into superpower crises, and limiting the nuclear arms race. Diplomacy would seek agreements for mutual benefit. While seeking superpower agreements, the administration continued to use internal balancing tools to augment U.S. strength to avoid a dangerous shift in the balance of power. Nevertheless, in the long run, the administration hoped, the Soviet Union's cooperative ties with the noncommunist world would transform it into a status quo power. In that sense, détente was a strategy of reassurance.

The second shift was an effort to move the world away from the bipolar balance toward a multipolar balance. The administration saw that superpowers' predominance was eroding. Europe, economically recovered from the war, was moving toward unification. Japan had become an economic power. Most important, China was emerging as an independent and powerful country. So the administration established relations with China, a dramatic reversal of the previous policy of ostracizing it because of its communist regime. For Nixon and Kissinger, what mattered was China's potential as a partner in balancing the Soviet Union. Its domestic system was simply not relevant. The administration wanted the United States to have closer relations with both of the major communist powers than they had with each other. The United States could then threaten to move closer to China (or the Soviet Union) in order to bring pressure to bear on the other.

The Nixon Administration's policy did not conform perfectly with realist logic. It opposed, for instance, any real independence of action for western Europe and Japan.[38] Balance of power arrangements were acceptable for adversaries, but not for allies. It also continued the commitment to stabilization in the Third World by relying on influential regional clients to act as U.S. proxies. This so-called Nixon Doctrine merely sought to make containment more of a low-cost commitment.

Nixon's strategy did not last past 1975. The Watergate scandal and Nixon's resignation eroded the political base for its foreign policy but the administration's political difficulties ultimately did not cause the policy to fail. Rather, the policy was undone when significant segments of the population rejected it on policy considerations. Two were most important. First, critics from both ends of the political spectrum condemned it for its amorality and its lack of concern for human rights abroad. Liberals denounced the administration's willingness to support anticommunist dictators; conservatives condemned it for implicitly condoning human rights violations in communist countries, especially the USSR.

Conservatives also rejected détente on realist terms. They claimed that it benefited the Soviet Union more than the United States and thus was creating an imbalance of power in favor of the USSR. A window of vulnerability was opening in which the Soviets would be able to commit aggression and the United States would be unable to take sufficient countermeasures. Therefore, they insisted the United States abandon détente and begin a crash program to strengthen itself and its allies. A build-up of military forces, more or less across the board, was the first priority.

Jimmy Carter's administration (1977–1981) went out of its way to distance itself from the foreign policy concepts of the Nixon and Ford administrations. It downplayed the realist-inspired focus on balancing Soviet power and emphasized building up international cooperation. Moreover, the administration denounced the amorality of realism and sought to replace it with a principled commitment to the protection of basic human rights.[39]

The Carter administration, nonetheless, carried vestiges of realism. From the start the administration split into two camps, with one camp, headed by national security advisor Zbigniew Brzezinski, viewing the world through realist lenses and especially seeing the struggle against Soviet power as the essential issue in world politics. In practice, the administration adhered to geopolitical rather than moral principles in its dealings with such influential states as the Soviet Union, China, and Iran. As the administration's term in office passed, moreover, the advocates of realism-inspired geopolitics gained influence while their antagonists lost influence and left the administration.

The administration of Ronald Reagan (1981–1989) likewise incorporated aspects of realism without it being the dominant logic. It continued and accelerated the "new Cold War" begun during the last two years of Carter's presidency. Its most fundamental concern was quite consistent with realist logic: Preventing the Soviet Union from gaining predominance. Toward that end it greatly increased U.S. defense spending, worked to degrade the Soviet economy, attempted to forge a global anti-Soviet coalition, and initiated covert operations and military operations against Soviet client states in Asia, Africa, and Latin America. All these undertakings were consistent with militant realism and balancing behavior in a bipolar system.

The Reagan administration deviated from realist logic, though, in two major ways. First, its stated intention was not to reestablish a bipolar equilibrium but rather to cause the collapse of the Soviet Union. It was a strategy for victory, not balance. The administration interpreted the Soviet Union as being dangerous not primarily because of its power but rather because of its ideology; communism made it aggressive, so safety required the ending of Soviet communism. The idea that a state's ideology and system of government determines its foreign policy is decidedly nonrealist. Second, the administration offered as an affirmative goal for U.S. diplomacy the expansion of freedom, democracy, and free market capitalism in the world, which also is not realist.

As with its predecessors, the foreign policy of George Bush (1989–1993) manifested a mix of realist and nonrealist tendencies. Qualities consistent with realism would include, first, its exceedingly cautious response to the end of the Cold War. Recognizing that Soviet domination had stabilized its sphere of influence in East Europe, it worried that the end of the Cold War and the collapse of the USSR could lead to increased violence in Europe. More generally, one of its guiding commitments was to maintain good diplomatic relations with those who held power in other powerful countries. It supported Mikhail Gorbachev, the last leader of the Soviet Union, until his loss of power was complete. It also took a decidedly low-key response to China's violent suppression of the prodemocracy movement in Tiananmen Square: It broke relations only because of severe domestic political pressure, secretly reestablished contact within a few weeks of the massacre, and steadfastly refused to punish China by suspending normal trading relations. This trait can also be seen in the administration's policy toward Iraq prior to the invasion of Kuwait. Despite Iraq's abysmal record of internal repression, the United States continued to sell it weapons and otherwise to treat it as a legitimate diplomatic partner because a strong Iraq was seen as a counterbalance to Iran in the Persian Gulf. The administration's realist tendencies were seen as well in its strong disinclination to intervene for humanitarian purposes. When brutal fighting broke out in Bosnia-Herzegovina, the administration took a hands-off stance, judging the Balkans not to be of great significance to the United States (it did not affect the balance of power) and to be the responsibility of the Europeans (that is, in their sphere of influence).

On the other hand, significant facets of the administration's foreign policy deviated from realist thinking. It continued Reagan's commitment to the expansion of democratic government and free trade. Its commitment to deal with the established leaders of other countries also did not extend to the Third World. The administration justified its invasion of Panama and its war against Iraq on the grounds that the leaders of those two countries were dictators. The most distinctive deviation, though, was the administration's response to Iraq's conquest of Kuwait. The administration addressed that invasion in terms of its implications not for the balance of power but for global stability. The invasion violated the basic principle of the international legal order and if it were allowed to stand, it would endanger the stability of the international system. It reflected, in other words, the logic of hegemonism. Hegemonism also informed the administration's main, though short-lived, postwar strategic concept: The "new world order" of collective security through the United Nations, revitalized by cooperation by the great powers behind the leadership of the United States.

The Clinton administration (1993–2001) displayed hardly any symptoms of realist logic. The dominant themes of its foreign policy were American leadership, expansion of democracy and free markets, international cooperation to promote a variety of common interests, and humanitarian intervention.

The administration of George W. Bush (2001–) returned the logic of realism to a position of importance in foreign policy. Until the war on terrorism, it was a dominant logic, if not clearly the predominant one. The administration was committed to strengthening American military forces as "an insurance policy that allows us to take risks."[40] The commitment to enhancing military power is reflected perhaps most clearly in one of the administration's highest priorities, the creation of a ballistic missile defense system. It is seen, too, in its insistence that U.S. armed forces personnel would never be charged and tried before the International Criminal Court for war crimes committed while serving in peace-keeping duties. Indeed, one way the administration sought to preserve military strength was to avoid using it in anything other than combat missions.

Another manifestation of realist thinking was the administration's disdain for international institutions, especially international law, but also international public opinion. The administration undercut the establishment of the international criminal court and refused to join the Kyoto Protocol for the reduction of gases that account for global warming. Its withdrawal from the Anti-Ballistic Missile Treaty with Russia was widely opposed by other countries. As is consistent with realism, the administration attended to power; international institutions, international law, and international public opinion lack power and so were ignored.

Since September 11, important facets of realism continue to inform the Bush administration's foreign policy. The war on terrorism has kept a focus on power and especially military power as the core of international relations. In conducting the war, moreover, the administration has been quite willing to align itself with undemocratic, and in some instances, unsavory, states. Finally, its refusal to be deterred from attacking Iraq by a lack of UN authorization shows the low value it places on international institutions in conceiving U.S. national interests. Nevertheless, in the post-September 11 world, hegemonism seems to have replaced realism as the administration's predominant foreign policy logic.

CONCLUSION

The logic of realism calls upon the United States to build up and maintain its power, especially its military power, in order to protect its national security in an inherently uncertain and dangerous world in which power is the ultimate and essential resource. The United States must act to preserve the balance of power but must eschew all other roles, especially those that would drain its power in pursuit of unattainable ends derived from ideology, morality, or an exaggerated sense of its power. Just as realism has been the predominant theory of international relations for millennia, so American diplomacy has largely conformed to realist principles throughout its history. Nevertheless, the logic has not dominated the way Americans conceive of their country's international role.

DISCUSSION QUESTIONS

1. Is realism right in portraying international relations fundamentally as an arena of conflict among self-interested and power-seeking states and war and the preparation for war as the most basic features of world politics? Or is that view extreme and applicable to only some places and some times?

2. What threats to its national security does the United States face at present and in the foreseeable future? Are war, force, and the threat of force necessary and sufficient for coping with those threats? Are there better options?

3. What risks, if any, are posed by a foreign policy designed to mobilize and use power in order to cope with possible threats? Might realism's expectations of conflict be self-fulfilling?

4. Is the logic of realism accurate in its analysis of the limits on the power of the United States and thus on the commitments it can undertake?

5. Is realism's analysis of morality applicable to a country as powerful as the United States? Might not the power of the United States free it from the constraints that bind other states and impose on it special obligations?

6. What might explain the contradiction between the pattern in history of U.S. foreign policy, which generally has conformed to realist prescriptions, and the rhetoric of U.S. foreign policy, which generally has not emphasized realist conceptions?

7. Is realism politically viable in the context of American democracy? Will the public be willing to accept over the long term a foreign policy based on realism's conception of the role of morality, especially if it employs the harshest and most unscrupulous tactics of internal and external balancing? Will the public be willing to accept over the long term a foreign policy premised on the notion that the United States is just an ordinary great power rather than the world's number one country?

ENDNOTES

1. House Committee on Armed Services, *Military Capabilities of the People's Republic of China: Hearings Before the Armed Services Committee*, 106th Congress, 2nd session, July 19, 2000, (online). Accessed July 2, 2003. Available at: www.commdocs.house.gov/committees/security/has201000.000_Of.htm.

2. John J. Mearsheimer, *The Tragedy of Great Power Politics* (New York: W. W. Norton and Company, 2001), 55–60; John Orme, "The Utility of Force in a World of Scarcity," *International Security* 22, No. 3 (Winter 1997/1998): 138–167.

3. Quoted in David Rieff, "Almost Justice," review of *To End a War*, by Richard Holbrooke, *The New Republic* (July 6, 1998): 32.

4. Henry Kissinger, *Diplomacy* (New York: Touchstone/Simon & Schuster, 1994): 705. The quotation is Kissinger's summary of Richard Nixon's view, but it is clear from the context that Kissinger agrees.

5. Mearsheimer, *Tragedy*, 12.

6. Kissinger, *Diplomacy*, 813.

7. Mearsheimer sketches a hostile alliance scenario on pages 142–43 of *Tragedy*.

8. Mearsheimer, *Tragedy*, 84.

9. Kissinger, *Diplomacy*, 809–810.

10. Richard N. Haass, *The Reluctant Sheriff: The United States After the Cold War* (New York: Council on Foreign Relations Books, 1997), 28–39.

11. Charles William Maynes, "America's Fading Commitment to the World," in *Global Focus: U.S. Foreign Policy at the Turn of the Millennium*, ed. Martha Honey and Tom Barry (New York: St. Martin's Press, 2000), 86–87.

12. See, for example, Thomas J. Christensen, "Posing Problems Without Catching Up: China's Rise and Challenges for U.S. Security Policy," *International Security* 25, No. 4 (Spring 2001):5–40.

13. George F. Kennan, *American Diplomacy*, expanded edition (Chicago: University of Chicago Press, 1984); Melvin Small, *Democracy & Diplomacy: The Impact of Domestic Politics on U.S. Foreign Policy, 1789–1994* (Baltimore: The Johns Hopkins University Press, 1996).

14. James R. Schlesinger, "Foreword" in Jonathan Clarke and James Clad, *After the Crusade: American Foreign Policy for the Post-Superpower Age* (Lanham, MD: Madison Books, 1995), ix, viii, xi.

15. Barry R. Posen and Andrew L. Ross, "Competing Visions for U.S. Grand Strategy," *International Security* 21, No. 3 (Winter 1996–1997): 18.

16. Mearsheimer, *Tragedy*, 4.

17. Samuel P. Huntington, "The Clash Of Civilizations? The Next Pattern Of Conflict," *Foreign Affairs* 72, No. 3 (Summer 1993): 22–50.

18. Kenneth N. Waltz, "Structural Realism After the Cold War," *International Security* 25, No. 1 (Summer 2000): 28.

19. Robert J. Art, "Geopolitics Updated: The Strategy of Selective Engagement," *International Security* 23, No. 3 (Winter 1998–1999): 113.

20. Thomas J. McCormick, *America's Half-Century: United States Foreign Policy in the Cold War and After*, 2nd ed. (Baltimore: The Johns Hopkins University Press, 1995), 6–7. Quotation from page 6. See also Paul Kennedy, *The Rise and Fall of Great Powers* (New York: Random House, 1987); Robert Gilpin, *War and Change in World Politics* (Cambridge: Cambridge University Press, 1981), Chapter 5.

21. Richard N. Haass, "Five Not-So-Easy Pieces: The Debates on American Foreign Policy," *Brookings Review* Vol. 18, No. 2 (Spring, 2000): 40.

22. See, for instance, Jonathan Clarke and James Clad, *After the Crusade: American Foreign Policy for the Post-Superpower Age* (Lanham, MD: Madison Books, 1995).

23. Paul Kennedy, "Will the Next Century Be American Too?" *New Perspectives Quarterly* 16, No. 1 (Winter 1999): 57.

24. The balancing techniques are exemplified in Samuel Huntington's discussion of how the West should act in dealing with the nascent civilizational conflict with the Confucian-Islamic axis. Huntington, "Clash of Civilizations," 22–50.

25. Kenneth N. Waltz, *Man, the State and War: A Theoretical Analysis* (New York: Columbia University Press, 1954), 222.

26. Excellent reviews of realist writings on ethics can be found in Steven Forde, "Classical Realism," in *Traditions of International Ethics*, ed. Terry Nardin and David R. Mapel (Cambridge: Cambridge University Press, 1992), 62–80, and in Jack Donnelly, "Twentieth-Century Realism," in *Traditions of International Ethics*, ed. Terry Nardin and David R. Mapel (Cambridge: Cambridge University Press, 1992), 85–103.

27. Max Weber, "Politics as a Vocation," in *From Max Weber: Essays in Sociology*, C. Wright Mills and H. H. Gerth (New York: Oxford University Press, 1958), 115–127; Gordon A. Craig and Alexander L. George, *Force and Statecraft: Diplomatic Problems of Our Time*, 3rd ed. (New York: Oxford University Press, 1995), 275–288.

28. Waltz, *Man, the State and War*, 207.

29. Kissinger, *Diplomacy*, 47.

30. Kennan, *American Diplomacy*, 100–101.

31. Kissinger, *Diplomacy*, 705.

32. Bradford Perkins, *The Creation of a Republican Empire, 1776–1865*, vol. 1 of *The Cambridge History of American Foreign Relations* (Cambridge: Cambridge University Press, 1993), 6.

33. On Roosevelt's realism, see Kissinger, *Diplomacy*, 29–45; Robert Endicott Osgood, *Ideals and Self-Interest in America's Foreign Relations: The Great Transformation of the Twentieth Century* (Chicago: University of Chicago Press, 1953), 67–70.

34. See Walter LaFeber, *The American Search for Opportunity, 1865–1913*, Vol. 2 of *The Cambridge History of American Foreign Relations* (Cambridge: Cambridge University Press, 1993) for one development of this thesis.

35. Osgood, *Ideals and Self-Interest*, 88–91. On the moralistic impulse in 1890s imperialism generally, see Walter McDougall, *Promised Land, Crusader State: The American Encounter with the World since 1776* (Boston: Houghton Mifflin Company, 1997), 109–121.

36. Osgood, *Ideals and Self-Interest*, 38–39.

37. Akira Iriye, *The Globalizing of America, 1913–1945*, Vol. 3 of *The Cambridge History of American Foreign Relations* (Cambridge: Cambridge University Press, 1993), 211.

38. McCormick, *America's Half-Century*, 175–176.

39. Jerel A. Rosati, *The Carter Administration's Quest for Global Community: Beliefs and Their Impact on Behavior* (Columbia, SC: University of South Carolina Press, 1987). 39–46; Richard A. Melanson, *American Foreign Policy since the Vietnam War: The Search for Consensus from Nixon to Clinton*, 2nd ed. (Armonk, NY: M. E. Sharpe, 1996), 95–110.

40. *Confirmation Hearings for Colin L. Powell* (online), Washington, D.C.: U.S. State Department, January 17, 2001. Accessed August 28, 2002. Available at: www.state.gov/secretary/rm/2001/443.htm.

CHAPTER 4

The Logic of Isolationism

On July 17, 1998, an international conference approved a treaty to establish an International Criminal Court (ICC). The ICC would try persons accused of crimes against humanity, such as genocide and violations of the laws of war. The United States was one of seven nations that voted against. Gary T. Dempsey, a foreign policy analyst at the libertarian Cato Institute, wrote an essay supporting the administration's controversial position. The ICC, he wrote, would eventually supercede the U.S. court system and thus "threatens to diminish America's sovereignty." As a consequence, " . . . many of the legal safeguards American citizens enjoy under the U.S. Constitution would be suspended if they were brought before the court."[1] In opposing international commitments because they endanger the domestic systems of the United States, Mr. Dempsey was making an argument inspired by the logic of isolationism.

INTRODUCTION

Overview

In presenting the logic of isolationism, this chapter makes the following main points:

- isolationism argues that interdependence does not create vital interests requiring political and military involvement;
- it holds that foreign commitments inflict serious domestic costs;
- it contends that the United States has sufficient power to protect its vital interests but not enough to undertake other objectives abroad;
- it insists that the United States has no binding moral obligations abroad; instead, its duties at home are put at risk by international commitments.

Isolationism was the most important foreign policy logic until midtwentieth century. According to conventional wisdom, it was destroyed with the fleet at Pearl

Harbor. Indeed, since 1941 there have been few self-identified isolationists. The conventional wisdom, however, overstates the case. Granted, few elites claim to be isolationist and public opinion generally rejects "isolationism" as a foreign policy option. Nevertheless, arguments reflecting isolationist logic continue to be raised in American foreign policy debates, especially by libertarians, some conservatives, populists such as Patrick Buchanan, many progressive Democrats, and political radicals. Because "isolationism" carries negative connotations, advocates of policies reflecting isolationist perspectives give their proposals different names, such as a republican foreign policy, offshore balancing, strategic independence, the strategy of restraint, and enlightened nationalism.[2]

Isolationist logic offers a doubly distinctive interpretation of U.S. interests. It fundamentally challenges the notion that its interests compel the United States to undertake extensive foreign policy commitments. It also condemns international activism for harming the U.S. society and constitutional order. By showing that foreign policy commitments are unnecessary and carry high costs and risks, the logic of isolationism makes a case for a substantial but selective retrenchment from international affairs.

Isolationism Defined

The nearly universal rejection of isolationism flows partly from its nearly universal misinterpretation. Usually it is misunderstood to mean cutting all contact with the outside world. Isolationism does not require such a stance. A complete withdrawal from the world, even if it were possible, would not be necessary to achieve the benefits it seeks.

Surveying the history of the idea of isolationism, one scholar found its essential meaning to be "diplomatic and military nonentanglement, as illustrated by President Jefferson's admonition in 1801 against 'entangling alliances.'"[3] Diplomatic and political nonentanglement aims, first and foremost, to secure the autonomy of the United States. Isolationism understood as *nonentanglement for the sake of autonomy* spawns seven corollary ideas. First, it seeks autonomy partly because it safeguards against being drawn, against U.S. interests, into other nations' wars. *Neutrality*, then, is a corollary of isolationism. Second, the United States must maximize *self-sufficiency* in order to be strong enough to protect its freedom. Third, to ensure safety, foreign powers must be kept from gaining a territorial foothold close to the United States. Isolationism, then, exalts *continentalism*, a focus on North America and the Caribbean and a correlative distancing from Europe and Asia. Fourth, in conducting foreign policy, isolationist diplomacy basically is *unilateralist*. Other things being equal, isolationists choose to go it alone, in order to preserve autonomy. Fifth, isolationists recognize, however, that sometimes the United States must collaborate with other countries. In those circumstances, isolationist logic dictates that coalitions be *ad hoc, limited to the particular problem at hand, and temporary*.

Nonentanglement and its corollary ideas are not ends in themselves, though. Rather, they are means to a specific end. Isolationism seeks to create a protective shell around American society so that the country can fulfill its most important mission, namely, achieving the purposes stated in the Preamble to the Constitution: "establish justice, insure domestic tranquility, . . . promote the general welfare, and secure the blessings of liberty. . . ." That implies the sixth facet of isolationism: The scale of foreign policy commitments must be compatible with what the Founders called "ordered liberty." Because excessive foreign policy commitments endanger the constitutional order, isolationism is a doctrine of *minimal commitment*.

Seventh, because wars and standing militaries endanger the Constitution's purposes, isolationism has a negative view of war. While not pacifist—it requires fighting wars that are necessary to protect vital interests—it seeks to *minimize war, preparation for war, and commitments that might require war or preparation for war*.

Within those constraints, isolationism is compatible with and even encourages foreign relations, through governmental channels and through the private activities of Americans. Among other things, an isolationist United States would still conduct normal diplomatic, cultural, and commercial relations, provide humanitarian assistance to the victims of disasters, and share tourism and cultural exchanges with the world.

Preserving autonomy has uncertain implications for international economic relationships. International economics divides isolationism into two distinct strains. One, which will be called *political isolationism*, views free economic exchanges as independent of politics; economic ties, because they do not entail political entanglements and do not erode American autonomy, are permissible. Indeed, one group of political isolationists, the libertarians, aggressively advocates free trade. The second strain, however, criticizes foreign economic ties, especially as they reflect the process and policy of globalization, which they see as eroding autonomy. This strain will be called *protectionist isolationism*.

Isolationism's rejection of foreign commitments, even entangling alliances, is more prudential than principled. It represents a judgment that, given the way the world works and how world power is distributed, the United States best promotes its core values and interests by minimizing its international commitments. Isolationism would endorse an expansive foreign policy if it were necessary and sufficient for removing a threat to vital interests and core values. Once the threat had disappeared, however, foreign policy would revert to one of minimal commitment.

U.S. NATIONAL INTERESTS

The sole purpose of foreign policy must be to protect *vital* national interests, those important enough to defend by war if necessary. Primary vital interests are those conditions necessary for independence as a political community: territorial integrity (freedom from military attack), sovereignty (freedom from political domination), maintenance of constitutional order, and preservation of economic and social stability. Secondary vital interests are those that have "a direct, immediate and substantial" connection to the primary ones.[4]

The United States can protect its vital interests without extensive foreign policy commitments. In both national security and economics, the United States is less interdependent internationally than is generally recognized. Furthermore, interdependence does not create vulnerabilities that require foreign commitments. Indeed, when all national interests are considered, weighing the costs of foreign policy commitments against the costs of isolationism, foreign disengagement best serves the national interests. This is so in both the security and economic realms.

Limited Interdependence in National Security

Protection of the United States does not require managing the international system, participating in alliances, or using force outside a narrowly drawn zone of national security that includes its territory, the oceans around it, and its neighbors Canada and Mexico.* This security zone is limited because the United States uniquely is an inherently secure country. For well over 150 years, it has not faced a serious military threat, nor is there a plausible scenario by which one could emerge.

American security rests on six pillars. First, the U.S. economy is by far the world's largest and has been since the turn of the twentieth century. It has not been challenged and is not likely to be challenged in the near future. Neither Germany nor Japan has the population base to match its economic production. Only China seems likely to have an economy as large or larger than that of the United States, though when and to what degree that transition occurs remains to be seen.

Second, economic strength has enabled the United States to create and sustain powerful military forces. Granted, during the periods before each of the world wars, the United States chose not to invest heavily in military preparations, so in the early days of those wars its enemies had temporary military superiority. Critics indict isolationism for that lack of military preparedness, but they miss the mark. In 1917 and 1941, the United States was prepared to defend its territory; it was unprepared to fight in Europe and Asia, and properly so. Furthermore, all parties understood that American military potential made it the decisive player whose entry would determine the eventual outcome. Therefore, Britain did its best to draw the United States into both wars while Germany sought to keep it neutral.

U.S. military dominance through most of the twentieth century greatly exceeded its national security requirements. To prevent military attack or intimidation, the United States need not be able to defeat its enemies in any conceivable war. Rather, it merely must be strong enough to deter an attack, that is, to deny any enemy hope of victory at an acceptable cost. Even China someday passing the United States economically and militarily would not endanger national security. The United States must continue to be well armed, but only to defend the zone of security and nothing else.

The third pillar of national security is geography: The United States "faces almost no discernible security threats. To the north and south are weak, friendly neighbors; to the east and west are fish."[5] The oceans are tremendous moats safeguarding "fortress America." Distance attenuates military power, especially over water. Large-scale

---

* Some isolationist writers would include the sea lanes and air space through which the United States engages in international commerce or Europe, but the latter only to the extent that the United States must prevent any rival hegemonic power dominating the Eurasian landmass.

amphibious operations, which an attack on the United States would require, are extremely complicated and require absolute control of the seas and the air. Combined with naval power and coastal air defenses, the oceans make the United States impregnable. Were Canada or Mexico to align with a hostile power, the protection provided by the oceans would be negated to a large degree and American vital interests would be threatened. But the odds of that happening are miniscule. Moreover, under the logic of isolationism, the United States would act to prevent such a shift.

Fourth, power balancing among the other major powers most likely will prevent the emergence of a dominant power in either Europe or East Asia. The rival nations of those regions will tie each other down, so none will be able to project power into the U.S. zone of security. The main obstruction to such balancing behavior, interestingly enough, is the United States. Its security guarantees to its allies relieves them of any need to take care of their own security. Thus acting as an offshore balancer to prevent the emergence of an Asian or European regional hegemon is both unnecessary and counterproductive.

Even if the first four pillars were to fail, the fifth would be sufficient: nuclear weapons. So long as the United States has them, no rational adversary would consider attacking it. The scenarios for fighting a nuclear war are absurd. Nuclear weapons, in other words, render the United States absolutely safe from military attack by another state.

Sixth and last, the United States is largely immune to the supposed dangers of instability abroad. The contagious effects of international instability are gravely exaggerated. "If history has taught us anything," write two scholars, "it is precisely the contrary of the lesson drawn by those who urge us to be the world's policeman. It is that peace is normally divisible and that conflicts, whatever their origin, are normally of merely local or regional significance."[6]

The proposition that the United States is fundamentally safe from foreign dangers defies conventional wisdom, which holds that the United States was sucked into the world wars, thus proving that it simply cannot stand aside while the world is in turmoil. But in 1917, the United States declared war primarily in response to Germany's program of unrestricted submarine warfare. Two alternatives could have allowed the United States to stay out of the war. First, it could have been truly neutral before 1917, rather than favoring the British. Then Germany might not have adopted unrestricted submarine warfare. Second, it could have kept American shipping out of the war zone. "After all, one logical if unlikely response to the submarine was to retreat to our shores."[7] Most importantly, national security did not require entry into World War I. The war would have ended within a year or two anyway, with either a German victory or a negotiated settlement. Either outcome would have left Germany dominating the European continent but not threatening the United States. Germany had neither the intention nor the means to act against U.S. interests, especially since it would still have had to contend with the land power of Russia on the continent and the naval power of Great Britain at sea.

Similarly, the United States could have stayed out of World War II.[8] It did so from the war's start in September 1939, until December 1941, when Japan and Germany blundered—Japan by attacking Pearl Harbor, Germany by declaring war on the

United States. The Japanese and German decisions, in turn, were made in response to prior American policy. The Japanese would not have attacked Pearl Harbor had the United States not made itself a virtual ally of China and adversary of Japan nor would the Germans have declared war had the United States not made itself a virtual ally of Britain. Nor did Japanese or German power endanger the safety of the United States. By December 1941, Japan's army was bogged down in China and Germany had failed to conquer all of Europe. Absent American entry to the war, "[p]robably World War II would have ended in some sort of draw and negotiated settlement, or would have continued on for a decade or two with occasional truces for breathing spells—not unlike the Napoleonic Wars."[9]

Limited Interdependence in Economics

Both political and protectionist isolationism deny that the economy requires extensive foreign policy commitments. Protectionist isolationism's reasoning is straightforward: Because international economic ties endanger U.S. sovereignty and well-being, they should be curtailed, not promoted by political commitments. Political isolationism takes a different tack: Economic interdependence is relatively insignificant, so it does not create dangerous vulnerabilities. Therefore, even expanded interdependence would not jeopardize U.S. autonomy. Because protectionist isolationism focuses on the costs of an internationalist foreign policy, its line of thinking will be presented in a later section addressing costs. The rest of this section develops the rationale of political isolationism.

One standard measure of economic interdependence is the volume of foreign trade. In absolute terms, such trade is substantial; in 2001 exports amounted to $731 billion and imports cost almost $1.2 trillion. But in relative terms, trade is less significant. The U.S. economy is huge; in 2002 it was about $10.5 trillion. Foreign trade constituted about 22 percent of the U.S. economy, a significant amount but still small compared to the total economy.[10] In the inconceivable worst case, if the United States suddenly were to be cut off from all trade, the economy would have to make a tough adjustment, but it would survive. During the Cold War, if the USSR had gained control over western Europe and Japan and then abruptly cut off trade, the U.S. economy would have shrunk by 3 to 4 percent.[11] That would have been painful but on average would not have seriously lowered the American standard of living.

Indeed, the United States could be self-sufficient. It has abundant resources and a huge internal market. Goods not sold abroad could be sold at home; domestically produced resources could be developed as substitutes for imported ones. Sectors of the economy that have become overly dependent on export markets—agriculture, higher education, and financial services, for instance—would suffer were those markets to be lost. Others, however, would benefit from reduced foreign competition. Adjustments would entail some expense for the entire economy, but the net cost would not be prohibitive, and after the period of adjustment had passed, perhaps not even noticeable.

Most importantly, though, economic interdependence does not necessitate political commitments to prevent serious disruption of foreign economic ties. Most trade is with friendly and secure countries. Canada is its largest trade partner, with about 21 percent of total trade. Mexico comes second and Japan third, both at about 11 percent. U.S. trade with other countries is highly diversified. China represents about 6 percent of trade; Germany and the United Kingdom are both at 5 percent; France and South Korea represent about 3 percent; about 2 percent of trade is with each of Italy, the Netherlands, Singapore, and Taiwan.[12] If some partners were to sever trade with the United States, others would fill the gap. Most countries, moreover, could not afford to cut trade with the United States; they are dependent on their trade ties with the United States.

Limited Petroleum Dependency

Economic interdependence does not require political protection even in the most difficult case: oil. Dependence on petroleum imports does not dictate that the United States maintain a political and military presence in oil-exporting areas of the world, the Persian Gulf in particular, nor did it warrant war against Iraq. Granted, imported petroleum plays a crucial role in the U.S. economy. A sudden disruption of oil imports would unsettle the economy and maybe trigger a severe recession. Fortunately, that will not happen.

First of all, it would be impossible to cut off oil exports to just the United States and a few other countries.

> Oil, like any other commodity, is fungible. In the same way that water in the bath flows around the duck, oil flows around embargoes. OPEC [Organization of Petroleum Exporting Countries] and anyone who chooses to join it in a production cut may succeed in lowering that great bath that is the international oil market for a time and in raising prices. But any act of hostility directed at a specific country or region by another does not achieve the desired isolating effect.[13]

When the Arab petroleum exporting countries embargoed the United States in 1973 they failed. The market redirected to the United States the petroleum that otherwise would have gone to other countries and sent those countries the petroleum that would otherwise have been sent to the United States. The flow of petroleum products to consumers was disrupted, but not because of a real shortage of crude oil. Refiners, distributors, and the government, thinking that the embargo would be successful, took actions that created shortages at various points in the production and distribution system.

Matters would be different, of course, if the petroleum exporting nations were to cut production. OPEC has done that several times, but with only limited success. Production cuts raise the price of crude oil, but that creates new incentives that subvert the production cuts. Pumping oil from less efficient wells becomes profitable, which brings forth increasing supplies from other countries. It also tempts OPEC members to exceed their production quotas. Many of them desperately need revenues from oil sales and increased prices create an overwhelming temptation to make windfall profits by cheating. Collective efforts to raise prices by cutting production, in other words, are successful, but only in the short term, and even then the price increase is tolerable; in the long run, they are self-defeating.

This position holds even for the worst case scenario offered in support of the 1991 Persian Gulf War: Without the war, Iraq would have controlled all the oil in the Persian Gulf. Even then, vital U.S. interests would not have been at risk. Assuming that Saddam Hussein wanted to maximize oil revenues, he would have cut Gulf oil production by 40 percent, a 7 percent decline in world oil production. Oil prices would have risen from $20 to $30 per barrel and gasoline prices would have risen by 24 cents per gallon; on average, it would have cost each American about $112 per year.[14] Those cost increases, though unpleasant, would have been something less than a disaster for the economy.

Furthermore, U.S. vulnerability to disruptions in petroleum imports is not an unavoidable fact. Nature dictated that the bulk of the world's known petroleum reserves would be located in the Persian Gulf region; policy choices, not nature, dictated that the U.S. economy runs on petroleum. The United States created its dependency; over time it can reduce it through policies to achieve energy independence.

Ultimately, U.S. policy has sought to ensure not access to supplies of oil, but access to supplies of cheap oil. The problem is, the policies designed to keep oil cheap are expensive. In addition to troops killed in combat, in training for combat, and by terrorists seeking to drive them out of the Persian Gulf, there is simply the financial cost of military preparations for protecting access to oil. The military force created for intervention into crises in the Persian Gulf "has cost more than $40 billion a year to protect $14 billion of current oil imports from the Persian Gulf."[15] Even in purely economic terms, that is a bad bargain.

Interdependence, Foreign Policy, and the National Interest

The United States can never be totally immune to harmful effects of interdependence. Global depressions or cuts in oil imports would cause economic pain; international terrorism endangers some American lives; the closing of international markets would cause some American firms to lose money and some American workers to lose jobs. Those effects, however, do not warrant political engagement in the world, for three reasons. First, the amount of harm from international economic disruptions is not fixed and uncontrollable. The level of U.S. interdependence substantially results from government policies that (sometimes unintentionally, but often intentionally) increased interdependence. For instance, reliance on imported oil results from support for industries that consume oil, especially automobiles. The volume of foreign trade also derives from foreign policy choices; for over a century, the United States has used diplomatic muscle, foreign aid, gunboat diplomacy, and other means to open foreign markets and increase exports. U.S. foreign policies increase vulnerability to terrorist attacks. Changing policies, then, can lessen vulnerability.

Second, when individual Americans or American firms find themselves threatened abroad, often it is due to their own choices. People who choose to travel or live abroad and businesses that choose to invest overseas place themselves in jeopardy. That does not oblige the community, acting through the foreign policy of the state, to protect them. "Certainly it was a terrible crime [for the British] to enslave American seamen," wrote Harry Browne, about the War of 1812. "But why was it the U.S.

government's business? Private companies had chosen to send those ships into foreign waters, and were responsible for the safety of their employees. If they couldn't provide safe passage (either by arming the ships or by negotiating with the British), they should have stayed out of the area."[16]

Third, the harms of insufficient foreign involvement pale in comparison to the harms of overinvolvement. Overinvolvement follows directly from an unwillingness to tolerate certain unfortunate events. Unless the United States carefully differentiates vital interests from other interests or purposes, it will have no basis for refusing international commitments. To consider every situation in which the United States, its citizens, or their interests might suffer harm as an occasion for some foreign policy response is a recipe for unlimited international adventurism. And that carries far greater harm to the community than the losses from foresworn involvement.

The Costs of International Commitments

The costs of internationalism cannot be calculated precisely because they vary with the type of internationalism. Moreover, political and protectionist isolationists would disagree vigorously over some of the costs listed here. Nonetheless, an inclusive inventory of the costs of internationalism would include these seven: the creation of new threats to U.S. security, the expense of war and preparation for war, the weakening of the U.S. economy, the exacerbation of social tensions, the diversion of resources from social needs, the erosion of constitutional order, and the loss of national sovereignty.

Creation of New Threats to U.S. Security

Internationalism makes the United States less secure. Ironically, internationalist strategies that most seek to increase security most degrade it. They make the United States a party to others' disputes. Because it is impossible to act in a way that is purely neutral (that is, does not benefit one party more than another) and that is seen by all as purely neutral, internationalism leads to the United States being seen as an adversary by one or even both parties to the dispute. Internationalism, then, creates enemies who, although unable to attack and conquer the United States, do serious harm. The phenomenon is called blowback; terrorism is the clearest example.

> Terrorism by definition strikes at the innocent in order to draw attention to the sins of the invulnerable. The innocent of the twenty-first century are going to harvest unexpected blowback disasters from the imperialist escapades of recent decades.[17]

The crimes of September 11 showed how great the danger of blowback can be; the danger is amplified by the proliferation of weapons of mass destruction with which those enemies can massacre Americans. American vulnerability also is increased by the globalization encouraged by internationalism, which gives enemies greater access to American society and to Americans abroad. Isolationism avoids that danger. "If nuclear threats are to be directed at the United States, there need be a reason.

Reasons plummet with the abrogation of entangling alliances. Maximum safety lies in getting out of harm's way."[18]

The Expense of War and Preparation for War

Ultimately, a foreign policy that does not eschew militarism means fighting wars. Even if the policy aims to create stability, "if the United States goes out into the world to prevent hypothetical wars, it will surely find some real ones."[19] So "we are almost always at war—cold or hot, but a conflict nonetheless—a war in which Americans will die, or a war that Americans will be taxed for, or a war that could easily erupt into wholesale destruction."[20] Indeed, the costs of war call into question the very meaning of security:

> More than 100,000 Americans died in Korea and Vietnam; over 300,000 were wounded. The extent of these losses cannot be mitigated, as they sometimes are, because they occurred abroad rather than at home, because they were suffered by soldiers rather than civilians. These enormous casualties detracted as much from our "physical security" as if they had been suffered in an attack upon the homeland.[21]

Weakening of the U.S. Economy

Foreign commitments harm the economy in four ways. First, they are expensive. Preparing for war in distant places adds tens of billions of dollars to the defense budget beyond what would be needed to defend the United States.[22] Isolationists of different political persuasions clash over what to do with savings from defense budget cuts. Those on the political left prefer that the money be put into domestic policy programs; those on the right want tax cuts. They agree, though, that the share of the defense budget devoted to supporting an expansive foreign policy "clearly constitutes an enormous amount of foregone national welfare."[23] Second, military spending draws top scientific, technical, and engineering talent away from the civilian economy, thereby hurting its competitiveness. Third, national defense costs get added to the tax bills of U.S. corporations, which gets tacked onto the costs of their products, which places them at a disadvantage with companies from countries who spend little on national defense because they are already protected by U.S. military might.[24] Fourth, the pursuit of influence leads the United States to give other countries trade concessions that also place U.S. businesses at a competitive disadvantage.[25] One summary finds that "the consequences of the sustained diversion of state monies to empire building over the past decade and a half for the U.S. national economy have been catastrophic: deteriorating social programs, disintegrating public health and educational sectors, rising homelessness, worsening unemployment, and spreading poverty."[26]

Exacerbation of Social Tensions

Because the costs and benefits of international involvement are shared unevenly across social classes, foreign commitments accelerate fraying of the social fabric at home. The uneven impact is clear in the case of trade. Free trade, whatever its long-term benefits, in the short term hurts workers in many industries. Placed into competition with workers in low-wage countries, they see their wages and benefits drop and often lose their jobs as factories are closed because the work is sent abroad. Whole cities can be devastated.[27] As class and regional differences are heightened, even a sense of membership in the same nation erodes. "Social stability depends on a rising standard of living for all our people, those who work with lathes as well as those who work with laptops."[28]

Diversion of Resources from Social Needs

Internationalism, furthermore, diverts resources from domestic needs. This concerns more than money. To some extent, government can increase the pool of money available for both domestic and foreign programs by borrowing or by raising taxes. Rather, the most serious cost is the drain on two absolutely limited resources: the time and attention of policy makers. No policy gets adopted unless the president and key legislators invest their time, energy, and political capital to get it adopted and implemented. When the government is seized with foreign policy matters, domestic policy making is put on automatic pilot. Virtually nothing gets done and problems fester and become more intractable.

Erasing Constitutional Order

Internationalism leads to the corruption of the constitutional order. As James Madison observed, "Perhaps it is a universal truth that the loss of liberty at home is to be charged to provisions against danger, real or pretended, from abroad."[29] An activist foreign policy necessarily leads, first of all, to a strengthening of the state over the private sector, with a consequent loss of freedom. For example:

- Individuals are liable to be conscripted into military service, a severe erosion of liberty;
- when the government imposes economic sanctions, it in effect forbids private firms from doing business with potential partners in targeted countries, an infringement on their economic liberty;
- individual liberties are abrogated when the state prohibits travel to enemy countries;
- freedom of the press is restricted when state secrets must be preserved.

An activist foreign policy also shifts power from the legislative to the executive branch.[30] It is widely believed that only the executive branch can act with sufficient dispatch, coherence, and, when necessary, secrecy to carry out international affairs. To the extent that the United States is committed to an activist foreign policy, Congress will abdicate its constitutional role and the executive will design ways around constitutional restrictions. Executive agreements will be struck when treaties would be politically difficult. Covert operations will be carried out when overt forms of pressure would be politically inopportune. Undeclared wars will proliferate as the "Commander in Chief" clause trumps the provision that Congress shall declare war.

Loss of National Sovereignty

Finally, an activist foreign policy feeds the erosion of U.S. independence from control by external forces. For protectionist isolationism, the loss of sovereignty is inherent in and an intended result of free trade policies. Patrick Buchanan develops this thesis most starkly: The United States, by its loss of self-sufficiency, is becoming "a colony of the world," its free trade policies amounting to "the surrender of national sovereignty" and "the potential loss of nationhood itself. . . . Once a nation puts its foot onto the slippery slope of global free trade, the process is inexorable, the end inevitable: death of the nation-state."[31]

Even were trade not to endanger national independence and identity, the multilateralism necessitated by internationalism erodes sovereignty. Beyond the protection of limited and vital interests, involvement in international affairs will require collaboration with others. The terms of collaboration—goals and objectives, strategies and tactics, burden-sharing arrangements—must be negotiated among the partners. The United States will not be able to dictate the terms of the partnership (if it could, it would not need partners), so it will have to adjust its goals and actions to conform to the wishes of other countries. Hence a loss of freedom of action.

Worse, multilateralism leads to treaties and to membership in international organizations. Treaties supercede the laws passed by Congress and state legislatures.[32] The decisions of international organizations bind the United States. Even giving the United States a veto does not protect its sovereignty, because of the pressure to make concessions to the majority in order to form a compromise agreement.[33]

> Like a shipwrecked, exhausted Gulliver on the beach of Lilliput, America is to be tied down with threads, strand by strand, until it cannot move when it awakens. "Piece by piece," our sovereignty is being surrendered. By accession to NAFTA, GATT, the UN, the WTO, the World Bank, the IMF, America has ensnared itself in a web that restricts its freedom of action, diminishes its liberty, and siphons off its wealth.[34]

U.S. POWER

While the United States has more than sufficient power to defend itself from organized attack by hostile states, its ability to achieve more ambitious goals is quite limited.* Two of the many limits on U.S. influence abroad are restrictions on the use of military power and the intractable internal sources of problems abroad.

---

* That logically has to be part of isolationist thinking: If the United States were to be strong enough to command obedience from other countries and accomplish its goals with little opposition, the costs and effort to influence international affairs would be quite small, the dangers would be proportionally reduced, and the rationale for limited involvement would be weakened.

Restrictions on the Use of Force

The logics of hegemonism and realism hit the mark in recognizing that national power rests on military power. They err in ignoring the real limitations on the ability of the United States to use its armed forces and thus the real limitations on its power. The limitations have both foreign and domestic sources.

Domestic Resistance

Resistance at home includes the military establishment, which opposes involvement in anything other than wars capable of quick and decisive victories. Public disinclination to use force abroad commonly is called "the Vietnam syndrome." That phrasing is misleading. The Vietnam War intensified but did not create such public resistance. Many political theorists have argued since the late 1700s that public opinion in a democracy would stop the state from going to war.* Much data from U.S. history conforms to that idea: Public opinion turned against the war to suppress the Filipino insurgency of 1899–1902; public opinion delayed U.S. entry into the world wars of the twentieth century; opposition to the war in Korea (1950–1953) grew as the war grew longer and stalemated and the number of dead rose; and in 1964, President Lyndon Johnson had to deceive the nation, contriving a crisis to maneuver the country into the Vietnam War.

Since Vietnam, the United States has successfully used military force in Grenada (1983), Panama (1989), the Persian Gulf (1991), Bosnia-Herzegovina (1995), Kosovo (1999), Afghanistan (2001–), and Iraq (2003). Each of those operations supposedly showed the end of the Vietnam syndrome; after each the syndrome's continued strength became clear. The Reagan and Clinton administrations terminated interventions in Lebanon (1982–1984) and Somalia (1992–1994) after spectacular incidents that killed U.S. troops.[35] The military operations in Bosnia-Herzegovina and Kosovo were delayed, small in scale, and designed to avoid U.S. casualties in order to avoid public opposition. Public opposition also deterred military action to stop genocide in Rwanda and East Timor. A substantial majority of public opinion supported the 2003 invasion of Iraq, but only after a concerted effort by the administration to shape public sentiment. Moreover, large numbers of people continued to lodge public protests against the war.

Foreign Resistance

There are two types of foreign resistance. The first is adverse public reaction that could inhibit foreign states from supporting U.S. efforts. Opposition from the publics of friendly Western nations is especially troublesome as it feeds domestic opposition.

The other and more important is armed resistance to U.S. military operations. The global spread of ideologies of resistance, such as revolutionary nationalism or radical Islam, and the diffusion of modern military technologies have robbed war and threats of war of much of their utility. Ideologies of resistance

---

* See the discussion in Chapter 5.

have transformed peoples and nations who previously were under the thumbs (or heels) of dominant nations. Instead of being submissive in the face of apparently overwhelming power, they have the will to resist, even at very high costs. The diffusion of modern military technologies has given them the means with which to resist.[36]

Together, those two changes have overturned the calculus of power. "Strong" states must anticipate that wars will be prolonged. They will achieve no decisive victory. Rather, their battlefield superiority will merely lead to guerrilla war and urban terrorism. As the war continues it becomes increasingly costly, in tangible resources, in lives, in international diplomatic capital, and in domestic political support. The "strong" state will be less willing to bear the costs of fighting over an extended period of time and therefore will make more political concessions sooner than the "weaker" one. The weak party wins. Having seen this pattern played out in Algeria and Indochina for France, in Vietnam and Somalia for the United States, in Afghanistan for the Soviet Union and Chechnya for Russia, and in Lebanon for Israel, powerful states are much less willing to use their forces. Moreover, targets of military coercion are much less likely to be cowed into submission. Superior military might becomes decoupled from actual political influence, and therefore much less valuable.

This point—that the use of military force is impeded—complements rather than contradicts the earlier point about the costs of war. In essence, foreign policy activism is caught in a dilemma. An effective activist foreign policy must be backed by force. If force cannot be used, policy will be less successful. If, on the other hand, force is used, then the costs of war must be borne, making the costs disproportionate with the policy's benefits.

The Intractable Internal Sources of Problems

The basic cause of many foreign problems is other countries' deficiencies. Civil wars grow out of racial, ethnic, and religious conflicts deeply rooted in their histories. The outside world cannot establish peace in those places. Other problems, such as poverty, famine, and environmental degradation, are caused by deficiencies in the governments of the countries that suffer them.[37] Indeed, many places lack a government that actually governs. In those places, the only hope would be for the United States, or the world community acting through the United Nations or a regional organization, to occupy them, to place them into receivership, and to effectuate imperial rule until the country is ready for independence. That is not going to happen. Other options are half-measures that cannot solve the problem and indeed are likely to make it worse.

The constraint imposed by the internal sources of problems is illustrated by the aftermaths of the successful wars in Afghanistan and Iraq. One year after the victory in Afghanistan, the U.S.-backed Karzai regime faces rising challenges from regional warlords and reorganized fighting units of Taliban.[38] Almost immediately after organized Iraqi military resistance ended, the United States faced widespread and fervent Iraqi political resistance to its forces remaining in the country and contributing to its political reconstruction. Most ominously, leaders of Iraq's majority Shiite Muslims mobilized to establish an Islamic republic. Evidently, compared to the task of creating a democratic Iraq, defeating Saddam Hussein's armed forces would be a cakewalk.

MORALITY

The United States has no moral obligations toward other people. It cannot and should not assume any responsibilities beyond the protection of its own vital interests. That conclusion rests on all the points made in the realist critique of morality in foreign policy plus one additional point.

The United States has only one compelling moral obligation: to preserve the experiment in "government of the people, by the people, and for the people" inherited from preceding generations, to improve domestic political, economic, and social institutions, and then to pass them on to future generations. Any activist foreign policy subverts that obligation in direct proportion to the degree of activism. An "imperial" foreign policy, write two scholars, "so often justified as a vindication of the American purpose, represents its betrayal. It prefigures, in fact, the end of American history. . . . The proud boast of American statecraft was once that . . . we would not forget the admonitions of the Founding Fathers and their successors, nor suffer the basic principles of the American experiment to undergo corruption. American history will come to an end when these sentiments no longer animate our political life."[39] Pat Buchanan goes further; he calls the sacrifice of national sovereignty for the sake of globalization "treason."[40]

This renunciation of moral obligations applies even to the hardest case: the Second World War. The United States was not morally bound to fight consummate evil. In 1941, the full horror of Hitler's rule was not known, nor was it known that the United States and its allies would manage to win a decisive victory and then reform the defeated enemies. The track record for moral crusades has not been particularly good. Indeed, had the United States not entered World War I there would have been no World War II. Nor were all the fruits of World War II sweet. Victory came too late to save 80 percent of Hitler's intended victims. While Nazism, Italian fascism, and Japanese militarism were all sent to the dustbin of history, Stalin's Soviet Union, hardly a model of humane government, came to dominate a larger chunk of the world. The war left the United States with a larger permanent military than it had ever had before; it also made the country confident it would get its way on the field of battle, which contributed to the tragedies of Korea and Vietnam; and the bombing of German and Japanese cities, ending in the atomic bombing of Hiroshima and Nagasaki, eroded the prohibition on directly attacking civilians, which culminated in the napalm bombing of villages in Vietnam.[41] Finally, if there was a moral obligation to fight in World War II, is there not also a moral obligation to go to war to stop the genocides and massacres in any of the too many places where men with power do evil against masses of victims? It is good to recall that those who led the United States into Vietnam justified that war on the moral grounds of protecting the people of Vietnam from a communist reign of terror.

ISOLATIONISM AND U.S. DIPLOMATIC HISTORY

Until the 1890s, American foreign policy was guided by the logic of isolationism.* The Founders articulated the doctrine and their successors implemented it. Isolationism did not mean inactivity. Indeed, the country had several periods of rather intense military and diplomatic activity, during which it expanded its commercial relations, fought wars, and acquired territory.[42] Those expansionist phases, however, respected the limits defined by isolationism and were followed by periods of lowered activism and greater attention to internal matters.

The thirty years between 1890 and 1920 saw a sharp departure from isolationist practice. Having acquired the resources of a great power, the United States began to think of itself as mandated to act as a great power. Largely as a result of the Spanish-American War of 1898, it seized a substantial empire in Asia and the Caribbean. It also began to play an imperial role within the Americas, intervening in several Central American and Caribbean countries. The United States built up its naval power in order to be able to participate in the balances of power in Asia and Europe. Finally, it joined World War I to restore a balance of power in Europe and to remake and reform the world order.

Nevertheless, isolationism influenced foreign policy debate and behavior during those three decades. Imperialism was severely criticized on isolationist grounds.[43] So were deviations from neutrality between the 1914 outbreak of World War I and the U.S. declaration of war on April 4, 1917. Six senators and fifty members of the House of Representatives voted against war, justifying their opposition with isolationist reasons. Isolationism even affected the conduct of the war: President Wilson refused to have the United States labeled an ally of Britain and France, insisting that it join the war as an "Associated Power."

Following the war, isolationism staged a comeback. The Senate rejected the Treaty of Versailles, which ended World War I, because it created the League of Nations, an international organization embodying the commitment to collective action to keep the peace. Isolationist sentiment inspired laws requiring scrupulous neutrality in any war. The neutrality acts severely limited the efforts of President Franklin Roosevelt (1933–1945) to help Britain in its war against Germany. Eventually, supporters of American involvement in the war were able to have the restrictions removed, but only incrementally and only after defeating vigorous resistance from large numbers of persons, like Senator Robert Taft, who opposed entering another European war on isolationist grounds:

---

* Chapter 3 claimed that the foreign policy of this period conformed to realism. That claim and this one do not contradict each other. During the nineteenth century, the distribution of power in the world led the logic of realism and the logic of isolationism to identical strategies.

> While I certainly do not consider myself an isolationist, I feel it would be a
> great mistake for us to participate in the European War. I do not believe that
> we could materially affect the outcome . . . and I do not believe we have shown
> any ability to make peace after the war is over. . . . In the meantime [by going
> to war] we would certainly destroy democracy in this country.[44]

Pearl Harbor gravely weakened isolationism for the next twenty years. Still, isolationism had not been extinguished. Senator Taft, for instance, led opposition to much of the infrastructure of containment, especially the North Atlantic Treaty Organization (NATO), a mutual defense pact that certainly constituted an entangling alliance. Also, Congress nearly passed the Bricker Amendment, which would have restricted the administration's capacity to use executive agreements with other countries to evade the Senate's authority to advise and consent on treaties.

The late 1960s saw the apparent resuscitation of isolationism. Policies adopted or seriously considered represented isolationist themes: withdrawal from commitments in Indochina, withdrawal of forces from Europe, ending conscription, and redressing the imbalance of power between the executive branch and Congress by, for instance, limiting the president's authority to commit forces, to undertake covert operations, and to make foreign policy commitments.

The shift, though, was far more complicated than simply a movement along a single isolationism-internationalism continuum. Studies of public attitudes found a complex structure with more than one variety of internationalism and, in some studies, more than one variety of isolationism.[45] The term neo-isolationism came into vogue, but that concept was misleading. Those who were labeled as neo-isolationists did indeed favor terminating or reducing of certain foreign policy commitments. At the same time, they reaffirmed other commitments and proposed the adoption of still others. Neo-isolationism, in other words, was a selective internationalism, not a principled isolationism.

The unambiguous end of the Cold War in 1989–1991 raised internationalists' fears of a surge in isolationism and a consequent U.S. withdrawal from international affairs.[46] The 1992 presidential election gave them cause for worry, given that Clinton's campaign indicted the Bush administration for emphasizing foreign affairs at the expense of domestic policy. The 1990s certainly saw less money devoted to international affairs, as the military shrank rather dramatically and foreign aid and other foreign programs received a smaller share of the government budget.

Still, it is hard to assess the degree to which isolationism is resurgent. Public opinion data are uncertain; the level of measured isolationism depends on how questions are phrased. For instance, questions asking about support in principle for international engagement find that large majorities of the public are internationalist, but ones posing a trade-off between domestic and foreign commitments uncover substantially lower levels of internationalism.[47] Moreover, fluctuations in those statistical data do not necessarily indicate fluctuations in the level of isolationism as the term has been defined in this chapter. The public could very well accept that the United States has to be involved in the world in the sense of trading with it, yet still be isolationist if trade were the only form of involvement they favored.

A prominent study makes the portrayal of public attitudes even more complex. It concludes that the public in reality is internationalist but appears to be isolationist only because they are misinformed. The public favors reducing the levels of U.S. involvement but only because it thinks that involvement is much higher than it actually is. For instance, the public favors cutting foreign aid, an attitude consistent with isolationism. But that does not mean that they are opposed in principle to substantial foreign aid programs. On average, Americans favor allocating about 5 percent of the federal government's budget to foreign aid. They favor cuts in foreign aid because they also believe, on average, that foreign aid consumes 15 percent of the budget. In fact, foreign aid is much less than 1 percent of the budget. So, if the public knew the facts, they would support substantial increases in foreign aid.[48] In principle, then, public opinion is internationalist, but in practice, it favors reductions in international commitments. The public's internationalism is latent and will continue to be, until the leadership class can get the public to attend to foreign affairs and provides the public with a clear and accurate portrayal of reality. In the meantime, though, the policies it favors are isolationist and elites perceive the public to be isolationist.

Protectionist isolationism was on the wane during the 1990s. With opposition to the North American Free Trade Agreement (NAFTA) as one of his main issues, presidential candidate Ross Perot won 17 percent of the popular vote in 1992. In 1996 and 2000, though, with the national economy functioning much better than in 1992, Perot and then Patrick Buchanan saw that support dwindle. Free trade advocates were able to push the Senate to ratify the World Trade Organization. On the other hand, Congress denied President Clinton his requested "trade expansion authority," which would have allowed him to negotiate an extension of NAFTA to other countries in Latin America without having to worry about Congress destroying the agreement by amending it. It did not give President Bush such authority until well into his second year.

CONCLUSION

The logic of isolationism calls upon the United States to minimize its political and military commitments abroad. One strain of isolationism—protectionist isolationism—also would have it reduce its economic involvement in the world, but the other strain—political isolationism—would not. Isolationism calls for pruning foreign commitments because they are unnecessary for protecting vital interests; the United States is powerful enough to take care of its vital interests by itself. Moreover, the United States lacks the power to bring about substantial improvement in the conditions of the world. Most important, curtailing foreign commitments is necessary to save the United States grievous harm to its social and political structures.

Isolationism was the dominant logic in the nineteenth century and strongly shaped American policy until World War II. Since then, it has largely been a marginal perspective in U.S. foreign policy debates.

DISCUSSION QUESTIONS

1. Is the United States as secure from foreign threats as the logic of isolationism contends?
2. Considering isolationism's renunciation of permanent alliances with other countries, does this logic offer a viable strategy for dealing with terrorism? While it allows war against states

that have attacked the United States or are responsible for such attacks, could such a war be effectively waged under this logic?

3. Does the logic's analysis of the restraints on the use of force have any continuing validity in the wake of the military victory in Iraq?

4. Does the logic of isolationism, by emphasizing safety from objective threats and ignoring the risks of subjective ones, construe national security too narrowly? How would Americans react if Asia or Europe were under the control of hostile powers?

5. How feasible would it be for the United States to retrench on its existing international political commitments? What obstacles would it have to overcome in making a significant disengagement? What harmful consequences might disengagement produce?

6. How politically viable would a foreign policy based on the logic of isolationism be? Would the U.S. public be willing to support a policy that renounces an exalted U.S. world role and foreign policy driven by moral principles?

ENDNOTES

1. Gary T. Dempsey, *Reasonable Doubt: The Case Against the Proposed International Criminal Court* (online) Washington, D.C.: Cato Institute *Policy Analysis No. 311*, July 16, 1998. Accessed May 20, 2003. Available at: www.cato.org/pubs/pas/pa-311es.html.

2. Michael H. Hunt, *Ideology and U.S. Foreign Policy* (New Haven: Yale University Press, 1987); Christopher Layne, "From Preponderance to Offshore Balancing: America's Future Grand Strategy," *International Security* 22, No. 1 (Summer 1997): 86–124; Ted Galen Carpenter, *A Search for Enemies: America's Alliances After the Cold War* (Washington, D.C.: Cato Institute, 1992); Eugene Gholz, Daryl G. Press, and Harvey M. Sapolsky, "Come Home, America: The Strategy of Restraint in the Face of Temptation," *International Security* 21, No. 4 (Spring 1997): 5–48; Patrick J. Buchanan, *The Great Betrayal: How American Sovereignty and Social Justice Are Being Sacrificed to the Gods of the Global Economy* (Boston: Little, Brown and Company, 1998).

3. Cecil V. Crabb, Jr., *Policy-Makers and Critics: Conflicting Theories of American Foreign Policy* (New York: Praeger Publishers, 1976), 8.

4. Carpenter, *Search for Enemies*, 7.

5. Gholz, Press and Sapolsky, "Come Home, America," 8.

6. Robert W. Tucker and David C. Hendrickson, *The Imperial Temptation: The New World Order and America's Purpose* (New York: Council on Foreign Relations, 1992), 207.

7. Melvin Small, *Was War Necessary? National Security and U.S. Entry into War* (Beverly Hills: Sage Publications, 1980), 208.

8. Hunt, *Ideology and U.S. Foreign Policy*, 145–150; Bruce M. Russett, *No Clear and Present Danger: A Skeptical View of the United States Entry into World War II* (New York: Harper & Row, Publishers, 1972), Chapters 2–3; Small, *Was War Necessary?*, Chapter 5.

9. Russett, *No Clear and Present Danger*, 30.

10. U.S. Department of Commerce, Bureau of Economic Analysis, *BEA News Release*, May 29, 2003 (online). Washington: Bureau of Economic Analysis. Accessed June 2, 2003. Available at: www.bea.doc.gov/bea/newsrel/gdp103p.htm; U.S. Census Bureau, *U.S. Trade in Goods and Services—Balance of Payments (BOP) Basis* (online). Washington: U.S. Department of Commerce, Census Bureau. Accessed June 2, 2003. Available at: www.census.gov/foreign-trade/statistics/historical/gands.pdf.

11. Eric A. Nordlinger, *Isolationism Reconfigured: American Foreign Policy for a New Century* (Princeton, NJ: Princeton University Press, 1995), 82.

12. U.S. Census Bureau, *Statistical Abstract of the United States: 2002* (Washington, D.C.: U.S. Census Bureau, 2002), 796–798.

13. Amity Shlaes, "Recycling the Oil Weapon," *The Chicago Tribune*, December 5, 2001.

14. Nordlinger, *Isolationism Reconfigured*, 85–86.

15. Ibid., 87.

16. Harry Browne, *Why Government Doesn't Work* (New York: St. Martin's Press, 1995), 139.

17. Chalmers Johnson, *Blowback: The Costs and Consequences of American Empire* (New York: Owl Books/Henry Holt and Company, 2001), 33.

18. Nordlinger, *Isolationism Reconfigured*, 131.

19. Barry R. Posen and Andrew L. Ross, "Competing Visions for U.S. Grand Strategy," *International Security* 21, No. 3 (Winter 1996–1997): 23.

20. Browne, *Why Government*, 141.

21. Nordlinger, *Isolationism Reconfigured*, 122.

22. Partial estimates are provided by Nordlinger, *Isolationism Reconfigured*, 220, 228; and Johnson, *Blowback*, 87.

23. Nordlinger, *Isolationism Reconfigured*, 220.

24. Buchanan, *Great Betrayal*, 80, 159.

25. Ibid., 29, 84, 233; Nordlinger, *Isolationism Reconfigured*, 224–227.

26. James Petras and Morris Morley, *Empire or Republic? American Global Power and Domestic Decay* (New York: Routledge, 1995), 63-64.

27. This case is made with amusing and appalling effects in Michael Moore's documentary film "Roger and Me."

28. Buchanan, *Great Betrayal*, 43. This problem is identified even by economists who favor free trade. See Robert Reich, *The Work of Nations: Preparing Ourselves for 21st Century Capitalism* (New York: Knopf, 1991).

29. Quoted in Miroslav Nincic, *Democracy and Foreign Policy: The Fallacy of Political Realism* (New York: Columbia University Press, 1992), 20.

30. Walter LaFeber develops this theme throughout his work *The American Search for Opportunity, 1865–1913*, vol. 2 of *The Cambridge History of American Foreign Relations* (Cambridge: Cambridge University Press, 1993).

31. Buchanan, *Great Betrayal*, 14, 71, 113.

32. Peter J. Spiro, "The New Sovereigntists," *Foreign Affairs* 79, No. 6 (November/December, 2000): 9-15; Ronald D. Rotunda, *Constitutional Problems with Enforcing the Biological Weapons Convention* (online) Washington, D.C.: Cato Institute, *Cato Foreign Policy Briefing No. 61*, September 28, 2000. Accessed July 16, 2001. Available at: www.cato.org/pubs/fpbriefs/fpb-061es.html.

33. Carpenter, *Search for Enemies*, 182–183.

34. Buchanan, *Great Betrayal*, 107.

35. Public support for the operation in Somalia actually was declining even before the disastrous firefight that killed 17 U.S. troops. See James Burk, "Support for Peacekeeping in Lebanon and Somalia: Assessing the Casualties Hypothesis," *Political Science Quarterly*, Vol. 114, No. 1 (Spring 1999): 53–78.

36. Richard Falk, *On Humane Governance: Toward a New Global Politics* (University Park, PA: The Pennsylvania University Press, 1995), 15.

37. P. J. O'Rourke, *All the Troubles in the World: The Lighter Side of Overpopulation, Famine, Ecological Disaster, Ethnic Hatred, Plague, and Poverty* (New York: Atlantic Monthly Press, 1994).

38. Carlotta Gall, "Taliban suspected in fatal attack," *The Chicago Tribune*, April 25, 2003.

39. Tucker and Hendrickson, *Imperial Temptation*, 211.

40. Buchanan, *Great Betrayal*, 230.

41. Russett, *No Clear and Present Danger*, 72-77.

42. Frank L. Klingberg, "The Historical Alternation of Moods in American Foreign Policy," *World Politics*, Vol. 4, No. 2 (January 1952): 239–273; Frank L. Klingberg, *Positive Expectations of America's World Role: Historical Cycles of Realistic Idealism* (Latham, MD: University Press of America, 1996).

43. Hunt, *Ideology*, 38–41; Walter A. McDougall, *Promised Land, Crusader State: The American Encounter with the World Since 1776* (Boston: Houghton Mifflin Company, 1997), 113; Robert L. Beisner, *Twelve Against Empire: The Anti-Imperialists 1898–1900* (New York: McGraw-Hill Book Company, 1968).

44. Quoted in David Fromkin, *In the Time of the Americans* (New York: Alfred A. Knopf, 1995), 385.

45. Ole R. Holsti and James N. Rosenau, *American Leadership in World Affairs: Vietnam and the Breakdown of Consensus* (Boston: Allen & Unwin, 1984); Ole R. Holsti, "The Three-Headed Eagle: The United States and System Change," *International Studies Quarterly* 23, No. 3 (September, 1979): 339–359; Michael Mandelbaum and William Schneider. "The New Internationalism: Public Opinion and American Foreign Policy," in *Eagle Entangled U.S. Foreign Policy in a Complex World*, ed. Kenneth A. Oye, Donald Rothchild, and Robert J. Lieber (New York: Longman, 1979), 40–42; Eugene Wittkopf, *Faces of Internationalism: Public Opinion and American Foreign Policy* (Durham, NC: Duke University Press, 1990).

46. Norman Podhoretz, "Strange Bedfellows: A Guide to the New Foreign-Policy Debates," *Commentary*, December 1999; Aaron L. Friedberg, "Are Americans Becoming Isolationist?" *Commentary*, November 1998.

47. Miroslav Nincic, "Domestic Costs, the U.S. Public, and the Isolationist Calculus," *International Studies Quarterly* 41, No. 4 (December 1997): 598.

48. Steven Kull and I. M. Destler, *Misreading the Public: The Myth of a New Isolationism* (Washington, D.C.: Brookings Institution Press, 1999).

CHAPTER 5

The Logic of Liberalism

In January 2002, Illinois Governor George Ryan, a Republican, visited Cuba with a delegation of executives from Illinois pharmaceutical and medical supply businesses. Their immediate purpose was commercial: to arrange the sale of medicines and medical equipment to Cuba in response to the devastation done by Hurricane Michelle two months earlier. Ryan's ultimate purpose, though, was political: to bring about the end of the trade sanctions the United States had imposed on Cuba in 1960 when its leader, Fidel Castro, expropriated U.S.-owned businesses and established friendly relations with the Soviet Union. "[I]t's time to end the embargo and welcome Cuba fully into the international marketplace," said the governor.

Ryan's initiative was part of a larger drama unfolding around U.S.-Cuba relations. A strong momentum had developed in Congress to ease restrictions on private relations with Cuba. President Bush had promised to veto any such bills, however. The governor was undercutting the policy of the president even though they were members of the same political party.

The governor's mission to Havana provoked a minor tempest back home. Chicago journalist Marianne Murciano chastised Ryan for his "questionable friendship" with Castro, who "heads one of the world's most repressive dictatorships" in "... a country that hasn't had a free election in more than 43 years..."[1] Not that Governor Ryan was unconcerned about human rights and democracy in Cuba. He too sought Cuba's liberalization. He simply thought that opening up relations with Cuba was a better way to reach that end. "I don't think isolation makes [Cuba] any freer," he observed. *The Chicago Tribune*, advocating termination of sanctions, agreed. "If an American bank or producer were to extend credit," it wrote, "Cuba would have to demonstrate its creditworthiness by opening up at least part of its finances and economy to foreign scrutiny. In effect, the U.S. would be promoting transparency in Cuba—and isn't that in part what we want?"[2] Trade, in other words, would hasten Cuba's freedom.

Beneath the disagreement over economic sanctions on Cuba, then, lays a stratum of consensus: The United States ought to foster democracy and human rights in Cuba. That agreement reflects the logic of liberalism.

INTRODUCTION

Overview

This chapter develops the following basic points about the logic of liberalism:

- It prescribes that the United States should seek the expansion of liberty because the United States and the world are better off when trade is free, nations are governed democratically, human rights are honored, and nations have self-determination because liberty promotes prosperity, peace, and cooperation;
- the logic of liberalism makes no specific assumptions about the power of the United States beyond the rather general assumption that it has the capability to increase liberty to some extent; however, any serious program actively to expand liberty necessarily makes expansive assumptions about U.S. power;
- promoting liberty is a moral obligation as well as a means to advance U.S. interests;
- the promotion of liberty has been a salient theme in U.S. foreign policy discourse since the country gained its independence; since the late 1800s, it has significantly shaped what the United States does abroad and plays a significant part in the foreign policy thinking of the Bush administration.

The logic of liberalism derives directly from classical liberalism, a strain of modern Western political and economic thought. Liberalism was developed by such luminaries as John Locke, Adam Smith, Thomas Jefferson, John Stuart Mill, and Immanuel Kant. At its core, liberalism is committed to political and economic freedom. The words liberalism and liberty have the same root, the Latin word for free. In the United States, the term's meaning has been muddied by the country's political history. It now is generally understood as support for government programs to regulate the economy, promote equality, ameliorate poverty, and so forth. That is not the sense in which the term is used in this chapter.

The international role of the United States, according to the logic of liberalism, is to increase individual and national liberty worldwide. It would expand liberty by promoting the expansion of free trade, the spread of democracy, the protection of human rights, and the national self-determination of peoples.

The means to be used could range along a wide continuum. At one end would be verbal advocacy, such as praising states for increasing freedom (perhaps by freeing political prisoners) and condemning states for decreasing freedom (perhaps by canceling elections, arresting political opponents, or dissolving the legislature). At the other end would be military interventions to topple dictatorships. Between these extremes would be many different kinds of behaviors, including: diplomatic initiatives to incorporate liberal norms in international law and United Nations resolutions; covert provision of financial support for prodemocracy political parties, newspapers, and labor unions; "constructive engagement," that is, diplomatic and political encouragement of friendly governments to undertake reforms leading to democracy; economic sanctions to punish the failure to reform; and covert operations to destabilize nonliberal regimes.

U.S. INTERESTS

Liberal political and economic institutions are superior to alternative forms of social organization and promote U.S. well-being and security. This can be seen in four key settings: the advancement of free trade or market economies, the expansion of democracy in the world, the protection of human rights, and the achievement of self-determination of nations.

Free Trade

The national interests of the United States are advanced when other nations follow liberal principles in their economic policies. Such policies are known by a variety of labels, including capitalist, free trade, open economy, and free market economy. They apply both to the organization and policies of the economy within the country and to its policies for economic exchange with the rest of the world.

Free trade is beneficial because it facilitates economic development of poor countries. Economic growth is natural; it results from myriad efforts by millions of individuals to improve their well-being by increasing their productivity. Therefore, "[w]hen a country does not grow, it is not because it lacks anything; it is because something is standing in the way. . . . [M]ost often it is actions of the government that prevent growth."[3] The key to effective economic organization and policy, therefore, is to get the government out of the way: "If the government is arranged so that individuals will receive most of the benefits they produce if they are able to become more productive, then many people will become more productive, and so will the country."[4] In a market economy, the government's proper role is to create the conditions under which individuals can profit from their initiative. Policies that would limit individual gain, such as high taxes, inflation of the currency, or nationalization of property, are forbidden.

Free trade not only promotes economic growth in poor countries; it also maximizes global and American prosperity. It removes tariffs, quotas, export subsidies, and other artificial impediments to international commerce. Such impediments, which are intended to protect domestic producers or workers or to secure a positive balance of trade (that is, the value of what one exports or sells exceeds the value of what one imports or buys), render the world economy less efficient and productive. In an open economy, buyers and sellers, adjusting their investment and consumption decisions in response to the lure of profits and bargains, steer the economy toward maximum production. When demand exceeds supply, sellers can and do raise their prices as buyers bid against each other for the scarce goods. Undersupply thus drives up profits in the short run. It also attracts investment, though, thereby bringing supply and demand into equilibrium in the long run. Overproduction, on the other hand, leads to declining prices and dwindling profits, which motivates producers to switch their investments into more profitable sectors. Supply then drops until it once again matches demand. Investment flows out of the production of goods for which there is insufficient demand and into the production of goods for which there is insufficient supply. Given a fixed pool of resources, a market economy ensures the greatest production of goods and services, thereby maximizing human welfare. However, government interventions in the economy provide direct or hidden subsidies for the unproductive and wasteful at the expense of the productive and efficient.

Efficient economic production maximizes economic growth and increases human prosperity. Increasing prosperity in turn expands markets for American exports and therefore increases the prosperity of the United States, its corporations, and its workers. "Trade may enable poorer nations to catch up, or to grow faster than we do; but this does not cause us to slow down. . . . We gain, too."[5] The rising tide lifts all boats.

Free trade not only is economically beneficial; it also fosters peace: "If commerce were permitted to act to the universal extent it is capable, it would extirpate the system of war."[6] The first way it does so is negative: Free trade precludes the strife-causing policies of imperialism. Under imperialism, strong states impose political control over weaker peoples so that the strong can exploit the weak. Imperialism begets war because victimized peoples rebel against its yoke and because empires, in conflict over control of territory, go to war. Under imperialism, political control is paramount, and wars must be fought to get it and keep it. Under free trade, however, political control is economically irrelevant. If states do not meddle in the marketplace, then the composition and disposition of foreign states bear no consequence for one's access to resources or markets: If one has the money to buy or attractive goods to sell, the market will guarantee the exchange.

The second way that free trade promotes peace is by creating a vested interest in peace. The nation's prosperity depends on maintaining its economic ties with other countries; war disrupts those ties; hence war brings economic loss. Free trade thus creates a peace interest for the economy as a whole. It also creates a class of persons whose interests are promoted by international commerce. International finance created the "peace interest" that made the nineteenth-century balance of power system effective.[7] Likewise, following World War II, free trade was integral to the plan to pacify Europe by creating a class of powerful interests who would oppose future movement toward war among the countries of western Europe.[8] *The New York Times* foreign correspondent Thomas Friedman observes that no two nations that both are home to a McDonald's franchise have ever gone to war against each other.[9]

Finally, free trade promotes peace by fostering democracy, which is a peaceable political system. As *Newsweek* editor Fareed Zakaria puts it, free trade "has a powerful effect on the politics of emerging markets, locking in reforms, forcing political openness and strengthening the forces of liberal democracy."[10] Moreover, the wealth created by market economics breeds democracy. "[T]he fact that essentially all wealthy countries are democracies is strong evidence that: (1) something about being wealthy makes a country likely to become democratic, (2) democracy may be a necessary (or almost necessary) condition to become wealthy, or (3) both."[11]

Three mutually reinforcing processes cause free trade to lead to democracy. First, as global prosperity increases, so does the prosperity of its member countries. Prosperity expands and strengthens the middle class, which demands reforms that lead eventually to democratic government. Second, market economies require independent judgment, which is inconsistent with authoritarian rule; as people develop the habit of thinking and deciding on their own in business, they come to reject the government doing their thinking and deciding for them on other matters. Third, free trade fosters democracy because of the interactions that are required by international commerce. Through contacts with people from the modern democracies, people from other countries learn democratic values.[12]

Democratization

Democracy is desirable because it is the best form of government. It provides the greatest protection for individual freedom and for civil and political human rights: "[D]emocracies have the great advantage that they can be counted on not to kill large numbers of their citizens or let them starve to death."[13] As Nobel Laureate Amartya Sen discovered, "no substantial famine has ever occurred in any independent and democratic country with a relatively free press."[14] Democracy fosters domestic justice, which in turn reduces the chances of the civil strife that leads to massacres and mass slaughters in much of the world.[15]

Democracy is also a superior form of government because it supports economic development. This is so for three reasons. First, democracy adjusts modes of thinking in ways appropriate for economic growth: The liberty that comes with democracy teaches the values necessary for rational economic decisions.[16] Second, democracy reduces the governmental corruption that impedes economic efficiency in many countries. Democratic government, of course, does not prevent corruption. But the political competition and individual freedoms that are inherent in democracy allow corruption to be revealed and for the guilty parties to be thrown from office. Third, democracy increases political stability, which is prerequisite to economic growth. Democracies are stable because they provide an outlet for public dissatisfaction during periods of economic distress. Autocracies, on the other hand, stifle dissent, which creates a false appearance of stability until unhappiness erupts in turmoil.[17] "Civil wars do not start because people lack food, but because they lack hope. They feel they have no power to change their political system and affect the course of their own future. In frustration they resort to changing things through the force of arms."[18]

Most importantly, democracy is the best form of government because it fosters peace. "Free people, where governments rest upon the consent of the governed, do not wage war on their neighbors," said President Reagan.[19] Democracy is intrinsically pacific because ordinary people, once they have political power, will apply the brake on the engines of war. "[I]t is very natural," wrote the philosopher Immanuel Kant, that the people in a liberal system "will have great hesitation in embarking on so dangerous an enterprise. For this would mean calling down upon themselves all the miseries of war. . . ."[20] In nondemocratic systems, on the other hand, political power can be held by social and economic groups that do benefit from war and thus propel their countries into wars for their own gain.

Social science strongly supports the thesis that democracies are more peaceful than are nondemocracies.[21] Although democracies historically have fought about as many wars as have nondemocracies, they are less likely to initiate or escalate crises or to start wars than are nondemocracies. Democratic aggression is not unheard of, especially against nondemocracies, but to a large extent, when democracies have fought wars, it has been as victims of aggression by nondemocracies.

The most important fact, though, is this: Democracies have peaceful relations with each other. They do not fight wars with other democracies; they even are inhibited against threatening to use force in their disputes with other democracies; they are likely to ally themselves with other democracies and to stay allied for longer; and they are relatively likely to use cooperative ways of solving their conflicts with each other. There is, in other words, a "*democratic peace*." Democratic countries have created for themselves a "zone of peace"[22] characterized by "the expectation that war is not a legitimate or likely recourse. . . ."[23]

The democratic peace suggests that Kant's explanation for why democracies are pacific is not completely true. Clearly, in their dealings with nondemocracies, the peoples of democracies can get riled up enough to support war, but not so against other democracies. The passions that can lead to war are tempered in relations between democracies. "Because widespread strong emotions are necessary to generate enough unanimity to authorize a war, democratic publics normally will only support wars against countries that they see as different and despicable. It is much easier for citizens of a democracy to hate a dictator than to hate a democratic government, and it is very hard to convince a democratic public that it should go to war against another democracy."[24]

Michael Doyle explains why: "The leaders and publics of domestically just republics, which rest on consent, presume foreign republics to be also consensual, just, and therefore deserving of accommodation. . . . At the same time, liberal states assume that non-liberal states, which do not rest on free consent, are not just. Because non-liberal states are perceived to be in a state of aggression with their own people, their foreign relations become for liberal governments deeply suspect. . . . In short, fellow liberals benefit from a presumption of amity; non-liberals suffer from a presumption of enmity." He calls this "mutual liberal democratic respect."[25]

The war-inhibiting role of public opinion only partly accounts for the democratic peace, however. It explains only why democratic countries don't go to war or threaten to use force against each other; it does not explain the more positive cooperative relations that go along with the democratic peace. Two other factors seem to buttress the democratic peace. First of all, democratic governance facilitates conflict resolution. Democracy breeds habits of compromise within the country, and those habits become generalized toward relations with fellow democracies. It affects the nature of leaders: "Democratic politics tends to reject people who are perceived to be combative and unwilling to compromise."[26] Democracies also have shared standards of fairness, which facilitates peaceful settlement of disputes via negotiations.

Second, democratic peace is reinforced by the pacific effects of international commerce. Democracies trade with each other more than they do with other countries, even after controlling for other variables that affect trade patterns. Commerce is conducive to peace. Not only must war be avoided; expectations of war must be avoided, too: "Since keeping open markets rests upon the assumption that the next set of transactions will be determined by prices rather than coercion, a sense of mutual security is vital to avoid security-motivated searches for economic autarky."[27] Commerce reinforces the democratic peace and the democratic peace facilitates commerce among democracies in what two scholars call a "virtuous circle."[28]

Human Rights

Two broad propositions establish the importance of human rights. First, human rights exist; they are not merely a form of Western cultural imperialism. Second, violations of human rights abroad harm the United States.

Universality of Human Rights

The existence of inalienable human rights was first established by liberal political philosophy. Individuals created the state, so the individual exists prior to the state. States, therefore, have no independent authority; the state derives its authority from the governed. The individual's rights, therefore, are inherent in her or his individual personhood, not in a grant from the government. Human rights, moreover, are universal: All people have them merely by being human. In the twentieth century, the universality of human rights was internationally recognized. They are inscribed in such key documents as the Universal Declaration of Human Rights, the Convention on Political and Civil Rights, and in human rights conventions adopted by regional groupings as diverse as the European Union, the Organization of American States, and the Organization of African Unity. Of course, not every right asserted by an individual or group or recognized by a government or international organization constitutes a universally recognized and inalienable human right. There is, nevertheless, a core set of rights that have been repeatedly acknowledged and therefore presumptively have legitimacy.

Civil and political rights, such as those in the U.S. Bill of Rights, have priority over economic and social rights, and individual rights have priority over group rights, for three reasons. First, they are intrinsically more important. Second, civil and political rights are prerequisite to the fulfillment of economic and social rights; civil and political rights inhibit the state from trampling economic and social rights. Third, as a practical matter, political and civil rights are more attainable than are economic and social rights. Civil and political rights are clearly addressed to the state; the state is the body that must assure them by not violating them itself. The agent for assuring economic and social rights, however, is not defined. If individuals have a right to work, for example, does that mean that the state is obliged to provide work? Moreover, for the state to assure economic and social rights, as they have been enumerated in various international documents, would require the implementation of programs far exceeding the resources of all but a few of the world's nations.

Finally, advocacy of human rights does not constitute cultural relativism. Cultural relativism contends that human rights are a construct of Western culture and that their imposition on the peoples of Latin America, Africa, and Asia therefore represents cultural imperialism and is illegitimate.* But that claim is wrong. Cultures are adaptable, not rigid. In every place on the globe, the existing culture is a blending of traditional and modern cultures. The politics of human rights, therefore, is far more subtle than is suggested by the term "cultural imperialism." That term connotes an image of a powerful outside force imposing its will on a unified victim population. In reality, though, the defenders of traditional culture usually are locked in battle with indigenous human rights activists. Finally, the cultural imperialism thesis is internally contradictory. Because human rights are contested within a country's political system, protecting the traditional culture means supporting a conservative or reactionary elite. The contradiction arises when the conservative elite controls the state, for the state (and often the definition of the nation) itself is an import from the West and thus in conflict with the traditional culture.

Human Rights and U.S. Interests

Protecting universal human rights promotes American national interests by enhancing the effective functioning of government and public policy. Violations of human rights create or intensify problems that, because of global interdependence, damage the United States and its citizens and their interests.** For instance, repression of activists prevents reporting of environmental problems and epidemics such as SARS that eventually affect the United States, repression leads to increasing immigration to the United States, and U.S. support for governments that violate human rights increases the likelihood that U.S. citizens will become targets of terrorist groups.[29]

Self-Determination

As the economic and political freedom of individuals must be promoted against the power of the state, the economic and political freedom of peoples must be freed from foreign control. A person cannot be free if she is a member of an enslaved people. Empires are illegitimate and must be dissolved as soon as practically possible. So, too, spheres of influence or other violations of the sovereign independence of states are wrong and must be stopped.

---

* This argument seems to be most intense about the rights of women in the Islamic world or against such practices as female circumcision.
** Concern with promoting and protecting human rights is one of the commonalities that link the logic of liberalism with the logic of liberal internationalism.

It is in the best interests of the United States to see the end of empires and spheres of influence. Foreign domination, formal or informal, contradicts the most powerful social force in the modern world: modern nationalism. Consequently, foreign domination of peoples is harmful to U.S. interests in three inter-related ways. First, it leads to wars of national liberation. The social unrest in such wars harms U.S. interests in stability. Second, internal strife is liable to be internationalized, so violations of the principle of national self-determination increase the risks of international war. Third, in the long run, the forces of nationalism are stronger than the forces supporting the status quo. If the United States fails to support national self-determination, or, even worse, supports the imperial power, when the nationalists gain power, they will see the United States as having been their enemy and act accordingly.*

All systems of foreign domination are illegitimate and contrary to American interests, even when the United States is the foreign power preventing self-determination.** The Vietnam War exemplifies the costs that can be incurred attempting to stifle revolutionary nationalism. The dangers of creating enemies might best be illustrated by the Iranian revolution of 1979. The United States had backed the Iranian monarch, the Shah, and Iran arguably was part of a U.S. sphere of influence in the Persian Gulf. When the Islamic revolution toppled the Shah, the people of Iran turned against the United States. A crowd attacked the U.S. embassy and took 66 Americans hostage, 53 of whom they held captive for over one year while huge throngs marched through the streets of the capital city, Teheran, chanting "death to the Great Satan." "By its support for the Shah," writes one scholar, "the United States got twenty-five years of good relations with Iran. In the fifteen years since he fell, Washington has felt the full blast of outraged Iranian nationalism."[30]

A Congenial International Environment

Liberal institutions require a supportive international environment. Ultimately, the long-term survival of liberty at home depends on there being liberty abroad. American leaders of all political stripes have shared that premise. Franklin Roosevelt, for instance, in 1941 tried to rally the American people to support U.S. assistance to the forces fighting fascist aggression, saying: "I tell the American people solemnly that the United States will never survive as a happy and fertile oasis of liberty surrounded by a cruel desert of dictatorship."[31] Two decades later, Lyndon Johnson's advisor Walt W. Rostow made the same point with a different metaphor: "It is difficult to envisage the survival of a democratic American society as an island in a totalitarian sea."[32]

---

*The same line of reasoning establishes another reason why the United States should promote democracy and human rights: When democratic forces overthrow U.S.-backed repressive dictatorships, they come to power antagonistic to the United States.

**Liberalism, in other words, implies a policy of anti-imperialism without calling upon a radical critique of the American political economy.

Freedom at home requires freedom abroad because, in economics, private U.S. businesses could not compete against foreign businesses that were backed by a national government. With regard to that nation's home market, the government would create two sets of rules, one applying to the U.S. firms and one to the national firms, with the rules discriminating against the U.S. firms. In other markets, the power of the government would give a decisive advantage to its firms. Only by forming an alliance with the U.S. government could U.S. firms compete against state-backed firms of other countries, and such an alliance would move the U.S. economy away from free market capitalism toward some form of state-regulated economy.

A world devoid of other liberal states, moreover, would be rife with threats to peace and national security, and American society, to protect itself, would have to become like a garrison state. Even if the United States continued to select its leaders by free and competitive elections, the institutions of the garrison state (high taxes, conscription, standing army, economic regulations, government secrecy, antisedition laws, executive branch dominance) would seriously erode the quality of American democracy.

The existence of other democratic capitalist nations also reinforces the American system's legitimacy. It bolsters public confidence that democracy and individual liberty are the best and most effective ways to organize social existence. Contrariwise, granting legitimacy to other forms of social organization encourages doubts. If socialism or benevolent despotism are good for China or Singapore, then why not for us? To the extent that such questions are widely held, they tend to erode the social consensus necessary for the preservation of American democratic capitalism.

U.S. POWER

As was noted earlier, liberalism is remarkably flexible about how the United States should promote freedom. Some tactics, such as praising democratic reforms or criticizing human rights abuses, use almost no resources and so are compatible with a conception of the United States having limited power. More assertive ways to promote liberal systems, though, require using resources and so must rest on the assumption that great power rests in the hands of the United States. At the extreme are those who favor the establishment of a liberal international order by the aggressive exercise of U.S. hegemonic power.

The power to promote liberalism, though, rests on more than U.S. resources. It is enhanced by the intrinsic attractiveness of democratic capitalism. All of the most successful countries in the world are capitalist democracies. Beginning in the 1970s, dictatorships began converting to democracies and closed economies began introducing market mechanisms. With the fall of communism in the Soviet Union, the last remaining ideological challenger to liberalism disappeared, leaving liberalism as the only viable coherent model for social organization.[33] Liberalism became international orthodoxy, as reflected in resolutions passed in the United Nations and the Organization of American States affirming democracy, human rights, and free trade. In promoting democratic capitalism, the United States is riding the wave of history, which greatly eases its task and improves its chances of success.

MORALITY

The logic of liberalism represents a serendipitous convergence of moral considerations and practicality. Free markets, democratic governments, human rights, and national self-determination not only promote U.S. national interests but also are moral imperatives.

The moral imperative is especially clear with regard to human rights. All violations of human rights are assaults on the dignity of persons and thus abhorrent. One simply cannot be aware of stories about people being tortured or imprisoned in degrading conditions for their political beliefs and not be appalled. Following the twentieth century, with its experience of totalitarian government and mass murder, extermination, and genocide, protecting human rights must be a fundamental requirement of conscience. As two journalists put it, "when somebody's spirit is crushed by tyranny, it is everybody's business at least to speak out and possibly to refuse to do business as usual with the crushers of that spirit. That is the idea . . . that should have animated the policy of the West when Germany was annihilating the Jews, but sadly it didn't."[34]

The moral imperative to promote national self-determination is nearly as strong. The global movement to end apartheid (South Africa's former system of legally required racial discrimination and oppression) sprang from the belief that White minority rule over the Black and Colored majority simply was wrong. The same moral sense fueled U.S. hostility toward Soviet domination of its satellites in East and Central Europe, as expressed in the 1952 Republican Party platform: "We shall again make liberty into a beacon light of hope that will penetrate the dark places. It will mark the end of the negative, futile, and immoral policy of 'containment,' which abandons countless human beings to a despotism and godless terrorism. . . ."[35]

Similarly, the expansion of free markets is a moral obligation. The Bush administration holds that free trade is a moral principle because it conveys "real freedom, the freedom for a person—or a nation—to make a living."[36] Clinton's national security advisor saw free trade as a moral imperative for fighting poverty: ". . . it is hard to see how the 1.3 billion people around the world living on a dollar a day will ever be able to live in dignity if we deny them the chance to sell the fruits of their labor and creativity beyond their borders. . . . [F]or the poorest countries, trade means growth and growth means improved working conditions. We don't want a race to the bottom in the international economy, but neither do we want to keep the bottom down. *It is not right* and it is not in our interest."[37]

LIBERALISM IN U.S. DIPLOMATIC HISTORY

Throughout its history, the logic of liberalism has influenced U.S. relations with the rest of the world. As a people whose revolution had freed them from monarchical rule and colonial domination, most Americans sympathized with republican and anticolonial revolutions, though their affection waned when revolutions took radical or violent turns.[38] The good feeling toward republican revolutions had strategic roots, too. "From the earliest days of the Republic, Americans had maintained that wars were caused only by the functioning of monarchies, and that there were no fundamental quarrels between peoples; if all countries were to become democracies, there would be no wars."[39] The Monroe Doctrine (1823), while motivated primarily by a realist concern to keep European powers out of the Western Hemisphere, also reflected a sense of support for self-determination in the Americas.

The people's sympathies, though, did not determine the government's policies. In an oft-quoted speech, John Quincy Adams, when he was secretary of state, declared that "America does not go abroad in search of monsters to destroy. She is the well-wisher to the freedom and independence of all. She is the champion only of her own."[40] The United States simply lacked the power to intervene decisively in revolutionary situations abroad and, had it tried, would have found itself drawn into wars it could not afford to fight.

Nevertheless, the United States was not indifferent to the struggle for liberty. In Adams's phrasing, its contribution would be twofold: it "will recommend the general cause [of liberty] by the countenance of her voice, and the benignant sympathy of her example." The latter was hardly a throwaway idea. From the first days they arrived, Americans conceived of their country as exceptional. It had a special mission: To establish political liberty on Earth, and, in doing so, to serve as an example (in biblical metaphor, to be the "shining city on the hill") for the rest of humanity, and thus to transform human history.

The logic of liberalism began to shape the foreign policy agenda in the late 1800s. The first important initiative was the Open Door policy, which advocated free trade in China as an alternative to China's being carved into spheres of influence by Japan and the European powers. The Open Door certainly served U.S. economic interests but it also appealed to U.S. liberal sensibilities. Similarly, liberal considerations played a role in the United States acquiring an empire during and after the Spanish-American War. Policy makers justified the war itself on liberal grounds: It freed Cubans and Filipinos from Spain's brutal colonial rule. Many offered that justification cynically, but that does not dismiss its importance. The policy had to serve anticolonial and liberal purposes if it were to be legitimate in the eyes of the public. Liberalism's anti-imperial strain also encouraged the early and abrupt abandonment of imperialism.

Liberalism first became the dominant foreign policy logic during the administration of Woodrow Wilson (1913–1921). Before the United States entered the First World War in 1917, Wilson had sent U.S. forces into Mexico, Haiti, and Santo Domingo because "I am going to teach the South American republics to elect good men."[41]

The logic of liberalism especially influenced Wilson's wartime diplomacy. It determined when the United States entered the war; so long as the czar ruled Russia and Russia was an ally of France and Britain, Wilson would have the United States stay on the sidelines, because it was not a struggle pitting the forces of democracy against those of autocracy. Only after the Russian Revolution toppled the czar did Wilson move toward intervention. Liberalism also framed his war aims. In his request for a declaration of war, he acknowledged the horrors of war and then proclaimed: "But the right is always more precious than peace, and we shall fight for the things we have always carried nearest our hearts—for democracy . . . [and] for the rights and liberties of small nations. . . ."[42] The war would "make the world safe for democracy." Liberalism, moreover, framed his peace aims. His program for peace, the famous "Fourteen Points," called for free trade and named the empires that were to be dissolved and the peoples who were to gain national self-determination.

The logic of liberalism next substantially influenced U.S. foreign policy during the administration of Franklin Roosevelt (1933–1945). Roosevelt abandoned U.S. efforts to shape the internal politics of other countries. He recognized the government of the Soviet Union and began normal diplomatic relations with it. He also quit U.S. meddling in the internal affairs of Latin American countries under his Good Neighbor policy. In both instances, the motivation was largely from realism: The United States needed to maintain good relations with those countries, which meant dealing with the governments that existed rather than ones we might have hoped to exist. In both instances, though, the policy reflected the national self-determination theme of the logic of liberalism. Consistently unsuccessful American attempts to dictate the form of government in other countries violated that principle and, having done so, created anti-American sentiment.

As the United States headed into World War II and during the war, the logic of liberalism inspired its vision of the postwar world. The first two of FDR's "Four Freedoms"—freedom of speech and expression and freedom of worship—are core values of liberalism. Liberalism also inspired the creation of international institutions for the postwar world. Article 1 of the UN Charter includes among its purposes "[t]o develop friendly relations among nations based on respect for the principle of equal rights and self-determination of peoples . . ." and "[t]o achieve international cooperation . . . in promoting and encouraging respect for human rights and for fundamental freedoms for all without distinction as to race, sex, language, or religion." Similar principles were incorporated in the Charter of the Organization of American States (1948). The International Monetary Fund and the World Bank were designed to create a viable international economic system based on open market principles.

National self-determination, too, was at the core of Roosevelt's stated war aims and much of his diplomacy. In 1941 he and British Prime Minister Winston Churchill included in the Atlantic Charter the right of all people to choose their own form of government. Both he and his successor, Harry Truman, pressed the Soviet Union not to establish puppet states in eastern and central Europe. U.S. insistence that Poland's government be democratically chosen and Soviet refusal to allow a free election or even a substantial role for Poles other than its stooges was a major source of the Cold War. The United States also clashed with its democratic allies, Britain and France, when it pressed them to dissolve their empires. According to one recent study, self-determination was the dominant strain of U.S. foreign policy during the 1940s.[43]

Nor was democracy ignored in the U.S. vision of the postwar world. As the occupying power of Japan and the dominant Western occupying power of Germany, the United States used its control to completely restructure their economies, social systems, and governmental structures in order to make them democracies so they could become peaceful contributors to the international order.

The logic of liberalism was central to the Cold War. The United States struggled against the Soviet Union and communism not just for reasons of national security. It placed itself in opposition to the Soviet Union immediately after the communists took power in Russia in 1917, long before it posed any real danger to U.S. security. The decisive impetus to Cold War antagonism was the clash of values. The Soviet system—with its denial of rights of property and economic freedom, its crushing of religious liberty and other basic human freedoms, its forceful imposition of its system on its satellites in eastern and central Europe—was the antithesis of liberal values. The dominant justifications for the containment policy were liberal. Even foreign policy professionals who thought in geopolitical terms found that they had to use the rhetoric of liberalism to persuade the U.S. population to support Cold War policies.

Policies toward the Third World during the fifties and sixties also reflected the application of liberal thinking to the problem of containment. Illiberal regimes—feudal in economics, authoritarian in politics—provided the perfect breeding ground for communist revolutions. To prevent the spread of communism in western Europe immediately following World War II and in Africa, Asia, and Latin America, the United States had to foster progressive social change through aid programs that built up economies and strengthened democratic forces. The Marshall Plan, foreign aid programs, and the Alliance for Progress grew out of that thinking.

The Cold War was marked by the anomaly (from the vantage point of the logic of liberalism) of the United States supporting dictatorships, and in several instances overthrowing elected governments and installing dictatorships in their place. Yet supporters of that behavior defended it on liberal grounds. First, the governments the United States overthrew were likely to cease being democracies in any case because communist elements in the government would seize power and turn them into dictatorships. Communist dictatorships would be long-lasting and resistant to reform, whereas a U.S.-installed dictatorship could be reformed and might even revert to democracy. Therefore, the short-term support for a Western dictatorship represented less of a deviation from democracy than did a long-term communist takeover. Second, a communist government would be more harmful to the freedom of the people than would a traditional dictatorship.[44] Third, communist acquisition of power in the Third World would strengthen the communist bloc. Given that the most important task of American diplomacy was to avoid losing the Cold War—a task required by the logic of liberalism—then the sacrifice of democracy in one country would advance the cause of democracy worldwide.

Supporting or even cooperating with dictatorships ceased to be acceptable to the American public by the late 1960s and into the 1970s. The left wing of the political spectrum rejected U.S. support for repressive right-wing dictatorships. The right wing rejected Nixon and Ford's policy of détente because it required the

United States to turn a blind eye to human rights violations in the Soviet Union and its allies.

What followed was a movement to make human rights a central criterion in U.S. diplomacy. The movement took hold in Congress and then, with the election of Jimmy Carter (1977–1981), moved into the White House. He created a bureau of human rights in the State Department to advocate human rights concerns in the making of foreign policy. The administration publicly censured governments that violated human rights and cut foreign aid to many of them. It jeopardized détente by inviting prominent Soviet dissidents to the White House. Nor was the promotion of human rights the only element of the logic of liberalism to serve as a central theme of his administration. He also disavowed supporting dictatorships as a way of containing communism and rejected U.S. intervention into the internal affairs of Latin America, the latter reflecting the spirit of the principle of self-determination. Carter's attempt to base U.S. foreign policy on liberal principles was unsuccessful, however, and contributed to his electoral defeat in 1980. His human rights policy especially seemed to be ineffective, internally contradictory, and harmful to other U.S. national interests.

Ronald Reagan's administration (1981–1989) jettisoned Carter's human rights emphasis as well as his disinclination to intervene in the internal affairs of other states. Reagan did not abandon liberalism as the guiding principle of his foreign policy, however. Instead, he shifted emphasis to two other elements in the liberal agenda: The promotion of free trade and, especially, the promotion of democracy. "No administration since Wilson's has been as vigorous or as consistent in its dedication to the promotion of democracy abroad as that of Ronald Reagan."[45]

The administration launched a full-scale ideological assault against communism. Reagan sought to win the Cold War by winning the ideological battle: To affirm democratic capitalism as the best social system, thus delegitimizing the Soviet model and causing its collapse. That would serve not only to spread democracy and capitalism, it also would serve to liberate the peoples captured in what Reagan called the "evil empire," thus also promoting national self-determination.

Reagan's liberal crusade went beyond policy declarations to include a wide array of actions to achieve its goals. For instance, it induced Saudi Arabia to raise its petroleum production substantially, thereby glutting the world oil markets and driving down oil prices, in order to create a cash crisis for the Soviet Union, which derived a substantial share of its export earnings from petroleum sales.[46] It collaborated with Pope John Paul II in funneling financial support through the Catholic Church to the Solidarity trade union in its battle against Poland's communist authorities. In a policy dubbed the Reagan Doctrine, it made war against communist and leftist governments: It supported anticommunist insurgents in Nicaragua and Afghanistan and it invaded Grenada with U.S. forces.

Although the administration's primary objective was to defeat international communism, its efforts to promote democracy were not limited to that objective. The administration applauded the transition to democracy as it occurred in various places in the world. It brought pressure to bear on South Korea and the Philippines to make a democratic transition. And it created the National Endowment for Democracy to foster the pluralism and civil society necessary for stable and effective democracy and to facilitate the conduct of fair elections. Other priorities sometimes compromised the administration's efforts to promote democracy. For instance, its policy toward apartheid in South Africa was called constructive engagement; the United States sought to have good working relations with the White minority government under the theory that it could then credibly prod it toward incremental reforms.

George Bush (1989–1993) was less of an enthusiastic spokesman for liberal values. Under the influence of the logics of hegemonism and realism, his administration emphasized stability rather than liberty. He took a decidedly cautious stance toward the collapse of communism, the Soviet sphere of influence in eastern Europe, and the Soviet Union itself, bolstering the status quo rather than seeking to accelerate the trends toward liberty. His preference for stability and for dealing with established authorities led to the administration's least glorious moment: Its hands-off reaction to the Chinese regime's brutal suppression of the prodemocracy demonstrations in Tienanmen Square.

Still, the influence of liberalism was not inconsequential. The administration continued to preach the gospel of liberalism. Moreover, its behavior showed the effect of the logic. It intervened to bolster new democratic governments in the Philippines and South Korea. It joined the Organization of American States and the United Nations in imposing economic sanctions on Haiti after a military coup removed its elected president. It continued to negotiate free trade agreements and to have the International Monetary Fund pressure countries into reforming their economies according to market principles. Twice Bush sent U.S. forces into battle: in Panama (1989) and in the Persian Gulf (1991). In both instances, in justifying his action, he emphasized that his adversaries were dictators.

In his campaign for the presidency, Bill Clinton savaged the Bush administration for failing to vigorously promote democracy and human rights abroad. Once in office, he made the promotion of the liberal agenda the central theme of his foreign policy. "All of America's strategic interests . . . are served by enlarging the community of democratic and free-market nations. Thus, working with new democratic states to help preserve them as democracies committed to free markets and respect for human rights, is a key part of our national security strategy."[47] Clinton himself made an even stronger claim: "In a new era of peril and opportunity, our overriding purpose must be to expand and strengthen the world's community of market-based democracies."[48] Democratization is more than a "key part" of a larger strategy; it is the country's "overriding purpose."

Several of the administration's actions reflected that commitment. It completed the negotiations, begun under Reagan and Bush, for the North American Free Trade Agreement (NAFTA) and the creation of the World Trade Organization (WTO). In the Department of State, it renamed the human rights bureau "The Bureau of Democracy, Human Rights and Labor." It continued and intensified Bush's support for Haitian president Aristide's return to power. In 1994, Clinton sent a delegation of three prominent Americans to persuade the regime to step down. When mere persuasion proved ineffective, he sent U.S. military forces to throw it out of power. Up to 20,000 troops then were deployed in Haiti in a peacekeeping role to facilitate the reestablishment of democracy.

Like his father, George W. Bush places greater emphasis on American military power and international stability than did Bill Clinton. That emphasis has only been enhanced since the terrorist attacks of September 11, 2001. Still, the administration continues to subscribe to the logic of liberalism. Three of the eight elements of its national security strategy—"Champion Aspirations for Human Dignity," "Ignite a New Era of Global Economic Growth Through Free Markets and Free Trade," and "Expand the Circle of Development by Opening Societies and Building the Infrastructure of Democracy"—embody liberalism. Its stated intention for postwar Iraq, moreover, following the successful Operation Iraqi Freedom, has been to reconstitute it as a democracy.

The logic of liberalism, then, has to one degree or another informed American diplomacy since the founding of the republic and, since the early 1900s, has defined "the greatest ambition of United States foreign policy."[49] The emphasis placed on the liberal agenda has varied across administrations, reflecting the strength of such countervailing forces as the condition of the international system and the power of the logic of realism in the administration's thinking. Since 1976, though, every administration has clearly and repeatedly subscribed to the logic of liberalism and to some degree shaped its foreign policy accordingly. Different administrations have emphasized different aspects of the logic and have used different strategies and tactics for promoting freedom abroad. That they diverged on how they sought to make good on their commitment to liberalism, however, does not negate the remarkable consistency of the commitment.

CONCLUSION

The logic of liberalism dictates that the United States seek to expand the realm of freedom in the world by promoting market economies and free trade, democracy, human rights, and national self-determination. It has been integral to most of U.S. foreign policy since World War I. Indeed, it seems that no foreign policy can attract long-term consensual support without being justified by liberalism. Nevertheless, the strategies for promoting a liberal agenda vary dramatically across administrations, reflecting the varying impact of other logics that are influential in different administrations.

DISCUSSION QUESTIONS

1. How can the logic of liberalism be integrated with other foreign policy objectives so that strong action to promote freedom does not alienate other actors whose cooperation is necessary for the achievement of other foreign policy goals?

2. Given that elites in other countries prefer to resist reform rather than lose their privileges or even their lives, how often and under what circumstances does the United States have sufficient influence to induce domestic reform abroad?

3. How universally attractive is the liberal model of democracy and capitalism? Is there a risk that promoting that model abroad will create conflicts with countries that have non-Western cultures?

4. Will it be possible to keep a liberal agenda limited to a relatively modest but feasible scale, such as reserving intervention for only the most severe of human rights violations or for when the United States has overwhelming power? Would not basing policy on principles create a strong pressure toward consistency and thus a loss of limits?

5. Given the complexity of the world, would a policy based on the logic of liberalism be rendered ineffective by inconsistencies in its implementation? Could the appearance of double standards be avoided? Would the appearance of double standards be fatal for the policy?

6. Why is it that the logic of liberalism's central goals of promoting human rights, democracy, and free markets have been embraced by virtually every recent presidential administration? Why are those goals so attractive to Americans? Must U.S. foreign policy incorporate the logic of liberalism if it is to attract public support? How willing is the public to support a liberal agenda? Will it be willing to move beyond verbal endorsements of democracy and human rights and begin to pay costs to promote those values effectively?

ENDNOTES

1. Marianne Murciano, "Ryan's Questionable Friendship," *The Chicago Tribune*, February 5, 2002.

2. "Put Cuba in Its Proper Place," *The Chicago Tribune*, January 29, 2002.

3. Max Singer and Aaron Wildavsky, *The Real World Order: Zones of Peace/Zones of Turmoil*, rev. ed. (Chatham, NJ: Chatham House Publishers, 1996), 52.

4. Ibid., 52–53.

5. Robert Samuelson, "Trade Free or Die," review of *The Great Betrayal: How American Sovereignty and Social Justice Are Being Sacrificed to the Gods of the Global Economy*, by Patrick J. Buchanan, *The New Republic*, June 22, 1998, 30.

6. Thomas Paine, quoted by Michael Doyle, *Ways of War and Peace: Realism, Liberalism, and Socialism* (New York: W. W. Norton & Company, 1997), 231.

7. Karl Polanyi, *The Great Transformation: The Political and Economic Origins of Our Time* (Boston: Beacon Press, 1944), Chapters 1–2.

8. Bruce Russett and John Oneal, *Triangulating Peace: Democracy, Interdependence and International Organizations* (New York: W. W. Norton & Company, 2001), 25–26.

9. Thomas L. Friedman, *The Lexus and the Olive Tree*, updated and expanded ed. (New York: Anchor Books/Random House, Inc., 2000).

10. Fareed Zakaria, "The New Face of the Left," *Newsweek*, April 30, 2001, 32.

11. Singer and Wildavsky, *Real World Order*, 19.

12. Ibid., 59.

13. Ibid., 59.

14. Amartya Sen, "Human Rights and Asian Values," *The New Republic*, July 14 and 21, 1997, 34.

15. Carnegie Commission on Preventing Deadly Conflict, *Preventing Deadly Conflict: Final Report with Executive Summary* (New York: Carnegie Corporation of New York, 1997), xxxiv–xxxv.

16. Avishai Margalit, "Rogini's Law," review of *Development as Freedom*, by Amartya Sen, *The New Republic*, September 11, 2000, 32.

17. William F. Schulz, *In Our Own Best Interest: How Defending Human Rights Benefits Us All* (Boston: Beacon Press, 2001), 77–81.

18. Dennis C. Jett, "Using Poverty As a Scapegoat," *The Chicago Tribune*, September 13, 2000.

19. Quoted in Tony Smith, *America's Mission: The United States and the Worldwide Struggle for Democracy in the Twentieth Century* (Princeton, NJ: Princeton University Press/Twentieth Century Fund, 1994), 270.

20. Quoted in Doyle, *Ways of War*, 280.

21. The literature is thoroughly reviewed in Russett and Oneal, *Triangulating Peace*, Chapter 2, and Doyle, *Ways of War and Peace*, 284–300.

22. Singer and Wildavsky, *Real World Order*.

23. Doyle, *Ways of War*, 293–294.

24. Singer and Wildavsky, *Real World Order*, 23.

25. Doyle, *Ways of War*, 282–283, 285.

26. Singer and Wildavsky, *Real World Order*, 23.

27. Doyle, *Ways of War*, 283.

28. Russett and Oneal, *Triangulating Peace*, 24–29.

29. Schulz, *In Our Own Best Interest*; Carnegie Commission, *Preventing Deadly Conflict*, 90–91.

30. Smith, *America's Mission*, 212.

31. Quoted in Smith, *America's Mission*, 124. FDR's reasoning is summarized in Frank Ninkovich, *The Wilsonian Century: U.S. Foreign Policy Since 1900* (Chicago: The University of Chicago Press, 1999), 124–125.

32. Quoted in Cecil V. Crabb, Jr., *Policy-Makers and Critics: Conflicting Theories of American Foreign Policy* (New York: Praeger Publishers, 1976), 178.

33. Francis Fukuyama, *The End of History and the Last Man* (New York: Free Press, 1992); Michael Mandelbaum, *The Ideas that Conquered the World: Peace, Democracy, and Free Markets in the Twenty-First Century* (New York: Public Affairs, 2002).

34. Richard Bernstein and Ross H. Munro, *The Coming Conflict with China* (New York: Knopf, 1997), 102.

35. Quoted in Smith, *America's Mission*, 189.

36. *The National Security Strategy of the United States of America*, September, 2002, 1.

37. Sandy R. Berger, *American Leadership in the 21st Century: Remarks at the National Press Club* (online) Washington, D.C.: U.S. State Department, January 6, 2000. Accessed April 17, 2001. Available at: www.state.gov/policy_remarks/2000/000106_berger.html. Emphasis added.

38. Michael H. Hunt, *Ideology and U.S. Foreign Policy* (New Haven: Yale University Press, 1987), 92–102.

39. David Fromkin, *In the Time of the Americans* (New York: Alfred A. Knopf, 1995), 120. See also Smith, *America's Mission*, 328–329, and Bradford Perkins, *The Creation of a Republican Empire, 1776–1865*, vol. 1 of *The Cambridge History of American Foreign Relations* (Cambridge: Cambridge University Press, 1993), 48–51.

40. Quoted in Walter A. McDougall, *Promised Land, Crusader State: The American Encounter with the World Since 1776* (Boston: Houghton Mifflin Company, 1997), 36.

41. Quoted in Ibid., 131.

42. Quoted in Ibid., 136.

43. Smith, *America's Mission*.

44. The classic statement of this argument is Jeane Kirkpatrick, "Dictatorships and Double Standards," *Commentary*, November 1979.

45. Smith, *America's Mission*, 304.

46. Peter Schweizer, *Victory: The Reagan Administration's Secret Strategy that Hastened the Collapse of the Soviet Union* (New York: Atlantic Monthly Press, 1994).

47. The White House, *A National Security Strategy of Engagement and Enlargement*. (Washington D.C.: Government Printing Office, February 1996), 96.

48. Quoted in Smith, *America's Mission*, 311.

49. Ibid., 4.

The Logic of Liberal Internationalism

On October 26, 2001, *New York Times* correspondent Thomas L. Friedman's column despaired of any meaningful help in the war against terrorism. "My fellow Americans," he wrote, "I hate to say this, but except for the good old Brits, we're all alone." In explaining the lack of support, he observed: "In part we're to blame. The unilateralist message the Bush team sent from its first day in office—get rid of the Kyoto climate treaty, forget the biological treaty, forget arms control, and if the world doesn't like it that's tough—has now come back to haunt us."[1] The real national interests of the United States, in other words, require cooperating with the rest of the world to frame agreements for the solution of a wide range of shared problems. That idea exemplifies the logic of liberal internationalism.

INTRODUCTION

Overview

Liberal internationalism is both an old and a new perspective on international affairs. It is intellectually and morally rooted in the "idealist" tradition of the period between the world wars. During the quarter-century following the outbreak of World War II, it was marginalized by the seeming triumph of realism and hegemonism. Events of the late 1960s and early 1970s, however, returned it to the center of American foreign policy debates. Indeed, some aspects of liberal internationalism are almost consensually accepted.

The essence of the liberal internationalist strategy is *cooperative multilateralism*: The United States should join others in devising common policy for solving shared problems. Its rationale rests on these main points:

- National security no longer is primarily a military matter but includes protecting the United States from dangerous side effects of interdependence such as

global pandemics and pollution, reducing the level of world armaments, and accelerating economic growth in poor nations;
- national security can only be promoted through global, multilateral cooperation;
- global cooperation requires effective international institutions, so the United States must work with and support international organizations and international law;*
- power is complex, involving different resources, actors, and hierarchies across different issues; military power has only limited utility and tends to be counterproductive; the power of the United States is, therefore, somewhat limited and dependent on situational factors;
- the United States has a legitimate leadership role but it must be leadership without dominance;
- the United States has a moral obligation to contribute substantially to solving global problems.

As with the logics presented in previous chapters, liberal internationalism seeks to promote the national interest, the well-being of the United States. It differs in stressing how the national interest depends on the common interest.

U.S. NATIONAL INTERESTS

Global changes have fundamentally altered the national interests of the United States. For the past two centuries, international interdependencies have increased in number and kind and grown exponentially in impact. This mushrooming interdependence has changed world politics in two ways. First, it has bred a new agenda of world politics emphasizing global issues of shared problems. Because the issues are global, their solution requires extensive international collaboration. No nation or limited coalition alone can deal effectively with these problems. Second, international institutions therefore have become increasingly competent and important. As the new global agenda has gained importance, the traditional agenda of military power and security has dwindling importance. Collectively, these changes add up to "a complex new calculus of the national interest."[2]

Interdependence

The past century has been revolutionary. Invention and widespread diffusion of communication, computation, and transportation technologies dramatically reduced the costs of moving words, images, data, goods, money, and people across the

---

* Liberal internationalism differs from what is sometimes called utopian globalism in that it does not seek to transcend the state system, but only to make it work more effectively. Examples of utopian globalism are Mel Gurtov, *Global Politics in the Human Interest*, 3rd ed. (Boulder, CO: Lynne Reinner Publishers, 1994) and Richard Falk, *On Humane Governance: Toward a New Global Politics* (University Park, PA: The Pennsylvania University Press, 1995).

globe. This fueled an amazing increase in international economic interdependence. International trade has grown at a much faster pace than other sectors of nations' economies, so that by 1999 exports and imports of goods alone represented over one-quarter of the value of the domestic production of the world's nations' economies. International flows of investment capital more than doubled in the decade after 1989 to constitute over one-fifth of the value of domestic production.[3] Foreign exchange trading (buying and selling different countries' currencies in world money markets) grew from $820 billion per day in 1992 to $1.5 trillion per day in 1998. The value of foreign direct investment (that is, ownership of economic assets in foreign countries) rose from $23 billion in 1975 to $644 billion in 1997.[4] Increasingly, any country's ability to control its economic fate has dwindled as its rates of economic growth, inflation, and unemployment are determined more by the rates of growth, inflation, and unemployment of the world's large economies than by its own political decisions. Economic sovereignty has become a wholly outdated notion. Modern telecommunications technologies and global economic interdependence also have facilitated the formation, propagation, and marketing of a nascent global culture.

The New Agenda of Global Issues

Interdependence has an ugly side, too, in addition to the erosion of national economic and cultural autonomy. The exponential growth of population and industrial production brought about scarcities of raw materials, depletion of fisheries, disruptions in the production and distribution of petroleum, famines, environmental catastrophes such as acid rain, and looming ecological dangers such as global warming and the depletion of the ozone layer.

The human consequences of globalization have political repercussions: intensified ethnic, class, and ideological polarization within countries and civil wars and massacres. These tragedies, along with famines and ecological disasters, have led, moreover, to unheard of movements of population. In 2001, 12 million people were refugees, four times as many as in 1976.[5] The total number of persons who had moved across national boundaries as refugees, asylum seekers, or legal or illegal immigrants was about 150 million.[6] Civil violence has driven millions more displaced persons from their homes into internal exile. In 1997, the total number of refugees and displaced persons was estimated to be over 35 million.[7] Rich countries spend billions of dollars to support asylum seekers in their countries; the costs of sustaining refugees and displaced persons fall disproportionately on the poor countries who host them.

The consequences of interdependence threaten the interests of all states. The power of the United States grants it no immunity. "Global menaces to an 'American way of life' may actually loom larger and more unpredictable in this crowded new world than did the danger of nuclear conflagration during the Cold War."[8] A State Department study concurred: "Global issues . . . directly affect the daily lives of Americans. There is no better definition of the national interest. . . ."[9]

The threats posed by global interdependence have changed the agenda of world politics. The old agenda of military security issues has been replaced by a new agenda of global issues in defining the most important political challenges facing human society. The agenda of global issues is large and diverse and constantly changing, so no definitive listing of its elements is possible. Its range is suggested by a 1992 special study by the State Department, which defined global issues as "transnational in origin, impact, and solution" and includes "the environment, population, human rights, refugees and migration, terrorism, narcotics, health issues such as AIDS, weapons proliferation, and international crime."[10] Another critical interdependence issue is coordinating macroeconomic policies among the large advanced industrial economies (the so-called Group of 7) so that all experience noninflationary growth.

The global agenda includes two other issues that impede the cooperation necessary to address other global problems. One is economic inequality. Economic globalization, while remarkably increasing the world's total wealth, has dramatically increased the gap between rich and poor countries. Moreover, the very technologies that drive globalization also remind those who are falling behind just how far behind they are.[11] Aside from being morally intolerable, global poverty must be addressed for two reasons. First, it exacerbates other problems. For instance, disparities in wealth contribute to ethnic and sectional violence and are major causes of immigration and refugee movements. Second, the poor countries "are also central to resolving global issues of the environment, energy, food, health, population growth, refugees and illegal immigration."[12] Those problems cannot be addressed effectively without their active cooperation, and they will be unlikely to cooperate while mired in poverty and inequality.

The other problem is externalized and polarizing regional conflicts. Such conflicts begin as disputes between a pair of nations or among a small number of nations. They become externalized when other countries support one side or the other. They are polarizing when intervening countries support different parties so that substantial power is placed behind both sides of the dispute. From the 1960s until its end in 1993–1994, the struggle over the apartheid system in South Africa was an internationalized and polarizing conflict. The most important current example is the stalemated struggle between Israel and the Palestinians, which divides Israel and the United States from much of the rest of the world. So long as that conflict endures, the Arab and Muslim countries will be unable fully to join with others, especially the United States, in addressing other issues on the global agenda.

Other regional and civil conflicts have a mixed impact on the world's ability to deal with global issues. On the one hand, violence exacerbates other problems: It diverts essential time and attention and "threatens global stability by eroding the rules and norms of behavior that states have sought to establish."[13] On the other hand, if it is not polarizing, then intervention by the global community can reinforce patterns of cooperation and strengthen recognition of common interests and values, thus increasing the community's capacity to address other problems.

Finally, although the global agenda ordinarily and understandably is considered as a set of threats to the world's well-being, it also presents opportunities for gains. The most obvious is the potential for commercial gain as solutions to problems in poor countries will fuel purchases of goods and technologies from the United States and other advanced industrial nations.[14]

International Institutions

As global interdependence has accelerated and the new global agenda has emerged, the number and variety of organizations engaged in world politics and international policy has exploded. Joining the some 190 states or national governments are:

- several hundred formal international organizations whose members are states, such as the United Nations, the European Union, and the Organization of American States.
- approximately 26,000 international nongovernmental organizations (NGOs), such as the human rights group Amnesty International, the environmental organization Greenpeace, and the relief organization Red Crescent.[15]
- countless transnational movements that collaborate toward some end without establishing any formal institution, such as the movement to ban landmines and the antiglobalization coalition.

This proliferation of transnational organizations is both consequence and cause of global interdependence. The technologies that allowed the growth in interdependence also support the functioning of organizations. People have created transnational organizations to address the new issues created by global interdependence. The growth of transnational organizations increases human awareness of our mutual dependence, which in turn facilitates growth of established organizations and the creation of new ones.

Although they increasingly share the global stage, states continue to be the most important international actors. Though some have predicted the state's demise, global interdependence has not made it irrelevant. It just has changed the environment in which it must operate.

The profusion of transnational organizations enriches and strengthens international civil society. The existence and growth of international society is one of the central facts missed by realism. The world is anarchic in that it lacks a central government, but it by no means is chaotic. Thomas Hobbes's famous description, in Chapter 13 of *Leviathan*, of the "incommodities" of the state of nature created by anarchy—"no culture of the earth; no navigation, or use of the commodities that may be imported by sea; . . . no arts; no letters; no society . . ."—clearly does not describe the world today, with its voluminous trade, travel and tourism, and cultural exchanges. While some states "are in continual jealousies, and in the state and posture of gladiators . . . ," many pairs of nations manifest deep confidence that they will not use force against each other.[16] Despite the lack of a world government, in other words, countries have established self-reinforcing patterns of cooperative behavior in their mutual interest.

Nor does the lack of a world government mean a lack of global governance. "At the global level, what we find is not world government but the existence of *regimes* of norms, rules, and institutions that govern a surprisingly large number of issues in world politics."[17] Those norms and rules can be thought of as international policy.[18] The regime-formation process is highly decentralized: It takes place in many settings, each attending to one or a small set of related issues. Regimes develop over time. They are partly embodied in formal documents, such as treaties and conventions, and formal institutions, such as the United Nations and the World Trade Organization, but also incorporate informal elements such as shared understandings and habits of behavior.

Effectiveness of International Institutions

These "islands of governance"[19] are effective because states and other actors voluntarily comply with the rules and norms of regimes most of the time. The rules and norms of behavior affect what international actors do despite the lack of any central enforcement mechanism in most regimes. They comply with rules and regulations for three reasons that reflect the complex, mutually reinforcing effects of morality and self-interest. First, as a general rule, states and other actors become parties to a regime voluntarily. States are not altruistic; they join a regime because they believe that it is in their best interests to do so. Regimes benefit their interests by placing limits on other actors, thus making an otherwise unruly environment more regular and predictable, thus making it easier to make subsequent decisions to advance their own interests. If a state were to renege on its obligations under a regime, it would weaken the bonds on others, and thus erode its self-interests. Therefore, in order to continue gaining the benefits of the regime, states are drawn to comply with the rules and norms that define the regime.

Second, states voluntarily comply with international policy because keeping promises is a basic principle of morality and behaving morally advances states' national interests. States have a vested interest in having an image for acting morally. States that violate basic moral principles come to be seen as purely self-seeking and untrustworthy. That image deters others from entering into relationships with them. One of the conditions necessary for relationships is equitable trust, that is, the judgment that the other party will not manipulate the relationship for its gain at the expense of its partner. Equitable trust is necessary because relationships entail depending on the decisions of the partner in unforeseeable circumstances. To enter into a relationship without equitable trust is to place one's self in jeopardy of predatory behavior by the other. Since no one wants to take on such risks if they can be avoided, states avoid relationships with states whose unscrupulous behavior in the past precludes equitable trust. So, compliance with moral principles promotes the state's long-term interest, which generally gives states a sufficient incentive to comply with the obligations of international policy.[20]

The impact of morality on self-interest feeds a third reason why states generally comply with their obligations. National interests are subjective, not objective realities. What states and other social actors do depends on what they think their interests are. Granted, certain interests—primarily sovereignty, territorial integrity, and security from attack—are so consistently held by states that they seem to be universal and therefore objective. But they are not, as recent history shows. In 1991 and 1992, the leaders of the Soviet Union and Czechoslovakia allowed their countries to dissolve rather than use force to keep them intact. Furthermore,

such supposed basic or vital interests as territorial integrity and security from attack only rarely are at stake in international affairs. Most of the time, the stakes
involve lesser concerns. Then, the subjectivity of the definition of interests is
much more clearly revealed. Among the subjective interests that states have (or
more precisely, that the people of a country have) is a sense of community with
other states with which they identify. One of the reasons why Poland, Hungary,
and the Czech Republic eagerly sought to become members of the North Atlantic
Treaty Organization is that they consider themselves part of the community of
western European nations and membership in NATO would embody that identity.
Similarly, some Americans are anxious when the United States is out of step with
the other democracies. Communities are defined to a substantial degree by the
values, principles, and ethical norms they share, that is to say, their common
morality. To violate that common morality, then, weakens the bond with the community, a condition that is uncomfortable for the deviant. That motivates the deviant to cease the violation of the moral code. Similarly, the interest in avoiding
separation from the community creates an interest in conforming to the demands
of morality.[21]

A National Interest in Strong International Institutions

Because the increasing effectiveness of international institutions enhances the
world community's capacity to cope with the problems of global interdependence,
the development of multinational institutions is a national interest of the United
States. "The next president and Congress," declared the president of the United
Nations Association, "must commit themselves to strengthening the United Nations system to handle these challenges. . . . [T]he United States has a vital interest in strengthening the U.N. system. Acting alone is not a sustainable option."[22]

International institutions are important mechanisms for international problem
solving. By providing established, institutionalized, and legitimate forums for conducting negotiations, they facilitate cooperation. Relative to developing a structure
for working out every new problem as it arises, international institutions lower the
transaction costs of diplomacy and cooperation and therefore contribute to the
management and solution of common challenges.

International institutions also provide a focal point for the development of international organization, which contributes constancy to international policy. International organization is informal, consisting of "multilevel linkages [among states
and other transnational actors], norms and institutions." The multilevel linkages
form networks, that is, regular patterns of communication and collaboration. These
change world politics. The networks, norms, and institutions become resources or
"organizationally dependent capabilities" for decision making and policy influence:
Networks create and reflect more or less established alliances, norms provide a basis
for persuasion, and institutions provide access. It is in the national interest of states
to conform to the rules of international organization. To disrupt them would sunder
the elite networks, which states are loathe to do, because of the loss of those resources. Hence the persistence of regimes and their rules.[23]

Declining Relevance of Military Power

That new interests have risen to the top of any well-ordered list of priorities is both a cause and a consequence of the lowered priority of traditional military security concerns. Such interests are much less important than they once were, and perhaps may even be virtually irrelevant if not harmful to the real well-being of the United States and its people.

Military security interests are devalued, first of all, because war and threats of war have lost their utility in the modern world. The analysis presented in the logic of isolationism is on the mark but incomplete. One additional reason must be mentioned: The development of a strong norm that states "refrain in their international relations from the threat or use of force against the territorial integrity or political independence of any state, or in any other manner inconsistent with the Purposes of the United Nations."[24] Force is permitted only in self-defense or as part of a collective defense against aggression.

Military might also is irrelevant to solving the problems on the new global agenda. Military strength is inherently unsuited, for instance, for solving global food or resource shortages, or for stimulating the global economy, or for caring for refugees. Thus "for many of the high priority items on the foreign policy agenda today, calculating the balance of military power does not allow us to predict very well the outcome of events."[25]

Indeed, the traditional agenda of world politics, with its focus on military security, actually hinders the management of interdependence-driven problems. Preparations for war consume (that is, waste) resources; money spent on arms cannot be spent on other purposes. The point goes beyond money, though; other inherently limited resources also are involved. Organizing international action requires an investment of time, attention, energy, and political capital by national leaders; spending them on military security questions denies them for work on the new agenda of problems. Therefore, addressing the new global agenda requires a corresponding decline in the political-military thinking of the old security agenda.

The old agenda obstructs the new agenda in one more way. As noted earlier, solving problems of interdependence requires collaboration, which in turn requires a generally cooperative attitude among nations. Preparation for war, however, goes directly against cooperative attitudes. It says to other states, "We expect war from you, and you should expect war from us. The bottom line is, we are enemies." By reinforcing conflictual expectations and inclinations, military preparations undercut the ability of the United States to advance its real interests. Needless to say, the actual use of military force has the same effect, only much worse.

Still, issues of security have not disappeared entirely. Indeed, large-scale violence within and between nations amplifies other problems on the global agenda and impedes effective political action. So security questions continue to require attention. But military action can be no more than part of a serious effort to create security. Such an effort would require significant action to address the root causes of the conflict, something that military force cannot do. Moreover, if military force must be used to deal with an immediate problem of ongoing violence, it should be undertaken multilaterally and through established institutions so that it is an undertaking of the community rather than one or a few leading countries. Otherwise, the unilateralism of the operation would erode the habit of multilateral cooperation on which so much depends. Over time, effective multilateralism will bring forth "a healthy and creative United Nations [which] will diminish the pressures for direct American intervention and allow for a much broader sharing of the costs."[26]

U.S. POWER

The United States continues to be a powerful country whose constructive involvement is absolutely necessary for managing global interdependence. It can and should play a leadership role. Nevertheless, its resources do not convert readily into actual power, that is, influence over others and control over events. The United States can influence but not dominate international affairs. Therefore, "our leadership must be of a new kind," one that "mobilizes collective action" because while "few great goals can be reached without America . . . America can no longer reach many of them alone."[27]

The decline in U.S. power and consequent change in the nature of its leadership result from the altered nature of power in a world of complex interdependence. Power has become complex and the distribution of power is pluralistic: "The world lacks a dominant axis of political alignment and antagonism; coalition partners in one arena of policy may be opponents in another arena; geostrategic, commercial, and ideological considerations often function at cross-purposes; and power rankings vary from arena to arena. . . ."[28]

Declining Utility of Military Force

Power rankings vary from arena to arena because military power no longer brings influence on nonmilitary issues. Military force, of course, still is potentially valuable. "[F]orce dominates other means of power," write Keohane and Nye in their seminal presentation of liberal internationalism, because "if there are no constraints on one's choice of instruments . . . the state with the superior military force will prevail."[29] If a militarily-superior state were willing to pay the costs, it could use force to impose its will. However, because constraints on the use of force have increased, states are more hesitant than they once were to use force to back up diplomacy. Despite its overwhelming military superiority, the actual power of the United States is much less because "it is becoming more difficult to translate military dominance into political influence."[30]

Limited Utility of Coercion

Indeed, coercion in general has lost much of its capacity to shape events. Most notably, economic sanctions have generally been ineffective in forcing changes in noneconomic policies. The optimistic assessment of the data found that sanctions worked in 33 percent of times they were used between 1914 and 1990. A pessimistic reading of the same history found that sanctions, when not combined with a threat of military force, worked in only 5 percent of the cases of coercion for noneconomic ends.[31]

Sanctions are unlikely to have significant economic effect if applied unilaterally, even by a state as economically powerful as the United States. To a large extent, other countries would replace the sanctioning country as markets and as suppliers of the target country. Even when sanctions have caused economic suffering in the target country, political influence has not followed, for three reasons. The first is exactly parallel to the reason why military coercion has lost its former effectiveness. "Pervasive nationalism often makes states and societies willing to endure considerable punishment rather than abandon what are seen as the interest of the nation, making even weak and disorganized states unwilling to bend to the demands of foreigners."[32] Second, the ruling elites in the target society can insulate themselves and their crucial supporters from economic pain; the suffering then falls on those, such as the general public, who lack the power to change the policy. Third, the ruling elites are able to blame those who imposed the sanctions for the economic pain the people are suffering; sanctions then have merely "bred popular hostility against sanctioners. . . ."[33]

Sanctions work best when imposed by the global community as a whole. Multilateral sanctions are more likely to have an economic effect. Moreover, elites in the targeted country would have a harder time blaming a set of enemies under those circumstances. Indeed, fully multilateral sanctions can work in some instances by the equivalent of shunning. They communicate that the target country has separated itself from the rest of the world, and thus create social and psychological pressure for it to adjust its policies.[34]

The Variability of Power by Issue Areas

In part because military and economic coercion have limited utility, no one source of power is applicable across all problem areas. Rather, different resources are relevant for different problems or issues. For military issues and problems, military resources continue to be most relevant. For global economic problems, having a large economy is the most relevant resource. For the problem of maintaining whale populations, possessing a whaling fleet is the key resource. It makes no sense to think about a single ranking of national power. Compared to the bipolarity of the Cold War, now there is "a more variegated lineup of 'movers and shakers,' with power rankings differing arena by arena."[35]

Nonstate Actors

For the new agenda of global problems, states no longer are the sole important actors. They share the stage with an enormous number of other kinds of transnational actors. Transnational actors have multinational membership and are organized primarily for international activities. Transnational actors fall into several categories, including: officials from the permanent secretariats of international organizations, such as the secretary general of the United Nations; international NGOs; movements such as the antiglobalization coalition; representatives of world religions, such as the Pope, the World Council of Churches, and the Dalai Lama; and transnational/multinational corporations, such as McDonald's, Disney, and Shell Oil.

These nonstate actors deploy various resources. Some provide key information because they are active in the field and close to the problems at hand. Others have great prominence and credibility and so are able to influence attitudes and shape public opinion. Multinational corporations, international banks, and international financial institutions move huge amounts of money around the world; the dollar value of private international investment is several hundred times greater than the total amount of foreign aid granted by all donor nations together. On economic issues, therefore, they may be more influential than most nation-states.

Characteristics of states enhance the impact of nonstate actors. First, no state has sufficient bureaucratic capacity to be purely self-sufficient in gathering information and implementing policies. Many states are terribly deficient. Nonstate actors, then, become indispensable extensions of government capacity and collaborators with governments. Second, government leaders depend on technical experts in their bureaucracies for guidance on policy. Bureaucrats in turn form their judgment through their interactions with other experts, including actors from international organizations and nongovernmental organizations. Third, the spread of democracy has increased the number of governments that must respond to a public opinion influenced by information from nonstate actors.

Power as Bargaining

Because coercion is prohibitively costly except in the most dire circumstances, influence means bargaining power. Moreover, the nature of global problems requires general cooperation for their solution. No one state or small group of states can manage the world's economy, stifle terrorism and the drug trade, constrain the international commerce in arms or endangered species, reduce pollution, and so forth. Attempts to do so unilaterally would be undone by those who would profit by acting in a contrary fashion. Therefore, power is the ability to form broad coalitions, to broker agreements to collaborate.

The coalitions required by complex interdependence differ from traditional alliances or internation bonds of friendship. Such traditional relationships were general purpose; they were partnerships on a variety of issues. Coalitions put together under complex interdependence, on the other hand, are *ad hoc* and issue-specific. Of course, having generally friendly relationships facilitates nations forming *ad hoc* coalitions. Most likely, though, the coalitions go beyond the set of friends. Moreover, the coalition is not constructed in order to strengthen the general bond among the parties. If relations in general are enhanced, that is a happy side effect of managing an immediate problem.

Bargaining power derives from several sources. It comes, first of all, from the ability to link issues together so that one side makes concessions on one issue while receiving concessions on others. Because of its tremendous and diversified resources, the United States has an unusually high capability to forge linkages and thus to have bargaining power. Indeed, were this the only criterion, the United States would have to be rated the world's greatest power. The other sources of bargaining power, however, make matters more murky. The capacity to form coalitions depends as well on the ability to persuade, to convince other states to adjust their thinking about, for instance, the causal dynamics of a problem, the likelihood that alternative policies would work, the cost-benefit ratio of various proposals, obligations and ethical responsibilities, and their chances of striking a better bargain. The ability to persuade depends, in turn, on the country's reputation for accuracy and truthfulness as a source of information and ideas and its reputation for looking out for the common interest.

Counterproductivity of Hegemonic or Unilateral Leadership

Because power under complex interdependence depends on being able to persuade and having a reputation for looking out for the common interest, hegemonic or unilateral leadership is self-defeating. Even if the United States were consistently to use its hegemonic power to implement policies that promoted the common interest, other states would resist its leadership because they would perceive it as exalting its self-interests over common interests.* Instead, in order to maintain the legitimacy of its leadership, the United States must foster "multiple leadership," in which it follows the leadership of other countries on some issues.[36]

A collective approach to decision making and problem solving requires that the United States avoid dictating policy. "We need to act more as catalyst than as commander, resorting more often to persuasion and compromise than to fiat and rigid blueprint."[37] Unilateral actions would degrade leadership in multilateral conditions because it would alienate other major actors.[38] It also would reduce America's moral authority.

Indeed, the United States must recognize that it is not "the indispensable country." The international community has been able to frame agreements—such as the Kyoto agreement on the reduction of gases that cause global warming, the treaty banning land mines, and the treaty creating the International Criminal Court—despite its opposition. By withholding its cooperation, the United States can weaken international initiatives, but it does not exercise a veto over global diplomacy.

---

* This point is essentially similar to the realist critique that hegemonism will provoke balancing behavior against U.S. hegemony.

Summary

Power is complex and widely distributed. Moreover the relative prominence of the United States necessarily has declined. It is only first among equals. Therefore its leadership must be conducted arm-in-arm with other important states. The United States must "seek ways to share not only the financial burdens represented by these problems, but also the burdens of leadership and responsibility as well."[39]

MORALITY

The United States must comply with the moral principles shared by the global community. It must do so not only because it is right but also because it is pragmatic. "[G]ood international citizenship is not a matter of charity. Good international citizenship is a matter of hard-edged national interest: A country's interest in being and being seen as a good international citizen is as important a national interest as the two traditional national-interest goals we always think of, namely security and economics."[40] In a world of complex interdependence, morality and national interest cannot be opposed categories. Conforming to moral codes defines and promotes the national interest.

Despite its instrumental benefits, "good international citizenship" also is a fundamental matter of right and wrong. The United States, because of its tremendous resources and because of the moral quality of the new agenda problems, is morally obliged to work together with other international actors to formulate and carry out policies that promote the common interest. This principle may be illustrated by the teachings of the Catholic bishops of the United States.

Basic facts reveal the moral significance of global problems. "Today there are 40 million people living with HIV/AIDS around the world. Of this total, 28.1 million live in Africa, 2.4 million of them children. 1.6 million Africans die each year from malaria and tuberculosis. . . . In the hardest hit African nations, between 1/3 and 2/3 of all 15-year-olds today are expected to die of AIDS. Over 12 million children have been orphaned in Africa alone as of 2000; 40 million orphans are projected by 2010."[41] Those appalling numbers clearly define a moral problem. The same would apply to the seeding of over 100 million landmines in the world. "Every 22 minutes someone is killed or maimed by an antipersonnel landmine; 500 people each week; 26,000 people each year; mostly civilians. . . . Children below 15 years of age make up 30–40% of mine casualties."[42] Global poverty also exemplifies the intrinsically moral character of the problems at hand. "Half of the world's people, nearly two and a half billion, live in countries where the annual per capita income is $400 or less. At least 800 million people in those countries live in absolute poverty, 'beneath any rational definition of human decency.' Nearly half a billion are chronically hungry, despite abundant harvests worldwide. Fifteen out of every 100 children born in those countries die before the age of five, and millions of the survivors are physically and mentally stunted." The bishops note that those facts give the elimination of world poverty "new moral urgency."[43]

National boundaries have lost their moral relevance; international ethics must be cosmopolitan; American action must promote the common good of all humankind. "Because of the blessings God has bestowed on our nation and the power it possesses, the United States bears a special responsibility in its stewardship of God's creation to shape responses that serve the entire human family."[44]

LIBERAL INTERNATIONALISM AND U.S. DIPLOMATIC HISTORY

Along with liberalism, liberal internationalism comprises what is commonly called Wilsonianism, after President Woodrow Wilson (1913–1921). Wilson was the first president whose foreign policy was heavily influenced by liberal internationalist premises. Nevertheless, elements of the logic appeared long before World War I made the world safe for Wilsonianism. Prominent European writers had advocated an international organization or world government to end the plague of warfare. Organized peace movements had formed in the United States as early as 1815. A strong movement for international law as the basis for world order had led to the establishment of a Permanent Court of International Arbitration in The Hague, Netherlands, in 1899. In 1878, the International Meteorological Organization was the first international body created to help states deal with a technical matter on which they shared interests. Although its attachment to isolationism precluded the United States joining either organization, it did join the Pan American Union in 1890 and the Pan American Health Organization in 1902. Support for international law and organization were part of the intellectual currents at the time and, in the first years of World War I, strengthened U.S. objections to German and British interference with shipping on high seas.[45] The normative impulse to improve the world, which enhances the attractive power of liberal internationalism, can be traced back well into the 1800s.[46]

Wilson took up these themes in his plan for restructuring international relations. His essential insight was that war must be eradicated by the working of effective international institutions. The cornerstone would be the League of Nations. The League would counter the warlike tendencies of the state system by contributing to the development of international law. It also could foster the peaceful settlement of disputes by hearing member states' grievances and suggesting diplomatic solutions. Most importantly, though, it would provide a mechanism of collective security to replace the balance of power. Acts that endangered international peace and security would be recognized as threats to all nations, and all nations would respond through the aegis of the League. Arraying the power of the world community against an aggressor would deter challenges to international order and, if deterrence failed, assured a lopsided conflict and thus a cheap and easy victory for the defenders of order. In proposing the League, Wilson was acting as spokesman for a substantial segment of U.S. public opinion. Indeed, his predecessor, William Howard Taft (1909–1913), had supported creating a "league to enforce the peace" in order to get rid of the balance of power.[47]

In addition to the League of Nations, Wilson's famous Fourteen Points included two other liberal internationalist proposals. One was the abolition of secret diplomacy by "open covenants, openly arrived at." Wilson reasoned that public scrutiny would keep states from striking the tawdry bargains that created an interest in joining wars. The other was his proposal for reducing armaments to the lowest possible level. Wilson assumed that states would fulfill their commitments under disarmament treaties because the pressure of international morality and public opinion would bolster their intrinsic interests in disarmament.

The Senate's failure to consent to the Treaty of Versailles, which included the Covenant of the League of Nations, did not signify a general renunciation of liberal internationalist thinking. Idealist and liberal internationalist thinking held powerful sway in the intellectual communities of the United States and Great Britain.[48] Even Wilson's Republican successors showed its influence. One of their major foreign policy initiatives was naval disarmament conferences, which one expert labeled "a monument to the Wilsonian formulation [of the new peace and international order]. The very fact that the United States took the lead is important. The Republican administrations that followed Wilson's presidency were just as committed to Wilsonian internationalism as he himself, at least insofar as disarmament was concerned."[49] World War II and the Cold War pushed liberal internationalism toward the margins of U.S. foreign policy thinking. Three factors trumped liberal internationalism during this period: The military instrument dominated all others, U.S. power superiority precluded any serious multilateralism, and the intensity of those conflicts meant world politics was dominated by security issues rather than complex trade-offs among many issues.

Liberal internationalism regained prominence in the early 1970s. Five developments brought this about. First, the Vietnam War made many Americans wary of using military force. Second, power became more diffuse and dispersed. Europe and Japan closed the gap that separated them from the United States. France and China asserted their independence from their former superpower protectors. Decolonization brought into existence nearly 100 new states that were more concerned with issues other than the Cold War. Third, the environmental movement, which began in the 1960s, the 1973–1974 Arab oil embargo, and predictions of resource scarcity drew notice to new threats. Fourth, these changes in international relations were duly noted in a wave of prominent academic writings. Fifth, the backlash against the amorality of the realism-inspired foreign policy of the Nixon administration fueled a more ethically motivated foreign policy.

Jimmy Carter's presidency (1977–1981) attempted to design a foreign policy based largely on liberal internationalist principles. President Carter himself observed that "in the near future issues of war and peace will be more a function of economic and social problems than of the military security problems which have dominated international relations since World War II."[50] The nature of the world's problems affected the nature of power. "In this [global] community, power to solve the world's problems—particularly economic and political power—no longer lies in the hands of a few nations. Power is now widely shared among many nations with different cultures and different histories and different aspirations."[51] It also amplified the need for cooperative diplomacy, for, as Secretary of State Vance noted, "each nation can surmount its own difficulties only if it understands and helps resolve the difficulties of others as well." He elaborated: "We cannot effectively promote multilateral diplomacy, control the proliferation of nuclear arms, fight international terrorism, reduce the levels of conventional weapons, or protect our interests in the oceans or space in a hungry, angry, embittered world. We are much more likely to achieve cooperation on these basically noneconomic issues if we can do our fair share in the long-term process of international development cooperation—if we are seen as furthering, not blocking, world aspirations." Indeed, according to National Security Advisor Zbigniew Brzezinski, "what is gradually, truly emerging [is] a global community." In this global community marked by diffusion of power and multiple issues, "leadership increasingly is in need of being shared. No nation has a monopoly of vision, of creativity, or of ideas."

Carter's experiment in liberal internationalist foreign policy was short lived. By early 1979, the administration's thinking and rhetoric had become dualistic. Secretary Vance and the State Department continued to see the world through liberal internationalist lenses. The White House, led by Brzezinski, seeing an upsurge of superpower rivalry and turbulence in Asia, Africa, and Latin America, returned to Cold War axioms. As time went on, the president became increasingly persuaded by Brzezinski's views. In 1979, he described the international environment as "a world of danger, a world in which democracy and freedom are still challenged, a world in which peace must be rewon day by day." U.S. foreign policy, then, must be "a quest for global stability in an increasingly turbulent world." As Brzezinski put it, "we have to play a stabilizing role, helping to provide a framework for orderly change, a framework of peace and stability."

The era of the Republican presidencies of Ronald Reagan (1981–1989) and George Bush (1989–1993) were guided by logics other than liberal internationalism. The only reflection of such thinking was Bush's concept of a "new world order" articulated after the collapse of communism, the undisputed end of the Cold War, and the successful coalition effort, under the aegis of the United Nations, to defeat Iraq in the Persian Gulf War. The new world order would have been an effective collective security system run through the UN. The administration's unilateral direction of the war itself, though, indicated that the new world order was a multilateral façade for hegemonism rather than a serious reflection of the logic of liberal internationalism. As one prominent critic put it, ". . . while praising multilateralism . . . U.S. policy toward multilateral diplomacy [is] at best, ambivalent and frequently hostile to that very process."[52] Another study came to a compatible conclusion: "On balance . . . the U.S. government has given insufficient priority to global issues."[53]

The Clinton administration (1993–2001) initially appeared to be strongly influenced by the logic of liberal internationalism. In its most important and extensive presentation of its national security policy, it recognized that "a number of transnational problems which once seemed quite distant, like environmental degradation, natural resource depletion, rapid population growth and refugee flows, now pose threats to our prosperity and have security implications for both present and long-term American policy."[54] It also made serious efforts to integrate global issues into the day-to-day workings of the foreign affairs bureaucracy, such as the creation of a Bureau of Global Affairs in the State Department.[55]

Liberal internationalism also was manifested in the concept of "assertive multilateralism," under which the United States would join with coalitions of other countries to stabilize places torn by conflict. However, assertive multilateralism was abandoned after disasters in Somalia and Bosnia, replaced by a hegemonism-inspired "doctrine of activism based on [Secretary of State] Albright's conviction that U.S. leadership is essential to calming upheavals of an unruly world."[56]

The current administration of George W. Bush, like that of his father, seems to be little influenced by liberal internationalism. It recognizes that U.S. well-being is endangered by nonmilitary challenges such as the environment and health crises such as AIDS and SARS. The administration's attention has been fixed on military security problems, though, even before September 11.

Indeed, one of the distinctive traits of the administration's foreign strategy was a continuation and intensification of the pervasive unilateralism that developed under Clinton. One critic, for instance, pointed to "a growing global dismay at what is widely perceived to be an escalating 'go it alone' tendency in U.S. foreign policy, an approach that dismisses the significance of multilateralism, international law, and the United Nations."[57] Examples of that unilateralism would be: the refusal to sign or ratify international agreements, such as the Convention on the Rights of the Child, the treaty creating the International Criminal Court, the Convention on Economic and Social Rights, and the Convention on the Rights of Women; the refusal to pay UN dues except as quid pro quo for UN agreement to U.S. demands; the withdrawal from ABM (anti-ballistic missile) treaty; and the refusal to negotiate a treaty banning biological weapons.

CONCLUSION

The logic of liberal internationalism prescribes a foreign policy of cooperative multilateralism under which the United States would play a limited leadership role in working with other members of the global community to adopt and implement solutions to the agenda of problems posed by global interdependence. Complex interdependence not only has changed the national interests of the United States, binding them closely with the common interest; it also has caused a diffusion of power in international relations and thus a reduction in the effective influence of the United States. Cooperative multilateralism thus is a pragmatic adaptation to a changed world. It also is dictated by the moral urgency of solving the world's problems.

The logic of liberal internationalism has played a sporadic role in shaping U.S. foreign policy. Aspects of it have been accepted by the political mainstream and it substantially shaped U.S. behavior during the Wilson and Carter administrations.

Aside from those two administrations, though, it has not been a dominant foreign policy logic and, given questions about its downplaying of the traditional agenda of security issues and its acceptability for the American political community, its chances of being the dominant logic in the foreseeable future seem slight.

DISCUSSION QUESTIONS

1. Is the premise that the new agenda of global problems has transcended the old agenda of security problems a factual claim about the relative importance of the two agendas or a normative claim about what it should be? What reasons can be given for assigning priority to the new agenda? What reasons can be given for assigning priority to the old one?

2. How would the logic of liberal internationalism diagnose the problem of international terrorism and what would be its prescription for dealing with it?

3. Does the profusion of international and transnational organizations and actors really indicate a relative weakening of the primacy of nation states?

4. Is the relative disutility of military power illusory in that it reflects the capability and willingness of the United States to deter the exercise of force by other states? If the United States were to reduce military spending and shift resources to other issues, would the use of force by other countries become more common?

5. Are the problems on the global agenda amenable to solution or management by international effort? Are the causes of those problems found at the international system level or in the internal workings of particular states? What would be the cost of solving global problems? Are they within or beyond the means of the international community?

6. Does the logic of liberal internationalism assign essentially the same global role to all the world's major actors? If so, is such uniformity a necessary or a good thing? Might not an alternative arrangement be for the United States to specialize in addressing the world's military security problems while other nations specialize in working on the problems on the new agenda?

7. Is liberal internationalism politically viable in the United States? Would the American people be willing to pay the substantial costs and make the necessary domestic adjustments required to solve global problems? Would the American people be willing to adhere in the long run to a perspective that minimizes the degree to which the United States is uniquely powerful and ascribed the role of world leader?

ENDNOTES

1. Thomas L. Friedman, "We Are All Alone," *The New York Times*, October 26, 2001.

2. U.S. Department of State, Management Task Force, *State 2000: A New Model for Managing Foreign Affairs* (Washington, D.C.: U.S. Department of State, 1992), 40.

3. Figures computed from World Bank, *2001 World Development Indicators*, Table 6.1, p. 320–322 (online) Washington: World Bank. Accessed February 22, 2002. Available at: www.worldbank.org/data/wdi2001/pdfs/tab6_1.pdf.

4. Thomas L. Friedman, *The Lexus and the Olive Tree*, updated and expanded ed. (New York: Anchor Books/Random House, Inc., 2000), xviii, 9.

5. Carnegie Endowment for International Peace National Commission, *Changing Our Ways: America and the New World* (Washington, D.C.: Carnegie Endowment for International Peace, 1992), 47.

6. Doris Meissner, "On the Fence: Interview by Moises Naim," *Foreign Policy* 129 (March/April 2002): 25.

7. Carnegie Commission on Preventing Deadly Conflict, *Preventing Deadly Conflict: Final Report with Executive Summary* (New York: Carnegie Corporation of New York, 1997), 3.

8. Carnegie Endowment, *Changing Our Ways*, 37.

9. Department of State, *State 2000*, 41.

10. Ibid., 40.

11. Friedman, *Lexus*, 70.

12. Carnegie Endowment, *Changing Our Ways*, 29.

13. Carnegie Commission, *Preventing Deadly Conflict*, 105.

14. Sandy Vogelgesang, "Annex D: The New Global Agenda," in U.S. Department of State, Management Task Force, *State 2000: A New Model for Managing Foreign Affairs* (Washington, D.C.: U.S. Department of State, 1992).

15. Robert O. Keohane and Joseph S. Nye, Jr., "Introduction" In Joseph S. Nye, Jr., and John D. Donahue, eds., *Governance in a Globalizing World* (Cambridge, MA: Visions of Governance for the 21st Century and Washington, D.C.: Brookings Institution Press, 2000), 22.

16. Thomas Hobbes, *Leviathan, or the Matter, Forme and Power of a Commonwealth, Ecclesiaticall and Civil*, ed. Michael Oakeshott (Oxford: Basil Blackwell, n.d.), 82–83.

17. Keohane and Nye, "Introduction," 20.

18. Marvin Soroos, *Beyond Sovereignty: The Challenge of Global Policy* (Columbia, S.C.: University of South Carolina Press, 1986).

19. Keohane and Nye, "Introduction," 20.

20. Robert W. McElroy, *Morality and American Foreign Policy: The Role of Ethics in International Affairs* (Princeton, N.J.: Princeton University Press, 1992), 1–13, 30–56.

21. Audie Klotz, *Norms in International Relations: The Struggle Against Apartheid* (Ithaca, NY: Cornell University Press, 1995).

22. William H. Luers, "Choosing Engagement: Uniting the U.N. with U.S. Interests," *Foreign Affairs* 79, No. 5, (September/October 2000): 9, 14.

23. Robert O. Keohane and Joseph S. Nye, Jr., *Power and Interdependence: World Politics in Transition* (Boston: Little, Brown and Company, 1977), 54–56.

24. Charter of the United Nations, Article II. See also John Mueller, *Retreat from Doomsday: The Obsolescence of Major War* (New York: Basic Books, 1989).

25. Keohane and Nye, *Power and Interdependence*, 225.

26. Luers, "Choosing Engagement," 14.

27. Carnegie Endowment, *Changing Our Ways*, 4. See also Department of State, *State 2000*, 4.

28. Seyom Brown, *New Forces, Old Forces, and the Future of World Politics*, post-Cold War ed. (New York: HarperCollinsCollegePublishers, 1995), 163.

29. Keohane and Nye, *Power and Interdependence*, 27; emphasis in original.

30. Carnegie Endowment, *Changing Our Ways*, 16.

31. Gary Clyde Hufbauer and Jeffrey J. Schott, assisted by Kimberly Ann Elliot, *Economic Sanctions Reconsidered: History and Current Policy*, 2nd ed., 2 vols. (Washington, D.C.: Institute for International Economics, 1990); Robert A. Pape, "Why Economic Sanctions Do Not Work," *International Security* 22, No. 2 (Fall 1997): 90–136.

32. Pape, "Why Economic Sanctions Do Not Work," 93.

33. Luers, "Choosing Engagement," 13.

34. Neta C. Crawford and Audie Klotz, *How Sanctions Work: Lessons from South Africa* (New York: St. Martin's Press, 1999).

35. Brown, *New Forces*, 141.

36. Keohane and Nye, *Power and Interdependence*, 229–234.

37. Carnegie Endowment, *Changing Our Ways*, 12.

38. Keohane and Nye, *Power and Interdependence*, 236.

39. George E. Moose, "Annex F: Multilateral Diplomacy," in U.S. Department of State, Management Task Force, *State 2000: A New Model for Managing Foreign Affairs* (Washington, D.C.: U.S. Department of State, 1992), 222.

40. Gareth Evans, "True Believer: Interview by Moises Naim," *Foreign Policy* 123, (March/April 2001): 29.

41. U. S. Conference of Catholic Bishops, Office of Social Development & World Peace, *Global Health Initiative, February 2002* (online) Washington, D.C.: Conference of Catholic Bishops, Office of Social Development & World Peace. Accessed June 6, 2003. Available at: www.usccb.org/sdwp/international/global1.htm.

42. U. S. Conference of Catholic Bishops, Office of Social Development & World Peace, *Catholic Campaign to Ban Landmines* (online) Washington, D.C.: U.S. Conference of Catholic Bishops, Office of Social Development & World Peace. Accessed June 6, 2002. Available at: www.commondreams.org/views02/0514-08.htm.

43. National Conference of Catholic Bishops, *Economic Justice for All: Pastoral Letter on Catholic Social Teaching and the U.S. Economy* (Washington, D.C.: National Conference of Catholic Bishops, 1986), 123.

44. United States Conference of Catholic Bishops, *Global Climate Change: A Plea for Dialogue, Prudence, and the Common Good* (Washington, D.C.: United States Catholic Conference, 2001), 2.

45. Akira Iriye, *The Globalizing of America, 1913–1945*, vol. 3 in *The Cambridge History of American Foreign Relations* (Cambridge: Cambridge University Press, 1993), 23.

46. Walter A. McDougall, *Promised Land, Crusader State: The American Encounter with the World Since 1776* (Boston: Houghton Mifflin Company, 1997), 173–174.

47. Iriye, *Globalizing of America*, 28.

48. E. H. Carr, *The Twenty-Years' Crisis: An Introduction to the Study of International Relations*, 4th ed. (New York: Harper & Row, 1964); McElroy, *Morality and American Foreign Policy*, 313.

49. Iriye, *Globalizing of America*, 79.

50. Robert D. Schulzinger, *U.S. Diplomacy Since 1900*, 4th ed. (New York: Oxford University Press, 1998), 316–317.

51. All the quotations in this paragraph and the next are taken from Jerel A. Rosati, *The Carter Administration's Quest for Global Community: Beliefs and Their Impact on Behavior* (Columbia, SC: University of South Carolina Press, 1987), 42–83.

52. Vogelgesang, "Annex D,"179–180.

53. *State 2000*, 41.

54. The White House, *A National Security Strategy of Engagement and Enlargement* (Washington, D.C.: Government Printing Office, February 1996), 1.

55. Thomas W. Lippman, *Madeleine Albright and the New American Diplomacy* (Boulder, CO: Westview Press, 2000), 279–283.

56. Ibid., 112.

57. Phyllis Bennis, *Global Affairs Commentary: Who's the Rogue State Now?* (online) Foreign Policy in Focus, August 2001. Accessed August 30, 2001. Available at: www.fpif.org/commentary/0108usunilat_body.html.

CHAPTER 7

The Logic of Radical Anti-Imperialism

In May 2002, the Bush administration sought to reorient U.S. military aid to Colombia, one of the world's most violent places. Previously, aid could be used only for training Colombia's armed forces to suppress drug trafficking. The administration proposed that it also be used against the two leftist groups that had been waging guerrilla war in Colombia for four decades. This would be an extension of the war on terrorism.[1]

One part of the U.S. political community rose in fierce opposition. "The Bush administration wants to escalate the conflict there, with U.S. soldiers digging in on the new Latin American front in the 'war on terrorism,'" was how journalist Laura Orlando phrased the news. She predicted "[e]ndless battles against a phantom enemy that is no threat to you and me. And the end result will be no end at all, just misery, economic and environmental destruction, with no chance for peace in Colombia."[2]

Other writers saw less of a shift than a continuation of policy. U.S. policy toward Colombia, according to Doug Stokes, was fully consistent with the real longstanding central purposes of U.S. foreign policy. "During the Cold War," he wrote, "the U.S. sold its counter-insurgency campaigns against social democrats, socialists, independent nationalists and even the Catholic Church, as part of a global struggle against the Soviet Union." In a post-Cold War world, the policy persists; only its rationalization morphs. Now the "narco-guerrilla and counter-terrorist pretexts [serve] as a useful PR mechanism for conflating U.S. 'official enemies' with drugs and terrorism." Thus the "U.S. terror war against Colombian civil society fits a consistent pattern within U.S. policy throughout Latin America, which has led directly to the death of hundreds of thousands of civilians."[3]

This critique of U.S. military aid for Colombia exemplifies core elements of the logic of radical anti-imperialism.

INTRODUCTION

Overview

This chapter presents the logic of radical anti-imperialism by making the following points:

- It opposes virtually every international undertaking of the U.S. government as being inherently exploitative;
- it diagnoses the United States as an imperialistic country, even though it has no significant formal empire; its empire is informal, long-standing, maintained by a plethora of instruments of intervention, and a necessary outgrowth of the system of capitalism;
- it rejects the concept of national interests because it distracts attention from the critical reality of class interests;
- it recognizes the United States as powerful enough to control international affairs on a day-to-day basis but sees its power as not absolute; it cannot prevent the eventual victory of revolutionary forces opposing capitalism;
- it is fueled by a powerful sense that imperialism is intrinsically and profoundly immoral;
- radical anti-imperialism has had little if any impact on what the United States does but has been an important voice in debates about what it ought to do.

Foreign Policy Position

The logic of radical anti-imperialism indicts U.S. foreign policy for being imperialistic. It contends that the United States, for at least one century, has engaged in a program of expanding domination over other countries in order to exploit them. The American empire has served economic and political purposes and has been created and maintained by intervention using economic, political, cultural, and military means.

In the United States, "radical" is a pejorative label connoting extremism. Radical anti-imperialism is so labeled here not to condemn it by implication, but rather because it is technically radical. The word radical derives from the same Latin word as radish: *radix*, which means root. That which is radical, then, goes to the root, that is, the origin or foundation. Rather than address immediate symptoms, radical analysis identifies fundamental causes and proposes fundamental corrections. Radical anti-imperialism diagnoses the problem—aggression against the world's poor— as a manifestation of a social and economic structure that fosters imperialism. That structure is capitalism, not as it is prescribed in theory but as it is carried out in practice.* The solution is to replace capitalism, either in the United States or globally, and to establish "an altogether new system based on a radically different distribution of power and assumptions as to its application."[4]

---

* Marxist interpretations of international relations naturally fall under the umbrella of radical anti-imperialism. I have been careful not to equate the two, however, because many radicals, while sharing the Marxist diagnosis of the maladies of capitalism, dissent from Marxist and especially Leninist prescriptions of those ills.

Radical anti-imperialism is only one strain of anti-imperialism in U.S. political culture. Indeed, three other logics—isolationism, realism, and liberal internationalism—are anti-imperialist. Radical anti-imperialism differs from those others on three grounds. First, it more consistently opposes the foreign policy undertakings of the United States. Isolationism, realism, and liberal internationalism identify limited but legitimate U.S. foreign policy strategies; radical anti-imperialism calls into question any U.S. foreign undertaking. Second, it locates the source of imperial impulses in the economic system, whereas the others blame psychological or cultural tendencies, such as a drive for power or glory. Third, radical anti-imperialism indicts U.S. foreign policy primarily for the harm it inflicts on other countries rather than for eroding U.S. national interest or damaging U.S. domestic values. For radical anti-imperialism, while sharing isolationism's indictment of imperialism's domestic harms, the main value is to protect the rest of the world from the United States.

Radical anti-imperialism's objective is not to be realistic, where being realistic is defined as taking positions likely to be seriously considered by the holders of power. For radical anti-imperialism, American imperialism is due to a deeply flawed social structure. A change in the essential orientation and objectives of policy could be possible only after fundamental changes in the U.S. economy and political system. Even policies that on their face sound like good things—such as human rights advocacy, foreign aid, and humanitarian intervention—are suspect because in practice they are corrupted into tools of imperialism to serve the purposes of empire.

The immediate objective of radical anti-imperialism is to build up the coalition of forces opposed to imperialism. This is a requisite step toward the long-run goal of effecting the fundamental social change needed to end imperialism. In the short run, by strengthening the forces of resistance, it may force the state to modify the details of policy to accommodate somewhat the demands of progressive forces. Also in the short run, building up the forces of resistance encourages individuals and groups to undertake their own foreign policy, for instance, by violating sanctions imposed on "enemy" nations.

IMPERIAL U.S.

Most Americans are under the illusion that the United States lacks an empire. It has, after all, no significant system of direct, formal control over other peoples, as the British and Roman empires did. Direct U.S. control is limited to 14 territories, all islands or island groups in the Caribbean or the Pacific, whose total land territory is about 1500 square miles, less than the area of Connecticut.

The lack of a formal empire is, however, beside the point. The American empire exists, but it is informal. It is a system of economic and political control that is no less effective for being informal. "When an advanced industrial nation plays, or tries to play, a controlling and one-sided role in the development of a weaker economy, then the policy of the more powerful country can with accuracy and candor only be described as imperial." The nature of the control is that "[t]he poorer and weaker nation makes its choices within limits set, either directly or indirectly, by the powerful society, and often does so by choosing between alternatives actually formulated by the outsider."[5] The United States seeks such control in order to preserve a system that benefits it and the other advanced capitalist countries, collectively called the North, at the expense of the people of the poor and weak countries of Africa, Asia, the Middle East, and Latin America, collectively called the South or the Third World.

The mechanisms of empire are many and varied; all serve to keep the countries of the South stuck in their particular niche in the international division of labor. Empire is, first of all, a rigged international economic system. The trading system is exploitative. The South sells three types of things to the North: agricultural goods, natural resources (petroleum, minerals, etc.), and industrial goods manufactured using labor-intensive and old technology production processes. Generally, what the South sells yields low-profit margins while what it buys from the North are high-profit margin manufactured goods. The system continues to serve the same purpose as the European empires established after 1492: It provides places from which to extract wealth, by theft or by unequal exchanges in trade.

For reasons spelled out later, imperialism must be expanded and maintained. Expansion incorporates ever more territory and people into the system. The primary mechanism for expansion has been the system of so-called free trade, which replaced both the system of preferences arranged under European colonialism and the option of self-sufficient (autarkic) development behind a wall of protectionism. In both instances, markets that would have been closed were opened to American traders. More precisely, they were forced open. As Woodrow Wilson said when he was merely the president of Princeton University, "[c]oncessions obtained by financiers must be safeguarded by ministers of state, even if the sovereignty of unwilling nations be outraged in the process. . . . the doors of the nations which are closed must be battered down."[6] Since the first famous instance of this policy—the "Open Door" notes of 1899 and 1900—some have called U.S. imperialism the policy of the open door.[7]

The "open door" does not imply, however, a sincere commitment to a system of free trade or open markets. Free trade is an ideology, a political tool used to remove impediments to U.S. exports of goods and investment capital. The United States does not adhere to free trade when it would harm U.S. interests. Rather, the state interferes in the market in order to steer it to the desired outcome. The government, for instance, helps some industries to export their wares by subsidizing research and development processes through contracts with the Department of Defense. In other instances, the government directly protects businesses from import competition, the protections rationalized as safeguards against unfair competition.

Imperialism, when it functions well, does not generally require overt political action to sustain it. It is self-reinforcing. The countries of the Third World must sell in order to earn hard currency (money that can be used in international economic exchanges) with which to pay for needed imports and repay debts. They must sell what the North needs to buy. To attempt to withdraw from the trading system is to court short-term economic disaster. Not that the elites in the South are inclined to withdraw from the system. They are enriched by the system and derive their power and status from it. It is the poor who are ground down by the system.

Because the economic exchanges are unequal, the countries of the South fall further and further behind those of the North. Often, their export earnings are insufficient to cover their import needs. To close the gap, they borrow. Their accumulated debts constrain them to stay in the trading system. When they are unable to borrow from the rich governments and international banks and financial institutions, they are forced to borrow from the International Monetary Fund (IMF), a branch of the UN system. IMF loans come with strings attached. Specifically, the IMF forces borrowers to accept so-called structural adjustment programs. Structural adjustment programs are designed to increase exports and to attract private investment. Typically, they require the borrowing government to reduce its role in the economy by such measures as balancing the budget by cutting expenditures, cutting domestic subsidies, and selling off government-owned enterprises. Such measures reinforce the system.

In their need for funds, the countries of the South open their economies to investment by corporations from the North. This investment further skews their economies toward serving the needs of the North. The investment generates profits that get repatriated to the corporate headquarters in the North rather than staying in the South.

> Whereas U.S. corporations in Europe between 1950 and 1965 invested $8.1 billion and made $5.5 billion in profits, in Latin America they invested $3.8 billion and made $11.2 billion in profits, and in Africa they invested $5.2 billion and made $14.3 billion in profits.[8]

The gap between the rich and the poor widens. The agents of the corporations become active players in the politics of the South, eroding the real independence of those countries.

Political control is achieved not only by constraining the policy options of Third World governments but also by convincing Third World elites that their interests are tied to those of the North. This is done by bribery, by cooptation, and by persuasion. Propaganda, educational exchanges, mass media, and other mechanisms of cultural influence facilitate such persuasion. Indeed, the single best insurance for the orderly functioning of the system is the belief that the market is the best and inevitable way to organize economic life. To the extent that "free trade" ideology becomes the consensus view, the system becomes immune from challenge.

Counterrevolutionary Intervention

The self-sustaining qualities of the system of imperialism are prone to failure, however. Rebellion against a structure of exploitation is a chronic possibility. Imperialism, therefore, necessarily entails intervention to preclude, stifle, or crush revolution. Such counterrevolutionary intervention has been the dominant strain of U.S. foreign policy for the last 100 years. Because the dynamic and trajectory of social movements are inherently uncertain, especially in their early stages, counterrevolutionary intervention has been employed against "perceived threats of revolution, including often what amount to rather minor reforms."[9]

Counterrevolutionary intervention has taken many forms. By providing covert financial support for "moderate" political parties, labor unions, and newspapers, the United States has acted to put "safe" (that is, subservient) governments in power and to reinforce their hold on power. This meant supporting fascist movements in Europe in the 1930s because fascism was anticommunist. The United States, despite its protestations, does not support democracy. Rather, it supports "formal democratic procedures" only where "civil society has either been demolished by violence or sufficiently intimidated and undermined to ensure an approved outcome."[10] As the singer/songwriter Tom Lehrer put it in explaining why the United States "send[s] in the Marines:" "They have to be protected/All their rights respected/'Til somebody we like/Can be elected."[11]

The United States has backed client governments by throwing its prestige behind them, by subsidizing them through foreign aid programs (there is almost no correlation between a country's objective need for development assistance and the amount it gets), by giving them information and advice, by pressuring them to reform in order to prevent a successful revolution, and by arming and training their militaries and secret police forces. The latter has made the United States in fact a sponsor of state terrorism and complicit in widespread massacres of hundreds of thousands carried out by its clients. It has intervened with U.S. armed forces to prevent successful revolutions or communist victories in civil wars in Korea (1950–1953), Laos (1961), the Dominican Republic (1965), and Vietnam (from the early 1960s to 1973). The Korea and Vietnam interventions led to long, bloody wars in which tens of thousands of Americans and millions of Koreans and Vietnamese were killed.

Imperialism also has required the United States to isolate, weaken, and try to destroy any government that poses a threat to the established order. For long periods it refused to establish normal diplomatic relations with communist governments in order to deny them the veneer of legitimacy. It has imposed economic sanctions on revolutionary governments in an effort to destroy their economies. In Iran in 1953 and Guatemala in 1954, the Central Intelligence Agency (CIA) organized the overthrowing of elected governments whose policies threatened the U.S. empire. It organized an invasion of Cuba at the Bay of Pigs in 1961 in an effort to overthrow Castro's government. When that failed, it began a four-year program of sabotage and terror in Cuba under the title Operation Mongoose. The CIA made several efforts to have Castro assassinated. Similarly, the U.S. government organized and financed a counterrevolutionary war against the Sandinista government of Nicaragua during the Reagan administration. U.S. armed forces have invaded countries to overthrow revolutionary governments (for example, Grenada in 1982) or clients that refused to toe Washington's line (for example, Panama in 1989).

Behind these specific actions lay the maintenance of the most powerful military in the history of humankind. Since the Second World War, when the United States took up from the British and the French the responsibility of policing imperialism worldwide, it has been prepared to fight major wars if necessary to stabilize its empire. This has included even developing the capacity to use nuclear weapons and a declared willingness to do so if necessary.

The United States does not avow an imperialistic foreign policy. Indeed, its stated intentions are quite different. The stated purposes of U.S. foreign policy, however, are deceptive. Intentionally so.* They serve to distract the public from

---

* The other foreign policy logics, especially the logics of hegemonism and liberalism, provide the system of rationalization.

being aware of what their state is up to. Moral or ethical justifications for policy are especially untrustworthy. The United States often claims humanitarian motives for its actions, but others of its actions directly violate those same humanitarian values, as when it supports governments that commit heinous violations of human rights, up to and including massacres and genocide. Foreign aid is given to bolster endangered clients, to reward docile clients, and to purchase political support; it is denied to those states that refuse to march to the cadence sounded in Washington. Even if some actions have moral or humanitarian motivations, as with the human rights initiatives of the Carter administration, they do not erode the fundamental nature of the policy: "these more liberal policies were designed to leave intact the power and influence of American military and American business in the world."[12]

Capitalism and Imperialism

The fundamental source of imperialism is the U.S. political economy. Capitalism generates imperialism. Capitalist exploitation under imperialism is highly profitable for the United States, and especially for the upper classes and the corporations that most directly are engaged in international commerce of various sorts. They, in turn, use their political clout to get the government to protect their interests abroad, which is not all that difficult to do, given that those who hold office in the United States share the belief that capitalism is the system that best serves the interests of the United States.

Empire, indeed, is necessary for American capitalism in three ways. First, the U.S. economy depends on imported raw materials. Oil is one obvious example. Manganese, a necessary component of steel, is another. Many of these raw materials come from the Third World. If supplies were to be disrupted by chaos in producer countries or by a politically motivated cutoff, important corporations would suffer and the harm would reverberate throughout the economy. Empire provides the political control that prevents such disruption of supplies.

Second, corporations, in their struggle to increase profits, seek to cut costs. Hence they seek opportunities to invest in countries that provide a "favorable business climate" of low taxes, low wages, and limited governmental regulations such as protections for labor or the environment. Empire opens the door for profitable foreign investment and deters the especially pernicious threat of state expropriation of the assets of foreign businesses.

Third, the economy needs expanding markets for its production. Productive capacity is greater than the domestic market can absorb. Without new markets, U.S. businesses would have to cut production, triggering a recession. As Truman's Secretary of State Dean Acheson put it, "we cannot have full employment and prosperity in the United States without the foreign markets."[13] Empire lays siege to the fortresses of tariffs and quotas that countries build around their economies to protect them from foreign competition.

That the empire ultimately exists to serve economic needs does not mean that each and every undertaking has an immediate economic rationale. Imperialism means maintaining economic and political control in order to maintain the system. The empire, once established, creates its own dynamic. Political disorder must be contained and corrected lest it disrupt trade. Indeed, empire subscribes to the logic of hegemonism; it is its "imperial creed."[14] Uppity states such as Iraq must be put in their place even if they pose no direct threat to U.S. economic interests. Otherwise, a bad precedent would be set, encouraging other states to defect from the empire, which, if allowed, would unravel the free trade order. In particular, the United States cannot tolerate nationalist revolutions, especially if they have a program of radical economic and social restructuring, because such movements by definition are hostile to the United States. Danger can even emanate from the establishment of an effective alternative model of social organization because it is likely to spread.

> The vision is totalitarian: nothing may get out of control. The doctrine has achieved near-total consensus. At the dovish extreme, Robert Pastor, Carter's Latin American adviser and a respected scholar, writes that 'the United States did not want to control Nicaragua or the other nations in the region, but it also did not want to allow developments to get out of control. It wanted Nicaraguans to act independently, *except* when doing so would affect U.S. interests adversely' [his emphasis]. We want everyone to be free—free to act as we determine.[15]

Economic needs, then, give rise to an imperial dynamic that acquires a life of its own and leads to foreign policy undertakings having no discernible economic rationale sufficient to justify the cost of the policy. Vietnam would be the clearest example. The empire exists, though, to serve the interests of the economic system. Capitalism calls forth the empire. Any effort to understand the empire much less to dissolve it without coming to grips with its economic foundation would be futile.

U.S. NATIONAL INTERESTS

Clarity begins by discarding the concept of national interests. National interests—that is, interests shared by society as a whole—rarely if ever define the stakes pursued by Washington. The very concepts of "nation" and "political community" imply strong bonds of common interests and concern: "We are all in this together. What hurts you, hurts me; what benefits you, benefits me." The United States as a capitalist system lacks such common interests. Rather, its social system is defined by class differences; the phrase "national interest" is merely a deceptive label for the interests of the class that dominates the state.

> The fantasy that *nations* are the actors in the international arena is the standard doctrinal camouflage for the fact that within the rich nations, as within the hungry ones, there are radical differences in privilege and power. . . . Any discussion of world affairs that treats nations as actors is at best misleading, at worst pure mystification. . . . [16]

American foreign policy, therefore, must be recognized as the international program advancing the interests of the dominant class. The president is "guardian and representative of corporate America . . . the top salesman of the system" who "tends to treat capitalist interests as synonymous with the nation's well-being."[17] The equation of corporate interests and national interests was most clearly enunciated in the confirmation hearings of General Motors Chairman Charles Wilson to be Eisenhower's secretary of defense, when he said "what's good for the United States is good for the General Motors Corporation *and vice versa*" (emphasis added). By promoting their own interests, they promote the interests of the nation. Or so they believe.

Policy is dictated by the class interests of the privileged because the United States is a democracy only in the formal sense. It has the institutions that are a necessary condition of democracy: political parties and elections. Those institutions, however, are not a sufficient condition for democracy. Actual control rests in the hands of the elite. The U.S. power structure consists, first and foremost, of "the industrial-financial-commercial sector, concentrated and interlinked, highly class conscious, and increasingly transnational in the scope of its planning, management, and operations."[18] It is complemented by the state. The government (that is, the executive branch) does not stand against the elite. Rather its members come from the corporate and military sectors of the elite, share the basic attitudes and beliefs of the elite, and are beholden to the elite for their continuation in power. Nor do members of Congress, who rely on the elites to contribute campaign funds and who, collectively, have little impact on the basic decisions of foreign policy.

Likewise, under ordinary circumstances, the general public cannot check the imperialistic tendencies of the elites. The public is ill-informed, so it cannot act intelligibly. It is ill-informed for a variety of reasons. It is uninterested in foreign affairs, so it does not seek out international information. It is uninterested, though, because it is in fact powerless. The day-to-day making of decisions takes place deep within the bowels of the bureaucracy, so the public has limited points of access for timely involvement in the making of policy. Too often it is able to respond to policy only after the fact, at which time the scope of choice is narrowed to next to nothing. The broad-based, mobilized resistance that radical anti-imperialism seeks to create could subject U.S. policy to real democratic control, but that describes the goal to be attained, not the condition that exists.

More importantly, when the public seeks to be attentive to foreign affairs, they are likely to become uninformed. What passes as news is in fact propaganda employed by the elites to keep the population under control. The government, for instance, can manufacture threats to rally the public into patriotic compliance, and even steer the country into a war. The Cold War, for instance, "provided easy formulas to justify criminal action abroad and entrenchment of privilege and state power at home" and thus "served very well the interests of those who held the reins."[19] The end of the Cold War created a need for new enemies, and the U.S. power structure went about the business of creating them: "It has been intriguing to observe the search for some new enemy as the Russians were visibly fading through the 1980s: international terrorism, Hispanic narcotraffickers, Islamic fundamentalism, or Third World 'instability' and depravity generally."[20] The state also intervenes in the flow of information to the public, both by creating a torrent of its own facts and spin on the facts and by preventing unfavorable information from coming out.[21] Government censorship is facilitated by the complicity of the mass media and the intellectual class, both of which are part of the power structure or dependent on it and thus in no position to bring the state's misdeeds to light.[22]

The concentration of control in the hands of the elite and the consequent evisceration of real democracy is not an accident. Rather, astute defenders of capitalism have always understood that the system can only be sustained if power is kept out of the hands of the masses.[23] When portions of the public mobilize and press demands on the state, the elite raises an alarm over the "crisis of democracy" as the society becomes "ungovernable."[24]

U.S. POWER

All radical anti-imperialists see the United States as an inordinately powerful, controlling country. One author, for instance, refers to ". . . the commanding position of the United States in global politics, military affairs, ideology, culture, information technology, trade and investment" and concludes that "America is the only country with the power and influence to shape the course of global affairs."[25] The power of the United States rests not only on its material resources and other sources of power. The United States acts in the interests of the other powerful nations in the international system, so, on the critical issues that determine the viability of the system of imperialism, the foreign policies of its allies converge with those of the United States, in broad outline if not in detail. Similarly, the United States generally can get the support of its clients; if they balk, the United States can twist their arms.

Limits on U.S. Control

Nevertheless, U.S. control over world affairs is limited. It cannot prevent revolution from being a chronic condition in the world. Moreover, it may not be able to change the international system, even if it were ever to be inclined to do so; the system of imperialism may be more powerful than the United States.

The first limit, then, is that the United States cannot eradicate permanently the potential for revolution. So long as the world economy widens the gap between the rich and the poor and grinds much of the world's population into abject poverty—that is, so long as capitalism is capitalism—the victims of injustice will be angry and ready to be mobilized against the forces accountable for their oppression. So long as the United States seeks to control the direction of social change in the world, it will be forced to violate the independence of other states and peoples, which also will breed anger and rebellious impulses.

The Weakness of the Neoliberal Consensus

A critic of radical anti-imperialism might answer this argument by noting the remarkable neoliberal consensus that developed in the late 1980s. State after state abandoned authoritarian governments and state-directed economic systems for popularly elected governments and greater freedom of the market. Mexico, through the

North American Free Trade Association (NAFTA), opened its economy to free trade with the United States and Canada. Other Latin American countries clamored to be let into NAFTA. The United Nations and regional organizations such as the Organization of American States (OAS) ceased passing resolutions calling for political regulation of the world economy, including elements of central planning, socialism, and redistribution, and instead began passing resolutions calling for open markets. It appeared that Adam Smith's disciples had routed their ideological adversaries permanently and that capitalist democracy had emerged as the unchallenged correct system for organizing societies.[26]

Such neoliberal triumphalism is wrong on three counts. First, it commits the fallacy of inferring the attitudes of the peoples of the Third World from the policies of their governments. Responding to the claim that in 1990 "Bush had 'organized the opinion of the world against Saddam,'" Noam Chomsky states: "This conventional formula too is grossly false—if the 'world' is taken to include its people. But it is correct if we take 'the world' to consist of its rich white faces and obedient Third World clients."[27] The neoliberal consensus, then, was shared by the elites of the world but not the world's people. Being shallow, it is liable to shatter when put under stress. An omen of things to come would be the 1998 election in Venezuela, which brought the populist Hugo Chavez to office. Chavez subsequently revised the Venezuelan constitution to weaken the power of the established elites and he courted friendly relations with Cuba's Fidel Castro, much to the distress of the United States. The class division in Venezuela was highlighted in 2002 by two waves of anti-Chavez agitation, predominantly carried out by the middle classes, while Chavez held onto power with the support of the poor.

Second, the late 1990s saw a remarkable growth in vigorous public opposition to capitalism under its contemporary moniker, globalization. Beginning in Seattle in 1999, antiglobalization protesters gathered at ministerial meetings of the World Trade Organization, the body established in 1994 to promote free trade worldwide. The protests drew heavy media attention because their size strained the resources of the local police and because they degenerated into violence; in Genoa, Italy in 2001 a police officer shot and killed one violent protester.[28] The antiglobalization coalition is momentous even though it is eclectic and inspired by other perspectives, including protectionist isolationism, in addition to radical anti-imperialism: All opposition to globalization under a capitalist system erodes the neoliberal consensus.[29]

Third, the neoliberal consensus has weakened even in the international organizations in which its victory was most prominently displayed. The UN and its bodies have begun once again to push an agenda of international economic reform, altering the rules of international trade in order to overturn the tendency of free trade to accentuate inequalities. In August 2002, the World Summit on Sustainable Development in Johannesburg, South Africa, provided one instance of this resistance from the bottom. South African President Mbeki, in his opening address, declared that "[a] global human society based on poverty for many and prosperity for a few, characterized by islands of wealth surrounded by a sea of poverty, is unsustainable." Not only is it unsustainable; it is morally intolerable. "We do not accept that human society should be constructed on the savage principle of the survival of the fittest," he proclaimed.[30]

Free market capitalism, then, has not won a complete and final victory over competitor ideas. If it had, then the privileged position of the United States and its corporations would be safe. There might be poverty and inequality, but they would not lead to revolution because there would be no viable alternative to the established order. But it has not, so the economic and social divisions created by capitalism will continue to cause revolutionary turmoil.

The Need for a Worldwide Anticapitalist Revolution

The second possible limit to the power of the United States concerns its ability to reform the international economic system if it were inclined to do so. The United States itself may be a captive of the capitalist world system. Although the United States is the most powerful of the capitalist states, it ultimately may be less powerful than the system itself and the corporations that constitute the system. Indeed, the capitalist empire may have evolved into an unprecedented structure, one in which there is no political center.[31] Were progressives and socialists somehow to take power in Washington, the system might very well defeat them. They would face huge, perhaps insuperable, difficulties putting into effect the kinds of policies necessary to bring about economic justice. Were they to attempt to do so, the immediate result would be capital flight as corporations and financial firms moved their money to safe "offshore" locations. The exodus of capital might cause a catastrophic collapse of the economy, followed by a deep and long-lasting recession or depression followed by an indefinite period of stagnation. The revolution, in other words, might very well have to be global; as the experience of the Soviet Union shows, Leon Trotsky was right: Socialism in one country is not possible.

MORALITY

Radical anti-imperialism's indictment of U.S. foreign policy rests primarily on moral grounds; there are, however, pragmatic grounds for rejecting the imperial tradition. Imperialism puts the United States against the interests of most of the people in the world. It creates enemies where they would not otherwise be, at considerable cost to the country and its citizens, with Iran being the clearest instance.* It also entails the expense of fighting and preparing to fight counterrevolutionary wars.

> [T]he cost of the war machine makes beggars of us. It seems there is not enough money to help handicapped children and impoverished families, but there is enough for a huge defense budget, the largest single item in the federal budget, allowing the military brass to enjoy a very good life indeed with its officers clubs, golf courses, polo fields, huge salaries, and fat pensions.[32]

---

* The information about Iran was summarized in Chapter 5.

Despite the practical harms of imperialism for the United States, the ultimate grounds on which imperialism must be condemned are moral. Imperialism is evil and requires evil acts. American foreign policy fosters oppression, exploitation, and war; that is wrong and must be ended. The demands of morality trump any argument about state interest or short-term diplomatic consequences. Even if imperialism were infinitely sustainable and maximally profitable, it is an abomination and must be ended.

The sense of moral outrage is best communicated by the words of anti-imperialist writers. One century ago, responding to the carnage being committed by U.S. forces suppressing the nationalist revolution in the Philippines, the Harvard University philosopher William James exclaimed, "God damn the U.S. for its vile conduct in the Philippines Isles."[33] More recently, political scientist Michael Parenti, noting that the U.S. military "constructs a technology whose goal is to intimidate and subdue people around the world and, if necessary, kill many of them so that their lands and labor can be better put at the disposal of rich owners and foreign investors," calls imperialism a form of social sin.[34] Noam Chomsky writes that imperialism's "operative principle" is "human life has value insofar as it contributes to the wealth and power of the privileged." U.S. policy toward Central America in the 1980s was a "shameful episode of imperial violence. . . ." After reviewing the evidence of the damage inflicted on Third World countries by imperialism, including illnesses that could be prevented were the West to take necessary means to provide the medical materials, he then says: "We would not hesitate to describe these policies as genocidal if they were implemented by some official enemy."[35]

Guatemala represents one compelling case. From 1960 through 1996, that country was devastated by a one-sided civil war in which more than 200,000 people, mostly Mayan peasants, died or disappeared. Most of the killing was carried out by the armed forces and by "death squads" associated with the ruling elite. The chair of the UN commission to study war crimes in Guatemala "emphasized that the U.S. government and private companies 'exercised pressure to maintain the country's archaic and unjust socioeconomic structure.'"[36] Chomsky comments: "The term 'exercise pressure' refers to years and years of massacres and slaughters and torture and mutilation and, in fact, genocidal attacks; it's describing 45 years of state terror."[37]

Radical anti-imperialism's moral analysis differs from that of liberal internationalism, with which it shares the sense of moral urgency to eradicate poverty in the world. For radical anti-imperialism, but not for liberal internationalism, the poverty of the poor carries with it the guilt of the rich. The poor are poor because the operation of capitalism has made them poor. Workers in the Third World accept low-wage jobs in the factories of multinational corporations because they no longer can support themselves in agriculture. The processes of imperialism cause the loss of work in agriculture. The flood of cheap imported food from countries like the United States destroys the market for domestically grown foods, throwing those farmers into poverty and driving them out of farming. Moreover, imported capital gobbles up the land and turns its use to growing for the export market in the United States and Europe. By its very nature, capitalism inflicts *structural violence* on the poor. Everyone who dies prematurely because of structural violence has been killed by the system as certainly as have been those murdered by security forces and death squads.

RADICAL ANTI-IMPERIALISM IN U.S. DIPLOMATIC HISTORY

Radical anti-imperialism has had little impact on the substance of U.S. foreign policy but has made an imprint on the policy-making process. The logic itself provides the explanation for its limited effect on policy substance. With rare exceptions, radical anti-imperialists are outside the mainstream of U.S. political discourse. They are neither elected nor appointed to positions of authority. Nor do they have the resources or numbers to be influential from the sidelines. Radical anti-imperialism, then, is a critical voice. It would have to be; if it were generally to be influential in the making of policy, it would to that extent be wrong: Either power would not have been monopolized by the elites or the elites would be making policy contradictory to their own material interests. Nevertheless, arguments from the radical anti-imperialist tradition have played a prominent role in U.S. foreign policy debates.

The moral revulsion against imperialism fed the anti-imperial movement of 1898–1900. Not all of that burst of anti-imperialism was radical.[38] Much of the movement grew out of isolationism's fear that empire would erode democracy. Other anti-imperialists were motivated by racist concerns not to dilute the American bloodlines by increasing the number of Latinos and Asians in the population. Still, some significant voices did attack the acquisition of Cuba and the Philippines on grounds consistent with radicalism. Mark Twain, to cite one prominent American, blasted the U.S. counterinsurgency war in the Philippines, which killed perhaps 100,000 Filipinos, for its savagery and for its violation of the Filipinos' right to independence. "We have pacified thousands of the islanders and buried them; destroyed their fields; burned their villages, turned their widows and orphans out-of-doors, furnished heartbreak by exile to dozens of disagreeable patriots; and subjugated the remaining ten million by Benevolent Assimilation," he wrote.[39]

Elements of radical anti-imperialist logic were integral to the progressive critique of the foreign policy of the Truman administration as the Cold War began. This critique was associated with one notable person, Henry A. Wallace. Wallace had been a cabinet member under both Franklin D. Roosevelt and Harry Truman and had been Roosevelt's vice president from 1941 to 1945. His public critique of the administration's foreign policy caused Truman to sack him as his secretary of commerce in 1946. In 1948, Wallace ran for president as the Progressive Party nominee.

Wallace blamed both the United States and the Soviet Union for the Cold War, which he condemned for unnecessarily polarizing world politics, for eviscerating the United Nations, and for threatening to lead to nuclear war. He indicted U.S. policy for failing to accommodate legitimate Soviet security concerns by allowing it a sphere of influence in East and Central Europe; he opposed the aid programs for Greece and Turkey and the Truman Doctrine because they would lead to the United States supporting dictators merely on the grounds that they claimed to be threatened by communists; and he condemned the policy as serving the interests of Britain in reestablishing its empire. His diagnosis of the genesis of that policy fits well within the logic of radical anti-imperialism. ". . . American foreign policy today is based on serving private corporations and international big business, rather than serving the great masses of people," he said; indeed, those whose interests were served by the Cold War were ". . . exploiters and misleaders of the people in this country and abroad." The Cold War served their interests by providing the "cover for their iniquitous machinations" and "the alibi for using the resources of our country to back up the same kind of cartels which contributed so greatly to the start of World War II."[40]

Following the freezing of the Cold War pattern between 1948 and the start of the Korean War in 1950, and the domestic crusades against communists and suspected communists, radical anti-imperialism moved to the margins of the U.S. political spectrum. Its main homes were the small communities of American communists and socialists and segments of the intelligentsia. It was from the intelligentsia, though, that the next wave of significant radical anti-imperialist activity was to emerge. Two academics wrote seminal and influential texts. One was C. Wright Mills, a sociologist at Columbia University. His classic work *The Power Elite* provided a powerful diagnosis of the gap between the U.S. political system and the ideal of democracy. He argued that a power elite had come into existence, composed of the holders of governmental office, corporate leadership, and the military. These three groups were joined by a common worldview reflecting their similar social backgrounds and their common membership in overlapping organizations.[41] The other was historian William Appleman Williams. His essay *The Tragedy of American Diplomacy* argued that since the 1890s the United States had pursued a consistent foreign policy of forcing other countries, by any means necessary, to accept the institution of free trade. He called it the Open Door policy. The Open Door policy would allow American traders access to markets abroad, markets necessary if the U.S. economy were to sell off otherwise-excess production and thus avoid economic collapse. The Open Door policy appeared to be anti-imperial in that it conflicted with other major powers' programs of formal empire and colonization, but it also served to create an informal American empire. *The Tragedy of American Diplomacy* was the first of a raft of historical studies that sought to blame the United States, wholly or in part, for the Cold War. Collectively, those scholars were called revisionists.

The radical critique of the United States and its diplomacy gained prominence in the 1960s. The self-labeled New Left was a primary agent for that shift. A seminal statement of New Leftism was the 1960 Port Huron Statement, the founding manifesto of the Students for a Democratic Society (SDS). In it, the SDS laid out a radical agenda of social transformation. Its treatment of international affairs was rather brief. It bemoaned the dangers of nuclear weapons and recognized the importance of anti-imperial revolutions that were breaking out around the world as the European colonial empires in Asia and Africa entered their death throes. It never named U.S. imperialism as a phenomenon much less as part of the problem. Still, the statement implied that the United States was an aggressor when it noted that "[t]he proclaimed peaceful intentions of the United States contradicted its economic and military investments in the Cold War status quo." Further, its analysis of American politics, reflecting that of Mills, found "its democratic system apathetic and manipulated," corrupted by "the dominating complex of corporate, military, and political power."

While the New Left was an important agent in drawing attention to the radical critique of U.S. foreign policy, U.S. foreign policy itself was the primary mover of that development. The Vietnam War was the key event. People's reactions to Vietnam varied. Some supported it to the bitter end, believing that it was a just and winnable struggle against aggression by the forces of totalitarianism. Others supported the war initially but turned against it when they decided it could not be won at an acceptable cost. Others opposed the war in principle but supported it in practice out of fear that the international position of the United States would be harmed if it were to lose or to renege on its commitment. For some, though, the war symbolized the evil of the American empire; they also were the most fervent of the opponents of the war, some turning to violence when nonviolent means of opposition seemed futile. Radical anti-imperialism moved from protests on Main Street into the political mainstream in the capturing of the Democratic Party and the nomination of George McGovern for president in 1972. McGovern himself was a more moderate critic of U.S. foreign policy, arguably influenced as much by the logic of isolationism as by the logic of radical anti-imperialism. Many of his supporters, though, did view U.S. foreign policy through radical lenses.

The closest that adherents to radical anti-imperialism have come to holding the levers of power came during the administration of Jimmy Carter, and the events of that administration showed how marginalized radicalism has been. Carter was the first president elected after the end of the Vietnam War. He brought into office several persons whose critique of that war grew out of a broader critique of antirevolutionary tendencies of U.S. foreign policy during the Cold War. The most notable and the highest ranking was Andrew Young, who Carter appointed to be ambassador to the United Nations. Young "blamed American Cold War policies for fostering 'an apparatus of repression' and 'imperialism, neo-colonialism, capitalism, or what-have-you.'"[42] Still, most radical anti-imperialists consider Young to have been closer to the political mainstream than to the mainstream of radicalism.

CONCLUSION

Radical anti-imperialism does not prescribe what the United States should do in the world so much as it prescribes what it should stop doing: Manipulating international relations and intervening in the internal affairs of other countries in order to maintain an empire that exploits the world's poor for the benefit of economic elites. Its fundamental and distinctive critique interprets U.S. foreign policy for the past century as having engaged in a campaign of establishing and maintaining an informal empire. The empire abroad, it argues, is a necessary condition for the preservation of capitalism at home. American foreign policy uses a wide array of tools of intervention to sustain the empire. The empire serves not the national interests of the United States but the class interests of the elites. Further, the empire is morally reprehensible: Its exploitation and the intervention necessary to sustain it are devastating to the poor of the Third World.

Radical anti-imperialism contributes a distinctive voice to debates about U.S. foreign policy but has had little direct impact on the content of policy nor does it seem likely to provide the guiding principles for policy in the immediate future.

DISCUSSION QUESTIONS

1. Don't members of social classes other than the economic elites benefit from the effective operation of the capitalist system and suffer when it is in crisis? For example, doesn't everyone in the United States, and not just the oil companies, profit from the importation of cheap oil? Don't recessions hurt everyone?

2. Does the existence and importance of class interests mean that there are no such things as national interests or a national interest?

3. How important are economic motives in shaping the foreign policy of the United States? Are there other motives—security interests or moral impulses—that also influence foreign policy and that cannot be explained as manifestations of economic interests?

4. Do foreign policy makers have legitimate concerns about national security in an anarchic world? Has the United States been absolutely safe from foreign threats and, assuming that it has been, did the country's leaders know it to have been so? Does the existence of economic motives prove that there were no security motives?

5. Is U.S. foreign policy as immoral and hypocritical as radical anti-imperialism contends? Is the failure to apply a moral standard consistently proof that it is irrelevant to foreign policy decision making? Might it be the case instead that moral considerations are relevant but only one factor of many that influence decision making? Would the United States have undertaken any humanitarian intervention or human rights advocacy or disaster relief if it were immune to moral considerations?

6. Do the economically powerful determine the public policy of the United States? Or does public opinion play a distinct role in directing foreign policy? Is public opinion itself manipulated by the elite to support policies of imperialism?

7. Would it be wise and proper for the United States to base its foreign policy on the pursuit of the interests of others, especially the world's poor and weak, rather than on the national interest of the United States?

ENDNOTES

This chapter profited much from the comments of my colleagues Mike Alvarez, Mike Budde, and Mike McIntyre, who provided detailed critiques of a first draft. In a couple of instances, I have taken phrasing from their feedback. I thank them and trust that they approve of my appropriating their words.

1. Howard LaFranchi, "U.S. Poised to Take Terror War to Colombia," *The Christian Science Monitor*, (online) May 31, 2002. Accessed August 24, 2002. Available at: www.csmonitor.com/cgi-bin/getasciiarchive?script/2002/05/31/p08s01.txt.

2. Laura Orlando, "Bush in Colombia: An Old War Gets a New Boost," Portland, Maine: CommonDreams.org, May 14, 2002. Accessed July 15, 2003. Available at: www. commondreams.org/views02/0514-18.htm.

3. Ibid.

4. Gabriel Kolko, *The Roots of American Foreign Policy: An Analysis of Power and Purpose* (Boston: Beacon Press, 1969), 134.

5. William Appleman Williams, *The Tragedy of American Diplomacy*, 2nd rev. ed. (New York: Dell, 1972), 55.

6. Quoted in Howard Zinn, *A People's History of the United States 1492–Present*, rev. and updated ed. (New York: HarperCollins Publishers, 1995), 353.

7. Williams, *Tragedy*.

8. Zinn, *People's History*, 556.

9. Michael Alvarez, personal communication, November 2001.

10. Noam Chomsky, *World Orders Old and New* (New York: Columbia University Press, 1994), 53.

11. Tom Lehrer, "Send the Marines" in *That Was the Year That Was*, July, 1965. Reprise Records, a Time Warner Communication Company, 6179–2.

12. Zinn, *People's History*, 555.

13. Quoted in Williams, *Tragedy*, 203.

14. Richard J. Barnet, *The Roots of War* (New York: Penguin, 1973).

15. Chomsky, *World Orders*, 76–77.

16. Ibid., 5.

17. Michael Parenti, *America Beseiged* (San Francisco: City Lights Books, 1998), 15–16.

18. Chomsky, *World Orders*, 1.

19. Chomsky, *World Orders*, 1.

20. Chomsky, *World Orders*, 3.

21. See Parenti, *America Besieged*, 149–158, for an inventory of techniques of information management.

22. Michael Parenti, "The Myth of a Liberal Media," *Humanist* 60, No. 2 (March–April 2000): 14–17.

23. Karl Polanyi, *The Great Transformation: The Political and Economic Origins of Our Time* (Boston: Beacon Press, 1944), especially Chapters 18–19.

24. Chomsky, *World Orders*, 93.

25. Tom Barry, "Challenges and Conundrums of a New Global Affairs Agenda," *Global Focus: U.S. Foreign Policy at the Turn of the Millennium*, ed. by Martha Honey and Tom Barry (New York: St. Martin's Press, 2000), xiv–xv.

26. Francis Fukuyama, *The End of History and the Last Man* (New York: Free Press, 1992).

27. Chomsky, *World Orders*, 21.

28. Alessandra Stanley and David E. Sanger, "Italian Protester is Killed by Police at Genoa Meeting," *The New York Times*, July 21, 2001.

29. One statement of the purposes of antiglobalization protests can be found in Lori Wallach, "Lori's War: Interview by Moises Niam," *Foreign Policy* 118, (Spring 2000): 29–54.

30. Quoted in Lori Goering, "Summit Host Says Trade No Boon to Poor," *The Chicago Tribune*, August 27, 2002.

31. William Hardt and Antonio Negri, *Empire* (Cambridge, MA: Harvard University Press, 2001).

32. Parenti, *America Besieged*, 42.

33. Quoted in Zinn, *People's History*, 307.

34. Parenti, *America Besieged*, 42–44.

35. Chomsky, *World Orders*, 23, 3, 131.

36. Quoted in Noam Chomsky, *Rogue States: The Rule of Force in World Affairs* (Cambridge, MA: South End Press, 2000), 94.

37. Chomsky, *Rogue States*, 95.

38. For a general overview of debate between imperialists and anti-imperialists, see Robert Endicott Osgood, *Ideals and Self-Interest in America's Foreign Relations: The Great Transformation of the Twentieth Century* (Chicago: University of Chicago Press, 1953), 47–54.

39. Quoted in Anna Manzo, "The Forgotten Legacy of 100 Years of U.S.-Philippines History" (online) *The Progressive*, June 5, 1998. Accessed August 28, 2001. Available at: http://www.progressive.org/mpmanzo698.htm.

40. Quoted in Graham White and John Maze, *Henry A. Wallace: His Search for a New World Order* (Chapel Hill: The University of North Carolina Press, 1995), 269, 283.

41. C. Wright Mills, *The Power Elite* (London: Oxford University Press, 1956).

42. Walter A. McDougall, *Promised Land, Crusader State: The American Encounter with the World Since 1776* (Boston: Houghton Mifflin Company, 1997), 197.

CHAPTER 8

Comparing the Logics

This chapter examines how the logics compare to each other. Although they could be compared on many dimensions, we will consider only eight, chosen for their importance. Five dimensions cut across the logics' foreign policy strategies: The degree to which they favor unilateral versus multilateral ways of acting, the degree to which they accept or oppose the use of military force, the degree to which they favor or oppose intervening into the domestic affairs of other countries, the degree of leadership they believe the United States must provide the world, and the degree to which they favor or oppose promoting corporate globalization. The other three concern the three causal variables that dictate foreign policy strategy: The degree to which they perceive the United States as being powerful, as having extensive national interests affected by international affairs, and as having moral obligations abroad.

UNILATERALISM-MULTILATERALISM

Figure 8.1 represents the logics' relative positions on the dimension of unilateral versus multilateral action.

Unilateralism					Multilateralism
	I	H	R	LI	

Key:
    H = Hegemonism   LI = Liberal Internationalism
    I = Isolationism   R = Realism

Figure 8.1   Placement of the foreign policy logics along a unilateralism-multilateralism dimension.

The logic of isolationism anchors the left end of the unilateralism-multilateralism dimension. Foreign policy must be unilateralist if it is to conform to isolationism's central objective: To maximize U.S. autonomy. Collaborative efforts would constrain the United States unless it was so powerful that it could dictate the coalition's strategy and tactics. Such circumstances, however, could hardly be called multilateral. Instead, they would be *false multilateralism*, that is, unilateralism disguised as multilateralism. According to the logic of isolationism, the United States is not powerful enough to dictate terms to allies. Moreover, even if it were, it would be able to act unilaterally and so would not need collaborators.

At the multilateral end of the spectrum is the logic of liberal internationalism. For liberal internationalism, collective efforts are both necessary, because of the limits on U.S. power and the nature of the issues on the new agenda, and intrinsically worthwhile, as means to create institutions of international cooperation.

The logics of hegemonism and realism occupy middle ground. Both can accommodate either acting alone or acting in conjunction with others. The logic of hegemonism, however, tends toward the unilateralist end whereas the logic of realism tends toward the multilateralist end. The logic of realism has a bias toward multilateralism because its diagnosis of the limitations of U.S. influence encourages collaboration in order to pool resources and efforts. That is especially so for diplomatic realism, with its emphasis on averting otherwise avoidable conflicts with potential partners against common foes. Nevertheless, the logic of realism would dictate unilateral action if national interests were endangered and collective action could not be organized quickly enough or at an acceptable cost. Many of the strategies for balancing power discussed in Chapter 3 are amenable to unilateral action and may even require it.

The logic of hegemonism, on the other hand, tends more toward the unilateralist end of the spectrum. Hegemonism, with its central purpose of providing leadership to the international system, requires collective action: A leader cannot be a leader without followers. Two considerations, though, draw it away from multilateralism. First, a hegemon faces the temptation to act alone because its power allows it to and it may feel compelled to act alone when action is urgent and collective action cannot be quickly organized. Second, hegemonic leadership in multilateral settings easily could turn into false multilateralism as the United States sets the terms and pressures others to concede to its position.

Two logics are excluded from Figure 8.1. The logic of liberalism is left off because it is completely compatible with any position on the spectrum. The placement of any particular adherent of liberalism would depend on his or her perspective on the power of the United States and its capacity to promote freedom acting alone. The logic of radical anti-imperialism is left off because of its critical perspective on any action taken by the United States as presently constituted. In principle, radical anti-imperialists would favor multilateralism. In practice, though, they interpret U.S. actions in multilateral settings to be false multilateralism. On the other hand, the logic cannot be placed at the unilateralist end of the spectrum because radical anti-imperialists oppose unilateral action as unquestionably undertaken to promote U.S. imperialist interests over the common good.

MILITARISM

Figure 8.2 shows the relative position of the foreign policy logics along a militarism versus antimilitarism dimension. This dimension represents the degree to which each logic accepts or rejects the necessity for military strength and the use of military force as part of the nation's foreign policy strategy.

Militarism							Antimilitarism
R	H	L	I	LI	RA		

Key:

H = Hegemonism   LI = Liberal Internationalism
I = Isolationism   R = Realism
L = Liberalism   RA = Radical Anti-imperialism

Figure 8.2   Placement of the foreign policy logics along a militarism versus anti-militarism continuum.

The logic of realism is the most militaristic. This is not because realists consider military power and the use of force to be good and attractive things in themselves. Some do, of course, but that attraction is not intrinsic to the logic. Rather, realists consider military power and the use of force to be inevitable consequences of the nature of world politics. States, including the United States, must attend to and nurture their power in order to avoid the disasters that follow from the atrophy of power: war and the loss of national security.

The logic of hegemonism comes next, it too lying near the militarist end. Hegemonism recognizes that military might is a critical resource and the United States as leader must have it and be willing to use it. This reflects the logic's membership in the broad realist tradition. On the other hand, for hegemonism, military power is only one of many sources of influence and control. Hence hegemonism's placement is somewhat away from the militarism end of the spectrum.

Right in the middle of the continuum is the logic of liberalism. It is placed there by default; there are no grounds for placing it closer to either end. It contains no arguments either opposing or favoring the use of military power to promote freedom. Liberalism, of course, has been used many times to justify wars and uses of force but it also has been used to justify completely pacific programs.

The logic of isolationism also occupies middle ground, but tending toward the antimilitarism end of the spectrum. Isolationism has an antimilitaristic strain; avoiding the domestic harms of wars and the costs of military preparations is, after all, one of the central goals of isolationism. Moreover, this logic contends that force has limited utility for accomplishing ends beyond national defense, narrowly understood. On the other hand, as part of the broad realist tradition, it also recognizes both the importance of military might to international affairs and the need for the United States to be strong enough to deter potential enemies and to fight if necessary to protect its vital interests. It cannot, therefore, be fully at the antimilitaristic end of the continuum.

Anchoring the antimilitarist end of the spectrum is the logic of radical anti-imperialism. Radical anti-imperialism is adamantly opposed to the use of force by the United States. War and military intervention are illegitimate because they are tools for maintaining the American empire. Moreover, war is wrong because of the damage it does to the victims of American aggression.

The logic of liberal internationalism, too, lies close to the antimilitarist end of the continuum. It belongs there because of its emphasis on nonmilitary problems, on peaceful cooperation for dealing with those problems, and on the limited effectiveness and counterproductive results of the use of military force. On the other hand, liberal internationalism, unlike radical anti-imperialism, is not opposed to the use of military power in principle. Its position is essentially pragmatic. Followers of this logic could support the use of force in the right circumstances. Liberal internationalism, therefore, is placed just to the left of the antimilitarist end of the spectrum.

INTERVENTIONISM

Intervention is action to influence or alter the internal affairs—domestic structures (such as the government or economic systems), policies, and actions—of other countries. The logics are arrayed along a continuum between those that prescribe intervention and those that prohibit it. The placement of the logics along this spectrum is presented in Figure 8.3.

Interventionism				Noninterventionism
	L	H	R	I
				LI
				RA

Key:
  H = Hegemonism   LI = Liberal Internationalism
  I = Isolationism   R = Realism
  L = Liberalism   RA = Radical Anti-imperialism

Figure 8.3   Placement of the foreign policy logics along an interventionism-noninterventionism continuum.

The logic of liberalism occupies the interventionist end of the spectrum and, indeed, is the only logic toward that end. The logic of liberalism is, at its very core, intrinsically interventionist. Its total purpose is to transform—reform—the internal structures of other countries: To convert them to market economies, democratic governments, and protectors of human rights, and to make them independent of formal external control. The logic is flexible about its means but any program undertaken under this logic by definition is intervention.

Three logics sit at the noninterventionist end of the spectrum. Radical anti-imperialism opposes intervention by the United States because intervention is a tool of imperialist subjugation. The logic of isolationism shares that judgment, but bases its opposition to imperialism on other grounds. Whereas radical anti-imperialism opposes intervention because it is unjust and damaging to its victim, isolationism opposes it because it is unnecessary, since internal conditions in other countries are irrelevant to U.S. national interest. Furthermore, intervention, according to isolationism, is harmful—it ratchets up the costs of international involvement to the United States. The logic of liberal internationalism opposes intervention because it risks alienating states whose cooperation is necessary for addressing the new agenda problems.

Realism strongly tends toward the noninterventionist position. Like isolationism, it sees intervention for the sake of reforming other countries as irrelevant to U.S. national interest, harmful in distracting attention and diverting resources from the protection of the real national interest, and dangerous in risking the alienation of countries whose membership in a power-balancing coalition might be needed. On the other hand, realism does permit, indeed, encourage, interference in other countries' internal affairs—for example, removing an adversarial government—if it is useful for power balancing purposes.

The logic of hegemonism is in the interventionist half of the spectrum primarily because its mandate to regulate international economic systems regularly draws the United States into efforts to get other countries to implement free market economic structures and policies. The logic of hegemonism offers ambivalent guidance about intervention for political reform. On the one hand, it could encourage intervention because successfully exporting American social, political, economic, and cultural systems would increase U.S. soft power and thus reinforce its primacy. On the other hand, intervention against the wishes of the government and elites in other countries could increase others' fear that the United States would misuse its power and thus encourage counterhegemonic balancing. While the logic of hegemonism in principle provides grounds for both interventionism and anti-interventionism, a country playing the role of hegemon likely would tend toward interventionism, for two reasons. First, exporting American domestic structures and values could be used to justify acting against another government that is obstructing the foreign policy purposes of the United States. Second, given hegemonism's expansive purposes, policy makers will be relatively susceptible to the temptation to see intervention as necessary or convenient.

LEADERSHIP ROLE

This fourth dimension of comparison addresses the logics' views about whether the United States should play a leadership role in international affairs. At one end are the logics that prescribe an expansive leadership role; at the other are those that reject it. Their placement is mapped in Figure 8.4.

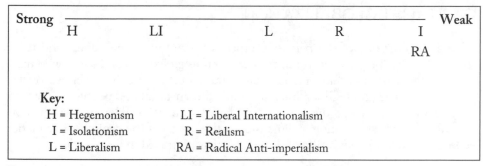

Figure 8.4   Placement of the foreign policy logics along a leadership dimension.

The placement of the three logics at the ends of the scale is fairly straightforward and self-explanatory. The essence of the logic of hegemonism is to provide leadership. The logics of isolationism and radical anti-imperialism, on the other hand, renounce any leadership role. Isolationism does so because a leadership role is a sustained, general commitment to international activism. Radical anti-imperialism does so because a leadership role in the extant international system, which it diagnoses as being an empire, is a sustained commitment to the preservation and extension of empire. In both cases, leadership is exactly what the logic opposes.

The other three logics occupy middle ground. The logic of liberal internationalism tends toward the strong end of the scale because the resources and prominence of the United States make it strategically well placed to exercise influence in a system of complex interdependence. Nevertheless, its leadership function necessarily is circumscribed. The lack of any single power hierarchy means that U.S. influence varies from issue to issue, and so does its capacity for leadership. Also, claiming a leadership role in a system of complex interdependence would tend to alienate other participants in the system and therefore would be counterproductive.

Very similar reasons underwrite the placement of the logic of realism. It too acknowledges that the United States may have to play a leadership role if it is necessary to organize a coalition to counterbalance a rising hegemon and no other state is willing to do so. On the other hand, the leadership role suggested by the logic of realism is quite limited. It arises only with regard to balancing power, rather than a wide array of issues, and then only under specified circumstances rather than as a general orientation. Those restrictions are implied by realism's diagnosis of the limits to the country's power and national interest. Moreover, any effort to claim a general leadership role will provoke counter-hegemonic balancing and thus be self-defeating.

The logic of liberalism occupies the middle for the same reasons that it did for the militarism scale. There is nothing in the logic itself that prescribes either playing or renouncing a leadership role. Where adherents to the logic of liberalism place themselves will depend on the other logics they hold. Of special note is that persons who subscribe to both the logics of liberalism and hegemonism will insist that the United States take a leadership role in the spreading of freedom.

CAPITALIST GLOBALIZATION

Globalization is one of the pervasive processes of international affairs and it has spawned a division between those who are seen as globalizers and those who make up an antiglobalization movement. That framing of the issue, however, is oversimplified and misleading. Globalization is multidimensional and people's views of it vary according to which dimension is under consideration. Here we will be concerned only with the economic dimension—the spread of the capitalist free market economic model. The position of the six logics is portrayed in Figure 8.5.

Support ————————————————————————————————————— Oppose
    H   I   LI   R   RA

    L

Key:
  H = Hegemonism   LI = Liberal Internationalism
  I = Isolationism   R = Realism
  L = Liberalism   RA = Radical Anti-imperialism

Figure 8.5   Placement of the foreign policy logics along a dimension of support for capitalist globalization.

The logics of liberalism and hegemonism are the most supportive of capitalist globalization. For both, their support of capitalist globalization is just another way of labeling their support for free trade.

At the oppositional end are the logics of radical anti-imperialism and realism. Radical anti-imperialism's opposition stems directly from its perception of capitalism as inherently exploitative. Realism's placement is more complicated. It rests, first of all, on that logic's lack of any justification for globalization. The policy imperative is to maintain the global balance of power. In no clear way does globalization advance that goal and, indeed, in some ways it can impede it. It impedes it if policy makers divert their attention away from the balance of power in order to tend to globalization. It impedes it also if globalization creates new enemies for the United States and thus gets in the way of it ensuring its own security. It impedes it, finally, if it obstructs the United States from using tools of economic statecraft, such as trade sanctions and protection of vital industries, to maintain the balance of power.

The logic of liberal internationalism is placed between the two ends but closer to the oppositional end for the following reason. Liberal internationalism is not opposed in principle to capitalist globalization. The spread of the market brings benefits, such as an increase in production and aggregate wealth, but also problems, such as social disruption, rising income inequality (at least in the short term), and pollution. Liberal internationalism favors economic globalization but with strong governmental and quasi-governmental regulations to mitigate the market's harmful effects.

The logic of isolationism is placed right in the middle because its two tendencies— political isolationism and protectionist isolationism—contradict and cancel out each other. Political isolationism favors capitalist globalization, or more precisely, it opposes regulations that would impede globalization. Protectionist isolationism, on the other hand, opposes corporate globalization (indeed, all forms of globalization) because of the putative harms done to Americans by their being thrust into competition with foreign producers and workers and to the independence of the American political system by its being entangled in the international institutions that foster globalization.

POWER

The logics disagree about the nature of U.S. foreign policy because they disagree about three factors that shape foreign policy. The first is the amount of power the United States has. At the one end are those who take seriously the notion that the United States is a superpower. They see it as having overwhelming power and thus is able to exert a great deal of influence on and control over international affairs. At the other end are those who see the United States as having considerably less, although still substantial, power. The location of the logics is presented in Figure 8.6.

Extensive			Limited
H	R	I	
RA	LI		

Key:
 H = Hegemonism   LI = Liberal Internationalism
 I = Isolationism   R = Realism
 L = Liberalism   RA = Radical Anti-imperialism

Figure 8.6   Placement of the foreign policy logics according to the amount of U.S. power.

The logics of hegemonism and radical anti-imperialism have the most expansive view of U.S. power. The superior power of the United States is a foundational premise of the logic of hegemonism. Similarly, the radical anti-imperialists ascribe great power to the United States; without great power there would be no empire. The two logics differ less in their diagnosis of the amount of U.S. power as in their normative evaluation of it: The logic of hegemonism sees it as a good thing whereas the logic of radical anti-imperialism sees it as very bad indeed.

The logic of isolationism has the least expansive view of U.S. power. According to isolationism, the United States is powerful enough to take care of itself but not powerful enough to change the world for the better. It is especially explicit about the limited value of military power for purposes other than homeland defense.

The logics of realism and liberal internationalism interpret U.S. power as falling short of superpower status but greater than what isolationism conceives it to have. For realism, the United States is powerful enough to be a decisive actor for the maintenance of the equilibrium of power. That is a significant accomplishment, reflecting the military and economic might of the country. On the other hand, American power is limited. It especially must avoid wasting it on frivolous undertakings; for powerful countries, overcommitment—imperial overstretch—is a dangerous trap. Its power is limited, too, by the need to focus on the global distribution of power and thus to leave alone all the other problems of the world.

Liberal internationalism's analysis of the limits of American power is almost the mirror image of realism's. For liberal internationalism, the United States has significant power on many if not most issue areas but does not hold a dominant position on any. The logic's interpretation of the limited value of military strength is especially crucial given the decisive effect that dominant military strength would otherwise have.

The logic of liberalism is excluded from Figure 8.6 because it is the one logic that does not address the question of U.S. power.

NATIONAL INTERESTS

The second factor that determines the preferred foreign policy strategy is the conception of U.S. national interests. Each logic has a distinctive understanding of American interests. This section abstracts from those descriptions a sense of whether the logics see U.S. national interests as being extensively involved in international affairs. The placement of the logics is shown in Figure 8.7.

Most				Least
H		R	I	
LI				
L				

Key:
H = Hegemonism   LI = Liberal Internationalism
I = Isolationism   R = Realism
L = Liberalism   RA = Radical Anti-imperialism

Figure 8.7   Placement of the foreign policy logics arrayed according to the extensiveness of national interests.

Three logics stand at the high end of the spectrum: hegemonism, liberal internationalism, and liberalism. For all three, the well-being of the United States depends on achieving expansive goals in the world: Leadership to regulate the international political and economic systems, collaboration for creating international institutions and solving the problems created by escalating interdependence, and the promotion of economic and political freedom around the world. All three logics' conception of U.S. national interests dictate extensive international activism around the world. They prescribe different levels of activism— hegemonism the most, liberalism the least, among these three—not because they define different levels of national interests, but because they assume different levels of resources to support activism.

The logic of isolationism falls at the low end of the continuum. In its view, the United States has quite limited interests in the world's affairs. Indeed, the United States would best promote its real interests by disconnecting as much as possible from the affairs of the world.

The logic of realism falls into a middle range. It diagnoses American interests, which though substantial, are more limited than those defined by hegemonism, liberal internationalism, and liberalism. The limits are threefold. First, realism circumscribes national interests by subject area: Only the military arena, and the supporting economic arena, matter. Second, it restricts U.S. interests geographically; its interests are engaged only in those regions of the world that control substantial amounts of the resources that underwrite national power. Third, realism includes principles that define limits of U.S. interests and engagement: The United States must avoid overcommitment and imperial overstretch.

Figure 8.7 excludes the logic of radical anti-imperialism because it rejects in principle the concept of national interests.

MORAL OBLIGATIONS ABROAD

This last dimension taps the extent to which the logics contain principles that articulate moral obligations beyond the national interest. Put another way, the issue here is whether the logics prescribe altruism toward other countries and peoples. The logics are placed along this dimension in Figure 8.8.

High				Low
RA	H		R	
	LI		I	
	L			

Key:
H = Hegemonism   LI = Liberal Internationalism
I = Isolationism   R = Realism
L = Liberalism   RA = Radical Anti-imperialism

Figure 8.8 Placement of the foreign policy logics along a moral obligation continuum.

At the highest end is the logic of radical anti-imperialism. Three other logics also tend toward that pole: hegemonism, liberal internationalism, and liberalism. Radical anti-imperialism rates highest because it is the only logic whose moral principles are purely altruistic. For hegemonism, liberal internationalism, and liberalism, altruism intertwines with self-interest: Promoting the good of others or the common good also benefits the United States. For radical anti-imperialism, advancing the interests of those outside the United States, especially the poor and marginalized, is a sufficient end in itself.

The logics of realism and isolationism, on the other hand, rest at the opposite pole. Both advocate that the United States should avoid making the promotion of others' interests a factor in the crafting of its overall diplomacy. For both, the promotion of the national interest is the only moral obligation.

CHAPTER 9

Logics and Foreign Policy Debates

This chapter illustrates the application of foreign policy logics for interpreting foreign policy debates. It examines two cases from the last years of the Clinton presidency: The debates over granting China Permanent Normal Trading Relations status and over military intervention in Kosovo. The next chapter includes a third case, the reactions to September 11.

TRADE RELATIONS WITH CHINA

Background

On March 8, 2000, President Clinton proposed that the United States grant China Permanent Normal Trade Relations (PNTR). Under normal trade relations, which used to be called Most Favored Nation (MFN) status, each country levies the same tariff rate on the other's exports as it applies to its other trading partners. Clinton's proposal came after agreements assuring China's membership in the World Trade Organization (WTO), thus assuring that its trade would increase. PNTR would enable the United States to share in the increase.

Prior to 2000, the United States had given China normal trade relations only on a year-by-year basis. Congress first approved MFN status for China in 1980 and until 1990 its annual renewal had been relatively uncontroversial. Beginning in 1990, though, following China's massacre of prodemocracy protesters in Tienanmen Square, proposals to extend MFN met intense opposition. From 1990 through 1993, they passed on condition that the administration certify that China had improved human rights conditions. In May 1994, Clinton reversed his policy and broke the link between MFN and human rights.

Debate over MFN/NTR extension always drew in a witch's brew of issues, with five being the most volatile: human rights, Taiwan, Chinese military sales, Chinese espionage, and the trade imbalance.

Human Rights

Significant segments of the American public and Congress have insisted on linking trade relations and human rights. Better trade relations would be granted to reward improving human rights conditions and withheld to punish worsening ones. Sensitive areas of violations included suppression of freedom of religion, destruction of the society and culture of Tibet, mistreatment of workers and the prohibition of independent trade unions, use of prison labor for export production, persecution of democracy activists, and imprisonment without a fair trial.

Taiwan

Taiwan is an island off the coast of mainland China and a province of China. At the end of the Chinese civil war, in 1949, nationalist forces fled to Taiwan after their defeat by the communists. The victorious communists called their country the People's Republic of China (PRC); its capital is Beijing. The United States allied itself with the nationalists on Taiwan at the time of the Korean War (1950–1953). For the next 20 years, the United States recognized Taiwan (the Republic of China) as the government of China. It had no ongoing formal diplomatic relations with the PRC. Taiwan held the China seat in the United Nations.

American policy toward China began to change in the late 1960s. In a spectacular bit of diplomatic theatre, in 1972 the Nixon administration began direct dealings with the PRC and allowed it to take the China seat in the UN. Seven years later, President Carter recognized the PRC as the government of China. The United States opened an embassy in Beijing and closed the one in Taiwan's capital, Taipei. Still, Taiwan in effect continued to be independent of China. It had its own government and an increasingly powerful market economy. Beijing insisted that Taiwan's separation from China was anomalous and impermanent and that Taiwan rejoin the rest of China under Beijing's leadership. It pointedly refused to rule out any means for the unification of China, including military force.

Although the United States recognized the PRC, it maintained relations with Taiwan. It kept a lower level diplomatic presence in Taipei. Trade burgeoned. It continued to sell advanced weapons to Taiwan. Indeed, the Taiwan Relations Act of 1979 committed the United States to provide sophisticated weapons systems to Taiwan. These relations angered Beijing.

Chinese Arms Sales

China's selling advanced military technology to its adversaries, such as Iran, angered the United States. Those sales also undercut U.S.-led efforts to establish nonproliferation regimes to control and curtail the spread of nuclear and ballistic missile technologies.

Chinese Espionage

China also had engaged in successful espionage against the United States. The spying, it was believed, had allowed China to upgrade its nuclear weapons capabilities. For some observers, the deeper concern was that China was seeking to replace the United States as the regional hegemon in East Asia, thus confirming their suspicions that China was, is, and increasingly will be an adversarial state.

The Trade Imbalance

In 1988, the United States exported $5 billion to China and imported $8.5 billion, for a $3.5 billion trade deficit. By 1999, exports had grown to $13.1 billion while imports had exploded to $81.8 billion, for a deficit of $68.7 billion.[1] This growing imbalance had many causes, but three were of greatest concern: China's government maintained impediments to U.S. imports; China's exports were facilitated by low production costs due to low wages; Chinese production costs also were depressed by China's lax environmental regulations. Policies to keep production costs down, such as repressing independent trade unions, amounted to subsidizing exports. Some economists were sanguine about the trade imbalance, seeing in China's low-cost exports a shift in material well-being from China's producers to America's consumers. Other economists and virtually all officeholders, though, considered the trade imbalance a serious problem requiring political solution. The flood of Chinese imports threatened U.S. workers' jobs without a compensating increase in jobs in export-oriented industries. The trade imbalance also had geopolitical implications; some analysts held that China was committed to running huge balance of trade surpluses as a means of shifting the balance of power with the United States.

The 2000 Debate About PNTR

Opponents of PNTR met President Clinton's proposal with demands for its outright rejection and its amendment to require Chinese reform in the areas of human rights, labor, and environmental regulations. The debate took place against a background of certain shared assumptions and goals, which Senator Joseph Biden enumerated: "[O]ne, there is going to be trade with China. There should be trade with China. Two, we should do something about the human rights, to the extent we can affect it. We should deal with proliferation to the extent we can affect it. And, three, we should be making it clear that we mean what we say about Taiwan. I mean, everybody . . . agrees on those three things."[2]

The Case for PNTR

Advocates of PNTR pressed four basic lines of argument: (1) Expanding economic ties would both enrich the United States and lead to Chinese domestic reforms; (2) engaging China in cooperative relations would foster international peace and security by building up institutions of international cooperation, whereas (3) rejecting PNTR would push U.S.-China relations toward conflict;

and (4) the United States had a responsibility as world leader to engage China so as to bring about those good things. Those lines of argument are based, respectively, in the logics of liberalism, liberal internationalism, realism, and hegemonism, though the connection to realism is debatable.

Liberalism

Advocates of PNTR advanced three arguments derived from the logic of liberalism. First, PNTR would advance U.S. economic interests because, in the words of U.S. Trade Representative Charleen Barshefsky, it would "open China's markets, what may become the world's single largest market to American exports of industrial goods and agriculture and services. . . . "[3] Estimates of increases in exports ranged from $2 billion to $13.9 billion per year.[4] Long-term benefits figured to be even greater as China's share of world trade more than tripled. "An open and prosperous Chinese economy will provide major export and investment opportunities for U.S. firms."[5]

Second, PNTR would encourage democratization and respect for human rights in China. This was a crucial issue. PNTR's supporters could not concede that China's mistreatment of its own people ought to condemn PNTR. Rather, they had to show that PNTR would not abandon liberalism's core values. So, asserted Commerce Secretary William Daley, who headed the administration's campaign, PNTR "does not mean a tacit endorsement of China's human rights policies."[6] The issue, according to Senator John Kerry, was this: "China is a dictatorship, it's authoritarian. We don't like it, we want it to be a democracy. We long for a change. But the question before us is going to be how best to achieve that."[7]

Withholding PNTR does not give the United States an effective lever for forcing China to democratize and respect human rights in the short run. China lacks a democratic tradition; transformation inevitably will be slow; so reformers must be patient.[8] "[T]he U.S. government has very limited direct influence over the regime's domestic behavior," wrote one expert.[9] Linking trade to human rights had not worked in the past.[10] Indeed, public pressure only makes China's leaders more rigid as they try to save face.

Fortunately, economic openness would speed China's political transformation in the long run. Trade and foreign investment feed economic growth, which "helps create a middle class with power and interests independent of the state."[11] Expanding China's economic relations with the world "will expand the flow of information, ideas, and business practices to China's emerging middle class and hasten the pace of political and economic reform."[12] The Committee for Economic Development concurred: "[U]ltimately, it will prove impossible to maintain a closed and regulated society in an open economy that is dependent on the free flows of information that increasingly drive productive enterprises."[13]

Third, PNTR also would promote international stability, especially in East Asia. Integrating China into the world economy will increase its stake in international order, making military conflict less attractive. "If both Beijing and Taiwan are in the WTO," President Clinton observed, "it will increase their interdependence and, therefore, the cost to Beijing of confrontation."[14]

Liberal Internationalism

Senator Biden's support for PNTR grew from his basic worry over China's trouble-some foreign policy; PNTR, he argued, would increase Chinese moderation.

> I do believe becoming a member of an international organization that has basic rules of the road and behavior moderates and/or ameliorates the conduct of the country joining. . . . So, I do think being a part of the WTO has an impact upon— may have an impact upon—Chinese behavior in the next two decades.[15]

In invoking the cooperation-inducing effects of multilateral institutions and the binding quality of international norms, Senator Biden drew on liberal internationalism.

So did Dr. Bates Gill, of the Brookings Institution. History, he maintained, shows that U.S. diplomacy must "[increase] China's integration into the international community. . . . The steady opening of China to the outside world over the past 25 years has had an undeniably positive effect on moderating China's approach to its foreign policy generally." Moreover, ". . . we should assure that we have multilateral support . . . as we attempt to curb Chinese activities of concern. Such an approach is far more likely to result in success than unilateral actions, which will end up isolating the United States rather than isolating China."[16] His emphasis on multilateral action reflects liberal internationalism's belief that the actual influence of any one nation, even the most powerful one, is limited, so action must be collective if it is to be effective.

Realism

President Clinton warned that rejecting PNTR "would have extremely harmful consequences for our national security."[17] It would, said Senator Biden, "convince China's leaders that we want to keep them weak and backward, and that we hope to contain them through our economic coercion."[18] Trade Representative Barshevsky spelled out the eventual danger: China "would be more likely to read hostile intent into our every move. This, in turn, would raise the prospect that our present disagreements would only escalate."[19]

That argument cannot be unambiguously classified as realist, however. It is consistent with realism in its focus on security competition. It also draws on diplomatic realism in warning against antagonizing powerful countries that are not already enemies. The argument, though, is not embedded in an analysis of the dynamics of the balance of power. Precisely, the argument does not claim that by alienating China the United States is losing it as a potential partner in a coalition to balance against another challenger. Conceivably those making the argument are concerned that China would challenge U.S. primacy in Asia. If so, the argument would represent the logic not of realism but of hegemonism.

Hegemonism

The support for PNTR drew heavily on the logic of hegemonism. Commerce Secretary Daley, for instance, testified: "As a world leader we have an obligation to foster further reform in China."[20] Agriculture Secretary Glickman invoked the U.S. leadership role equally explicitly: "If the United States' status as a world leader is to remain undiminished . . . then the U.S. must fully engage China, and approving PNTR is an essential course of action."[21]

The Committee for Economic Development related U.S. leadership to the maintenance of the international system. It observed that "a refusal to normalize our trade relations with China . . . could be interpreted abroad as a rejection of the global trading system by the United States" and would ignore "the continuing need for U.S. economic leadership in the global economy." They elaborated:

> Realistically, there is no alternative to U.S. leadership. . . . No other large . . . country has demonstrated a strong commitment to these principles and a willingness and capacity to step out front and take the lead . . . [T]he United States must project a coherent strategy to advance the common interest, and inspire and induce collective action by its own example and by patient consultation with its principle trading partners in both the industrial and developing world.[22]

The Case Against PNTR

Critics opposed PNTR on four grounds: (1) It would mean losing a valuable lever for promoting reforms in China; (2) it would strengthen an adversary state; (3) it would destabilize world politics; and (4) it would harm the U.S. economy and democracy. These arguments reflect the logics of liberalism, realism, hegemonism, and isolationism, respectively.

Liberalism

Critics vigorously and repeatedly brought up China's shortage of democracy and surplus of human rights violations. Activist Lori Wallach's indictment was quoted in Chapter 1.[23] People at the opposite end of the ideological spectrum made exactly the same point. For instance, conservative republican Senator Jesse Helms intoned:

> Now, I do not believe the American people will countenance a foreign policy, which looks the other way . . . when the Chinese dictatorship throws into jail, members of the China Democracy Party with no semblance whatsoever of due process; and when the Chinese dictatorship detains and tortures thousands of harmless followers of the Falun Gong spiritual movement. So when the Chinese dictatorship brutalizes the underground Christians and Roman Catholic priests by arresting, torturing and in some cases throwing them out of the windows, when the Chinese dictatorship occupies and suppresses Buddhist Tibet . . . , when the Chinese dictatorship permits no labor unions, except those labor unions which it can control, when the Chinese dictatorship subsidizes State enterprises with the confiscated savings of low-income workers. . . . [24]

Although Senator Helms framed his argument as a prediction about what the American people would tolerate, he clearly also was articulating his views about what they should tolerate.

Critics denied that the United States could rely on the long-term liberalizing impact of commerce. They insisted, rather, on direct action to press China toward reform because policy cannot be based on the assumption that commerce will bring reform. As Wallach told Congress, "greater trade links and economic liberalization with China have not resulted in improvement in China's human rights conduct nor promoted the growth of democracy in China."[25]

China's dictatorial government, moreover, poses a security threat that requires a more active policy response with a shorter time horizon. The argument is the mirror image of the democratic peace thesis: Just as democracies are intrinsically peaceful, dictatorships are intrinsically belligerent. According to Elliott Abrams, the Chinese government is dictatorial, so it is inherently aggressive. Lacking legitimacy, its "leaders will always be tempted to use foreign adventures as a means of boosting nationalism and their own popularity. . . . Threats against Taiwan are the foreign side of the crackdown on Falun Gong—two sides of the same coin—again, force as a substitute for consent, legitimacy, respect for human rights."[26]

Human rights, finally, are a matter of moral urgency, so efforts must be made to induce reform immediately; the long run is not soon enough. Critics of PNTR were especially clear about the moral imperative embedded in the logic of liberalism. "Now, this debate is not merely about how to increase exports to China or about maintaining dialogue with China," declared Senator Helms. "It's about what America stands for as a nation. . . . Morality is still an integral part of America's identity. . . ."[27]

The sense of moral obligation to stand against Chinese violations of human rights was not restricted to the political right. It is seen, too, in the comments of the late Senator Paul Wellstone, a democrat from Minnesota:

> To me, Mr. Chairman, if we're living in a global economy and we care about human rights, then we can no longer concern ourselves just with human rights at home. If we live in a global economy, we're concerned about human rights throughout the world.
>
> If we truly care about religious freedom, we can no longer just be concerned about religious freedom at home. . . We care about religious freedom in other nations.
>
> If we truly care about the right of workers to organize and bargain collectively, and earn a decent living for themselves and their family, then we can no longer just be concerned about labor rights at home.[28]

In contrast to the supporters of PNTR, opponents held that U.S. policy can decisively influence the internal behavior of the Chinese government. The size of its market, which absorbs 40 percent of Chinese exports, gives the United States economic leverage to influence China's internal policies.[29]

Realism

The logic of realism draws attention to the prospect of conflict over the distribution of power, especially military power, in the international system. It calls on the United States to weaken its known adversaries lest they surpass its power. We have already seen in Chapter 3 the realism-inspired warnings about China's growing military might and the dangers that it will act aggressively against it neighbors and U.S. interests in Asia. In that context, the logic of realism underlays three arguments against PNTR.

The first can be found in the testimony of George Becker, president of the United Steelworkers of America. Recalling that industrial capacity in general and steel in particular had been decisive in winning World War II, he warned: "We are losing that industrial capacity today in the steel industry, in the electronics industry, in textiles, across the board. These are the plants that are leaving the United States for other countries."[30] PNTR, in other words, would harm the U.S. economy in ways devastating to its military potential; it would ease industry's exporting of U.S. productive capacity, thus depriving the country of the potential to muster the military supplies necessary to fight the next war.

The second realist-inspired argument against PNTR denies that entangling China in treaty commitments and multilateral organizations will alter its behavior. "If one looks at China's behavior as a member of the Security Council of the United Nations," observed Joseph Bosco, "the prospect is not that the organization changes China, but the danger is that China changes the organization."[31]

The last realist argument is that fully normalizing trade relations with China when it is vigorously augmenting its military strength and putting pressure on its neighbors would increase the chances of Chinese aggression. The Chinese would interpret PNTR as showing that the United States values increasing trade so much that it will tolerate Chinese aggression. That perception would encourage such aggression.

Not every critic relied on the logic of realism to argue that PNTR would weaken U.S. security. Some, such as Senator Helms and Elliott Abrams, saw China as a danger because of its undemocratic political system. Were China to democratize, it would cease to be a threat. That analysis reflects liberalism, not realism. Still other analysts predicted security problems following from PNTR, but their arguments more closely manifested the logic of hegemonism.

Hegemonism

Some critics of PNTR drew on the logic of hegemonism to argue that PNTR would create a Chinese threat to U.S. security. "I think that China needs to see some limits, some constraints on its behavior, particularly internationally," testified foreign policy analyst Joseph Bosco. "And obviously, the United States is the main player on the international scene. And unless we start drawing some lines and hopefully lead other nations to join us in that approach, I think China will see green lights all over the place and will tend to move aggressively where it thinks it can . . . succeed."[32] The United States, by its power, must lead the international community in preserving the international political system, specifically by constraining the disruptive actor, China. Expressions of the logic of hegemonism rarely come any clearer.

An intriguing perspective melded the logics of liberalism and hegemonism. It held that China threatens stability because it is undemocratic (liberalism) and the United States has a responsibility as leader of the international system (hegemonism) to convert China to democracy. Robert Kagan advanced this view. He insisted that policy toward China must not be based on the best case assumption that China, with or without PNTR, will democratize. "The United States," he wrote, "has an interest in a democratic China" because "the looming confrontation between the United States and China has a powerful ideological component. The international democratic order that we uphold is inherently threatening to Chinese dictators clinging to power. . . . They must either force us to change (or make an exception to) the rules of that international order, or they must succumb to it."[33] If China's authoritarianism represents a threat to international peace and stability, his argument goes, and if its democratization cannot be assumed to be inevitable, then the United States must apply maximum pressure on China to change. Cutting a trade deal, therefore, contradicts the most important U.S. national interests and moral obligations.

Isolationism

The logic of isolationism supported two criticisms of expanded trade relations with China, primarily caused by its joining the WTO. Both reflect the antiglobalization strain of isolationism. First, expanded economic relations with China "will gradually increase U.S. imports of Chinese labor intensive products like textiles and toys, putting more downward pressure on wages in general, and the wages of unskilled U.S. workers in particular."[34] The net result is liable to accentuate divisions within the United States because "Wall Street wins, main street loses; high-tech and finance win, light industry loses. The highly skilled win, the low skilled lose. If you are lucky enough to keep your job and avoid a drop in your real wages, you will be able to buy more (Chinese made) toys to put under your Christmas tree. If you lose your job or, like most Americans, if you continue to fail to get wage increases commensurate with inflation, Christmas will be all the more bleak for you and yours when China enters the WTO."[35]

Second, expanded trade relations with China could harm the United States domestically and erode its sovereignty. Antiglobalization activist Lori Wallach clearly stated her position: "As the past five years of WTO jurisprudence have shown, plaintiffs generally win cases at the WTO and each and every domestic environmental, health, or other public interest measure brought to the WTO has been ruled an illegal trade barrier. Thus . . . a full U.S.-China WTO relationship would mean U.S. laws would be newly exposed to WTO attack by China, whose government has been very vocal in challenging the legitimacy of U.S. laws and policies."[36]

Radical Anti-imperialism

The forces opposed to corporate globalization predicted that WTO and PNTR would be devastating to the people of China as well. "[H]undreds of millions of Chinese peasants will lose their jobs to international food imports . . . [and] hundreds of millions of Chinese workers in state owned enterprises will lose their jobs as 'downsizing' Chinese-style makes the last ten years of downsizing in the U.S. look like a proletarian picnic." The loss of jobs will mean destitution and misery because the Chinese "social safety net" had been gutted by China's embrace of markets. Not that there won't be winners in China. The elites who command political power will gain because they now will have a larger number or more lucrative opportunities to enrich themselves via corruption. That hundreds of millions are impoverished while the privileged few accumulate fabulous wealth will present a familiar problem of social control with a heinous outcome: "the Chinese political repressive apparatus will set new standards for brutality and effectiveness at the beginning of the new century." The only alternative is for China to sever itself from the global market so that "the feast of the Chinese and international corporate elites at the expense of hundreds of millions of Chinese peasants and proletarians will prove mercifully short lived."[37]

Comparison

Both sides employed the logics of realism, liberalism, and hegemonism. Supporters offered arguments from the logic of liberal internationalism while opponents offered criticisms derived from isolationism and radical anti-imperialism. A closer examination of the debate indicates four additional differences.

First, the proponents showed a general confidence in the processes of globalization. They favored economic and political liberalization of the world as beneficial to the United States and to the human community in general. They also were optimistic about the development of international political institutions, including international law and international moral norms. Expecting such development to promote human well-being, they favored policies to encourage it. Opponents, on the other hand, saw globalization as fraught with dangers and sought to slow its expansion.

Second, in offering arguments grounded in the logic of realism, proponents and opponents divided over whether the United States and China are doomed to be strategic adversaries. Opponents, reflecting the perspective of the militant school of realism, were fatalistic. They assumed that China will commit aggression in Asia, and perhaps beyond, as its economy grows and fuels a corresponding growth in its military capabilities. Proponents, on the other hand, were more hopeful, as would be consistent with diplomatic realism. They saw China's path as not predetermined. Further, the United States may decisively influence China's strategic future. If the United States and the international community, following the U.S. lead, treat China as an adversary and seek to contain it, then China will indeed become an adversary. If, on the other hand, China is engaged in cooperative relations, it will choose a constructive path. One might well question whether, at this point, the arguments of the proponents did not reflect more the rosy world view of liberal internationalism than the darker lenses of realism.

Third, both sides invoked U.S. leadership responsibilities under the logic of hegemonism, but they differed in their conception of U.S. power. For the opponents of PNTR, the United States is capable of acting unilaterally and coercively to contain and transform China. For proponents, American leadership would consist of mobilizing multilateral action toward cooperative ends.

Fourth, both sides employed the logic of liberalism. Each strove to establish that its preferred policy would best promote the democratization and liberalization of China. They differed over how to achieve that end. Opponents preferred the direct route: The United States demanding Chinese reforms. Proponents preferred to rely on longer-term and indirect processes of transformation. This difference correlates with their divergent conceptions of U.S. leadership, where the opponents favored a more assertive notion of U.S. leadership and proponents favored a more integrative and collaborative approach. Proponents and opponents differed in one more way in their take on liberalism. Opponents placed much more emphasis than did proponents on the moral obligation to promote democracy and human rights in China.

MILITARY INTERVENTION IN KOSOVO

Background

Kosovo is a province of Serbia, the largest of the units that had made up the Federal Republic of Yugoslavia. Kosovo's population is predominantly of Albanian ethnicity. The Albanians of Kosovo are called Kosovars. For decades, the Kosovars had sought change in Kosovo's relationship to the rest of Serbia. Their demands ranged from a greater degree of autonomy within Serbia to full independence.

To Serbia, the Kosovars' agenda was anathema. Kosovo was integral to Serbian identity. Indeed, Slobodan Milosevic, Yugoslavia's dictator from 1989 to 2000, rose to power by whipping up Serbian nationalism, and he began his nationalist campaign with a trip to Kosovo to pledge that it would always be part of Serbia.

Events in Kosovo took place against the background of earlier events in another part of former Yugoslavia: Bosnia. Stirring up Serb nationalism had helped Milosevic gain power in Yugoslavia, but it also led to secession of other parts of Yugoslavia, first Slovenia, then Croatia. Bosnia's declaration of independence in 1991 led to a nasty war. The Serbs of Bosnia waged a campaign of terror against the Bosnians, who were predominantly but not exclusively Muslims. Serbian tactics included massacres and widespread raping of Bosnian women, all intended to drive the Bosnians out of the part of Bosnia that the Serbs intended to take for their own. They laid siege to the capital, Sarajevo, and for months fired artillery shells into that city. Snipers picked off civilians moving about Sarajevo. They massacred some 3000 Bosnian men and boys at Srebrenica.

When these atrocities were prominently reported in the news media, the world recoiled with revulsion. It was widely believed that Milosevic was behind the Serbs' campaign of terror. Demands that the Serbs cease and desist were ignored. Eventually, the United States and its European allies, acting through NATO (the North Atlantic Treaty Organization), intervened militarily and the American diplomat Richard Holbrooke brokered an agreement to end the fighting, the so-called Dayton Accords, signed December 14, 1995.

Less than three years later, the tension shifted to Kosovo. In order to regain control of territory lost to the Kosovo Liberation Army [KLA], Milosevic unleashed a military campaign against the Kosovars' independence movements. Although not as brutal as the ethnic cleansing in Bosnia, it was brutal enough, and an exodus of Kosovars fled into refugee camps in neighboring countries. Again, the Western community demanded cessation of the campaign and again Serbia ignored those demands. Eventually, as winter weather made military operations infeasible, Ambassador Holbrooke negotiated a ceasefire and the withdrawal of most Serb forces.

Few expected the 1998 ceasefire to hold. U.S. intelligence predicted resumption of the Serbian campaign in the springtime. In January, Serb forces massacred 45 Kosovars at Racak and killed another 24 in an attack on a suspected KLA base. In order to prevent a repeat of Bosnia, the United States and France hosted a diplomatic conference at Rambouillet, France, in February. Secretary of State Madeline Albright represented the United States. After much effort, she got the Kosovars to agree to a set of proposals that meant a delay in the earliest date of their independence. On March 18, though, the Serbs rejected the proposals.

On March 24, 1999, air forces of NATO members, including the United States, began bombing targets in Kosovo and Serbia. The goal was to coerce Serbia into accepting a peace agreement under which NATO forces would be deployed in Kosovo to protect the Kosovars.

President Clinton's decision to commit the United States to an undeclared war over Yugoslavia prompted considerable reaction in the Congress. Over the next six weeks the legislature acted on a number of conflicting proposals that gave members of Congress ample opportunity to take a stand on the Kosovo intervention and to articulate reasons for their stand. On balance, congressional actions lacked any simple consistency and left the administration with a free hand in its actions in Kosovo. The debate in Congress was matched by a vigorous debate in the public arena.

On June 3, Milosevic accepted a peace plan and on June 10 Serb forces began withdrawing from Kosovo. On June 20, 1999, American and NATO forces stopped bombing Serbia.

The Case for Military Intervention in Kosovo

The case for intervention rested primarily on three main propositions: (1) Intervention would promote U.S. security interests by preventing the spread of instability from the Balkans; (2) the United States had a responsibility to take charge; and (3) intervention would promote self-determination, democracy, and human rights, with a special moral obligation to end the Serb program of terror. A fourth proposition, of lesser importance, invoked the value of international cooperation. The first two arguments reflect the logic of hegemonism, the third reflects the logic of liberalism, and the fourth, the logic of liberal internationalism.[38]

Hegemonism

The logic of hegemonism bred two arguments raised repeatedly in the Kosovo debate: The violence endangered the stability of international affairs and the United States had responsibility to provide leadership in the situation.

Experts across the ideological spectrum predicted that turmoil in Kosovo would destabilize Europe. Secretary of State Albright stated that the "great lesson of this century is that when aggression and brutality go unopposed, like a cancer, they spread. And what begins as a treatable sickness in one part of the body can rapidly endanger the whole".[39] Indeed, Balkan instability would cause disruption not just in Europe but worldwide. Senator Orrin Hatch warned that events in Kosovo would teach lessons to dictators outside Europe, such as Saddam Hussein, who would be "taking notes. Seeing the survival of Slobodan Milosevic, he and others will challenge us again and again. I predict . . . that with the survival of Slobodan Milosevic, the security of this country will be increasingly challenged."

That the United States bears leadership responsibilities was directly stated by Senator Charles Robb. "I am deeply concerned about our unwillingness to accept responsibility for our position of world leadership," he said, adding: "I regret that fewer and fewer of our citizens are willing to take necessary risks. There are beliefs and principles that our founders were willing to die for, and we cannot shrink from the challenge that we face today."

The logic of hegemonism was especially clear in the arguments that linked stability to leadership. President Clinton, for instance, claimed that "we have a security responsibility to prevent a wider war in Europe. . . ."[40] Similarly, Senator Hatch asserted that "the United States must lead. . . . We cannot afford to ignore instability in other key regions."

Liberalism

The logic of liberalism suggested three values that intervention would support. The first was the autonomy of the Kosovars. Secretary of State Albright, for instance, stipulated that "[t]he people of Kosovo must be able to govern themselves democratically without interference from Belgrade. . . ." All the various ethnic groups in Kosovo "must be able to control, without government interference, their identities and cultural life."[41] Autonomy and multicultural respect are not identical with national self-determination. Nevertheless, as critics argued, the autonomy and rights of the Kosovars could be protected only by the separation of Kosovo from Yugoslavia. In fact, then, advocacy for autonomy meant advocacy for self-determination, one of the core values of the logic of liberalism.

The second value was democracy. President Clinton, for instance, proclaimed as a goal the establishment of "a progressive, democratic, multi-ethnic Balkans region."[42] Likewise, Congresswoman Jackson-Lee urged "a durable peace that prevents further repression and provides for democratic self-government for the Kosovar people."[43] Supporters of intervention frequently labeled Milosevic a despot or dictator, which would be relevant only if the undemocratic quality of his rule either accounted for its aggression and oppressiveness or stripped it of legitimacy. Both presumptions are integral to liberalism. The references to Milosevic's authoritarian rule, then, were implied arguments based on the logic of liberalism.

The third and critical value was human rights. Serb rule was indicted primarily for violating the human rights of the Kosovars, as Secretary Albright made clear: "Behind these images is a reality of people no different in their fundamental rights or humanity than you or me. . . ."[44]

The most compelling argument for intervention was grounded in the ethical component of the logic of liberalism. In essence, Kosovo presented a human rights problem in the extreme, a situation "in which war and crime are often indistinguishable, in which crime segues into massacre, and massacre into humanitarian emergency, in a vast Moebius strip of horror."[45] Faced with such enormities, "we have," in President Clinton's words, "a moral responsibility to oppose crimes against humanity and mass ethnic and religious killing and cleansing where we can."[46]

The decisive impact of these moral considerations is clearest in the justifications offered by persons who ordinarily were inclined to oppose military action. One was Senator Wellstone. During debate, he stated his "foreboding" in supporting the intervention because ". . . I knew once unleashed, a bombing campaign . . . to put a stop to violence would likely lead to more violence." Nevertheless, Kosovo was one of "those extremely rare occasions when our moral judgment dictates that [force] is the only remaining course available to us." Alternatives had been tried and found wanting; "without military action by the United States, a humanitarian disaster was about to occur. . . ." The senator had no doubt that evil was afoot. He reported a conversation with two people who "told me of four little children they had met in a refugee camp. The children had bandages over their eyes. They thought perhaps they had been near an explosion. That was not the case. The Serbs had raped their mother. They had witnessed the rape, and the Serbs cut their eyes out. . . ." Facing such evil, only military action in this instance could "prevent the imminent slaughter of thousands, if not tens of thousands, of innocent civilians. . . . Inaction in the face of unspeakable, imminent, and preventable violence is absolutely unacceptable."

Liberal Internationalism

During Senate debate, Senator Christopher Dodd emphasized that "this is not a unilateral effort on behalf of the United States. There are 18 other nations that make up the NATO strategic alliance. As a result, it is essential that we act in concert with them." Other intervention supporters noted that NATO would be harmed were the United States not to participate fully. Those arguments employed two core concerns of liberal internationalism: Multilateral cooperation and enhancing international institutions.

Liberal internationalism, however, provides at best an ambiguous and unconvincing foundation for support for intervention. The policy was inconsistent with that logic in three important ways: (1) It reflected the primacy of the security agenda over the new agenda of nonsecurity issues, (2) it reflected the primacy of Europe over other regions where humanitarian interventions had not been undertaken, and (3) it acknowledged the primacy of military means in international affairs.

The Case Against Intervention

Opponents of intervention had two tasks. They first had to refute the propositions that morality and the danger posed by Balkan instability required intervention. They then had to show that intervention created its own dangers and evils. The central claims against intervention, therefore, were: (1) Morality did not compel intervention, (2) instability in the Balkans did not endanger U.S. national interests,

(3) intervention in Kosovo would degrade U.S. power and exacerbate threats to its security, (4) military action violated the U.S. Constitution and diminished resources for domestic needs, and (5) military action in Kosovo inflicted severe suffering on the people of Kosovo and Yugoslavia. The first claim derived from three logics: realism, isolationism, and radical anti-imperialism. The second conformed with the logics of realism and isolationism. The third reflected the axioms of the logic of realism. The fourth represented the concerns of isolationism. The fifth claim was rooted in radical anti-imperialism.

The arguments made to support the first and second claims derive from several different logics. This convergence makes perfect sense. In debunking the strategic implications of hegemonism for Kosovo, realist and isolationist logics necessarily would use the same grounds, given that they both represent the broader realist tradition in international affairs. Similarly, although they begin from fundamentally different assumptions and propose fundamentally foreign policy strategies, realism, isolationism, and radical anti-imperialism oppose imperialist projects and question the professed idealistic motives of the United States.

The Moral Question

According to Senator Hutchinson, the key question is "What will guide our national security policy? Will it truly be our vital national security interests, or will it be that guided by understandable humanitarian concerns?" The question was rhetorical; his answer was national interests. Similarly for Senator Jim Bunning, a Kentucky republican, who said "we have no national security interest to intervene in this civil war." This privileging of national security to the exclusion of moral considerations conforms to the dictates of realism and isolationism, both of which deny that foreign policy ought to seek morality-based goals.

Four points were raised to buttress the claim that moral considerations in fact played little or no role in the policy of intervention. First, it was inaccurate to equate the Serbs with oppression and the Kosovars with victimization. Both parties were guilty of abusive behavior. For instance, Senator Inhofe recalled that some years ago while touring Kosovo he had observed that "the KLA was doing all the raping and looting and burning, and not the Serbs" and concluded that "there are bad guys on both sides."

Radical anti-imperialists joined in rejecting the simple moral polarity underlying the case for intervention. In fact, Serbia initiated its program of repression in 1998 in response to a KLA "terror campaign against a variety of Serbian targets in Kosovo, including dozens of police stations, police vehicles, a local headquarters of the Socialist party, and Serbian villagers, farmers, officials, and professionals."[47] The KLA was a violent faction with fascist tendencies that no more wanted a democratic, multiethnic Kosovo than did the Serbs. The perception that the Serbs were the bad guys derived not from reality but from an effective propaganda campaign in support of intervention.

Second, the critics denied that morality motivated the intervention because states—for radical anti-imperialism, capitalist states—generally seek to maximize interests, not righteousness. Radical anti-imperialism rejects so-called humanitarian intervention in general because its history "is replete with invocations of humanitarian intentions by strong powers or coalitions to conceal their own geopolitical interests."[48] Realists and isolationists would concur.

Third, the insignificance of moral considerations is shown by American refusal to intervene in cases of even worse atrocities. Senator Inhofe made the point: "For every one person who has been killed, ethnically cleansed, killed in the Kosovar Albanians, for every one, there have been 80 killed in just the two countries of Angola and Sierra Leone. . . . For every one that has been killed in Kosovo, there have been 300 killed in the one country of Rwanda." Noam Chomsky juxtaposed the supposed moral justification for the Kosovo intervention with U.S. inaction in other horrifying situations and concludes that the real U.S. policy is to intervene in humanitarian crises defined as "when the interests of rich and privileged people are endangered."[49]

Fourth, the intervention itself was poorly designed to achieve its supposed moral purpose. Bombing could not stop Serb military and paramilitary units from victimizing the Kosovars. It only could coerce Milosevic into ordering a stoppage, which took about six weeks. Until then, it was "the worst policy of all," wrote one correspondent, "one that makes promises it fails to keep, backing off when things become difficult." Taking the moral rationale at face value, he continued: "NATO's intervention in the Balkans makes no sense if it cannot prevent more ethnic violence. NATO . . . can stop the violence. The United States holds the key to what NATO does. As matters stand, it is failing its responsibility."[50] The failure to fulfill a self-claimed moral responsibility suggests that the moral considerations were unimportant in the first place.

Indeed, the gap between professed motives and actual results was even greater. The bombing not only failed to stop Serb violence, it provoked them into accelerating their attacks on the Kosovars. This is fully consistent with the core realist belief that injecting ethics into international affairs has unintended and unwanted consequences. The radical anti-imperialists were even harsher. In general, U.S. policy is "to act in such a way as to escalate the violence, with exactly that expectation."[51] They count the bombing, which killed "upwards of three thousand women, children, and men" and contributed substantially to the flight of refugees from Kosovo,[52] as part of the violence in the region.

Realists, isolationists, and radical anti-imperialists, in sum, deny that morality motivated the Kosovo intervention. Realists and isolationist further argued that morality should not have been the motivation.

The Issue of Instability

Realist and isolationist criticisms also rebutted the strategic rationale that the United States had a compelling interest in stifling instability in the Balkans. They emphasized that in general the United States had no national interest in Kosovo. Congressman Bonilla defined U.S. interests in a pristinely realist way: "Our interests in the Balkans are limited. . . . Our interests are solely limited to preventing any other outside power from increasing its threat to America by dominating the region."[53] Because the problem in the Balkans would not lead to an outside power dominating the region, the United States had no interests there. Senator Hutchinson went further, denying a strategic interest under any circumstances: "The Balkans, of course, are not in the heart of Europe. They are a backwater separated from the European heartland by mountain ranges and salt water. They are entirely unastride the major routes of communication and/or axis of invasion, and they are strategically and economically unessential."

Nor did instability create a security interest. Senator Hutchinson, for instance, challenged the argument that the Balkans are important because both world wars began there, quoting from what he called "an impressive article": "[T]he beginning of World War II had nothing to do with the Balkans, World War I began at a time when the interests of three vast empires collided in the region, making it one of extraordinary geopolitical sensitivity. That is no longer the case." Furthermore, treating the Balkans as important actually could create a security risk. "In citing them as the origins of the First and, incorrectly, Second World Wars, and therefore as justification for his policy of internationalizing their conflicts," Senator Hutchinson pointed out, "President Clinton seems not to comprehend that one of the reasons for the First World War was that the great powers of the time stupidly, mistakenly and fatally internationalized the conflicts there."

Even if by some chance instability would spread from Kosovo, it would not necessarily be an American problem. "But if there should be any immediate intervention into this civil war," said Senator Bunning, "let it come directly from those European neighbors where this tragedy is occurring. This is happening in Europe's backyard. . . ." Kosovo, in other words, lies within a European sphere of influence, another classically realist principle.

Realism

In addition to denying that Kosovo threatened real U.S. national interests, the logic of realism suggested that intervention was dangerous. It meant "we will be pulling our troops and weapons out of regions where we truly have an interest," Senator Bunning warned, and thus left the United States less able to use force to protect its real interests. His critique conforms exactly to a basic premise of realism: The United States has limited power. Not only were U.S. military resources finite, at best they were barely sufficient to protect important national security interests. Moreover, NATO air attacks would fail to coerce the Serbs and force would fail to pacify Kosovo; in other words, the actual ability of the United States to influence or control events abroad was limited.

Moreover, the intervention in Kosovo risked alienating Russia and making it an enemy. NATO meddling in the Balkans intruded into what many Russians consider its sphere of influence. Moreover, Russians historically have considered themselves to be Serbia's fraternal protector. Therefore, NATO intervention would be threatening and offensive to many Russians, leading to a more confrontational Russian foreign policy.

Isolationism

In addition to sharing realism's conviction that Kosovo did not impinge on U.S. national interests, the logic of isolationism fueled three criticisms of the intervention.

First, arguments highlighting the opportunity costs of intervention reflected isolationist logic. Congressman Duncan, for example, pointed to the "money that will have to be taken from other programs and from American taxpayers, and if we have to stay in there to preserve the peace for many years to come, the costs could become unbelievable."[54] Congressman Ewing pointed out that the financial costs "will be of a major detriment to our efforts to save Social Security and Medicare."[55]

Second, opponents raised concerns about the integrity of U.S. political institutions. Congressman Rohrabacher spoke about what "our Founding Fathers wanted us to have, and that is the legislative branch must have a check and a balance to the decisions of the Federal branch when it comes to foreign commitments and military operations, and this is something that is part of our Constitution. We are demanding that the Constitution be followed."[56] Senator Arlen Specter observed that "we have seen a significant erosion of congressional authority, as mandated in the Constitution, to declare war. . . ."

Third, the logic of isolationism fueled worries that multilateral intervention would erode U.S. sovereignty. Senator Inhofe made the point most explicitly: "I have to say that sometimes the NATO interests do not necessarily coincide with our interests. I wonder sometimes what has happened to sovereignty in the United States of America, why we have to take on all these other obligations at the expense of our ability to defend ourselves." Senator Bunning, however, stated the underlying emotional impulse most bluntly. "It is an insult," he said, "to ask an American soldier to serve as a policeman under the umbrella of some international organization instead of the American flag."[57]

Liberal Internationalism

The logic of liberal internationalism generated several reasons for opposing military intervention in Kosovo, all neatly stated by Senator Feingold. He denied that the choice was either inaction or war. "I am not sure all the other options have truly been explored," he said. He then listed a few options, such as arming the Kosovars, and continued: "Are there further diplomatic efforts that could be taken? What about the United Nations? Have we fully explored all of the options available working with Russia?" This criticism reflects liberal internationalism's general distrust of military means. It also reflects its respect for international law and institutions. The problem was partly that intervention was undertaken by a U.S.-dominated military alliance rather than the United Nations. It also was partly that, by violating Yugoslavia's sovereignty, it showed a "cavalier attitude" toward international law. "I am also concerned," Senator Feingold continued, ". . . about what I consider to be a somewhat inconsistent application of international law. . . . Our country recognizes Kosovo as being part of Yugoslavia, and yet we proceed with this action without a real explanation of how this comports with the rules of international law."

Radical Anti-imperialism

The radical anti-imperialist critique of the Kosovo policy rested on two main arguments: (1) The goal was not to end human rights violations but to establish political dominance over Yugoslavia for economic ends; (2) the military operation itself was morally abominable.

If humanitarian concerns did not motivate the Kosovo intervention, what did? Noam Chomsky claimed that the United States was acting to solidify its political domination: ". . . violence is Washington's strong card. It is necessary to guarantee the 'credibility of NATO'—meaning, of U.S. violence: others must have proper fear of the global hegemon."[58] Political scientist Michael Parenti offered a different interpretation. The crisis in Kosovo, he contended, can only be understood in the context of the long-term U.S. policy toward Yugoslavia: "The motive behind the intervention was not NATO's newfound humanitarianism but a desire to put Yugoslavia—along with every other country—under the suzerainty of free-market globalization."[59] The United States and its capitalist allies created the crisis in Yugoslavia and in Kosovo in order to have a pretext for military intervention.

Not only was this aggression against Yugoslavia unjust in its genesis, it was unjust, too, in its execution. It violated international law because it was undertaken by NATO without approval by the United Nations and because it used prohibited weapons, such as cluster bombs, and prohibited tactics, such as systematic destruction of civilian infrastructure. According to Parenti, it violated basic moral norms in the killing of "upwards of three thousand women, children, and men." He concluded, "Such a massive aggression amounts to a vastly greater war crime than anything that has been charged against Milosevic."[60]

CONCLUSION

In both cases, the policy debate incorporated arguments from all the logics. In both, as well, hegemonism, realism, and liberalism seemed to be the most powerful of the logics for shaping the arguments and thinking about the problem. In the Kosovo debate, though, the other logics played a relatively more substantial role than they did in the China debate.

The cases differed in the degree to which the logics lined up on one side or the other. In the China debate, advocates on both sides drew inspiration from the logics of hegemonism, realism, and liberalism. Apparently those three logics carry the most weight in setting the direction of U.S. foreign policy. That those three logics undergird arguments on both sides of the debate also suggests that each suffers from lines of internal incoherence. The debate within realism reflected the split between the militant and diplomatic schools of realism. The debate within liberalism reflected that logic's indeterminacy about its assumptions about U.S. power and, therefore, about the best way to promote liberal causes.

In the Kosovo debate, unlike the China debate, the logics fell more cleanly on one side or the other: Intervention was supported by arguments from hegemonism and liberalism while opposition came from realism, isolationism, and radical anti-imperialism. Liberal internationalism was the only logic that fueled arguments on both sides of the debate. Perhaps they divided neatly in this instance because of the immediacy of the stakes in a humanitarian crisis and military intervention. Perhaps it also derived from the relatively short-term nature of the problem, which meant that preferences for short-term or long-term strategies did not come into play.

Arguments about morality were important to both debates, but especially for the Kosovo debate. It probably was the decisive issue for Kosovo, at least for supporters;

indeed, the arguments from the logic of hegemonism may have been merely a pragmatic justification for an action motivated primarily by principles.

Liberal internationalism seemed to have the least influence on the substance of either debate. That may have been an artifact of the choice of these two cases. In the Kosovo case, many people of liberal international tendencies would have been severely cross-pressured as their humanitarian sensibilities conflicted with their general aversion to the use of military force. Moreover, the logic of liberal internationalism's contribution to foreign policy debate primarily is to urge that the policy-making agenda be expanded or revised to emphasize different issues. The decision to examine debates about high-profile issues on the traditional agenda biased the research away from the contributions of the logic of liberal internationalism.

The most important finding of the cases studies, though, is that the foreign policy logics do seem to structure the rhetoric, and probably the thinking, of the foreign policy-making community. The relationship is complex; there is no simple one-to-one correspondence between logics and policy preferences. Nevertheless, the arguments made to advocate alternative foreign policies do seem to draw on and reflect deeper divisions about the nature of the world and the consequent interests, power, moral obligations, and appropriate policy for the United States.

ENDNOTES

1. "Trade Issues," *Congressional Digest*, June-July 2002, 165.
2. Senate Committee on Foreign Relations, *Giving Permanent Normal Trade Relations Status to Communist China: National Security and Diplomatic, Human Rights, Labor, Trade, and Economic Implications*, 106th Congress, 2nd session, July 18-19, 2000, 19.
3. House Committee on Agriculture, *Administration's Proposal for Permanent Normal Trade Relations with China*, 106th Congress, 2nd session, May 17, 2000, 63.
4. Committee for Economic Development, *The Case for Permanent Normal Trade Relations with China* (online). Washington, D.C.: Committee for Economic Development, May 2000. Accessed January 25, 2002. Available at: www.ced.org/docs/report/report_pntr.pdf; U.S.–China Business Council, *The Case for Permanent Normal Trade Relations with China* (online). Washington, D.C.: U.S.–China Business Council. Accessed January 25, 2002. Available at: www.uschina.org/public/wto/b4ct/normalpntr.html.
5. Committee for Economic Development, *The Case for PNTR*, 2.
6. *Congressional Digest*, 174.
7. Senate Committee on Foreign Relations, *Giving*, 54.
8. See, for instance, the testimony of Dai Qing, in ibid., 68–69.
9. David Shambaugh, "Facing Reality in China Policy," *Foreign Affairs* 80, No. 1 (January/February 2001): 58.
10. *Congressional Digest*, 186.
11. Michael A. Santoro, "Global Capitalism and the Road to Chinese Democracy," *Current History* 99, No. 638 (September 2000): 264.
12. Laura D'Andrea Tyson, "The Most Important Vote Congress Will Cast This Year," *Business Week*, May 1, 2000, 34.

13. Committee for Economic Development, *The Case for PNTR*, 9.

14. President Bill Clinton, "Statement on Permanent Normal Trade Relations Status for China," *Weekly Compilation of Presidential Documents*, April 17, 2000, 791.

15. Senate Foreign Relations Committee, *Giving*, 20.

16. Ibid., 10–11.

17. Clinton, "Statement on PNTR," 791.

18. Senate Foreign Relations Committee, *Giving*, 3.

19. House Committee on Agriculture, *Administration's Proposal*, 25.

20. *Congressional Digest*, 170.

21. House Committee on Agriculture, *Administration's Proposal*, 71.

22. Committee for Economic Development, *The Case for PNTR*, 8–9.

23. *Congressional Digest*, 181.

24. Senate Foreign Relations Committee, *Giving*, 33–34.

25. *Congressional Digest*, 177.

26. Senate Foreign Relations Committee, *Giving*, 6.

27. Ibid., 33.

28. Ibid., 60–61.

29. Senator Paul Wellstone, Ibid., 62.

30. Ibid., 43.

31. Ibid., 29.

32. Ibid., 24.

33. Robert Kagan, "The Money Trap. Review of *The Coming Conflict with China*, by Richard Bernstein and H. Ross Monro," *The New Republic* (April 7, 1997): 36.

34. Robin Hahnel, "China & the WTO," *Z Magazine* (online), January 2000. Accessed August 22, 2002. Available at: www.zmag.org/ZNEThtm.

35. Ibid.

36. *Congressional Digest*, 181.

37. Hahnel, "China and the WTO."

38. The following analysis draws heavily on the speeches made in debate in the Senate on May 3, 1999. Unless otherwise noted, quotations are from the transcript of that debate. *Congressional Record* 2000d, S4516-S4546.

39. Secretary of State Madeleine Albright, *Commencement Address at Georgetown University, School of Foreign Service*, May 29, 1999 (online). Website of Federation of American Scientists, accessed June 26, 2003. Available at: http://www.fas.org/man/dod-101/ops/docs99/990601-kosovo-usia2.htm.

40. President Bill Clinton, "Commencement Address at the United States Air Force Academy, 2 June 1999," *Weekly Compilation of Presidential Documents*, June 7, 1999, 1018.

41. Secretary of State Madeleine Albright, *Remarks by Secretary of State Madeleine K. Albright at the U.S. Institute of Peace, February 4, 1999* (online). Washington, D.C.: U.S. Institute of Peace. Accessed August 24, 2002. Available at: www.usip.org/oc/events/Albright_020499.html.

42. Clinton, "Air Force Academy Commencement," 1018.

43. *Congressional Record*, 106th Congress, 1st session, Vol. 145, No. 59 (April 28, 1999): H2449.

44. Secretary of State Madeleine K. Albright, *U.S. and NATO Policy Toward the Crisis in Kosovo: Statement before the Senate Foreign Relations Committee, Washington, D.C.*, April 20, 1999 (online). Website of Lower Hudson Regional Information Center, accessed August 24, 2002. Available at: http://www.lhric.org/validation/war/articles/albright.html.

45. David Rieff, "Almost Justice," review of *To End a War*, by Richard Holbrooke, *The New Republic* (July 6, 1998): 28.

46. Clinton, "Air Force Academy Commencement," 1018.

47. Michael Parenti, *To Kill a Nation: The Attack on Yugoslavia* (London: Verso, 2000), 99.

48. Jules Lobel and Michael Ratner, "Humanitarian Intervention: A Dangerous Doctrine," in *Global Focus: U.S. Foreign Policy at the Turn of the Millennium*, ed. Martha Honey and Tom Barry (New York: St. Martin's Press, 2000), 113.

49. Noam Chomsky, *Rogue States: The Rule of Force in World Affairs* (Cambridge, MA: South End Press, 2000), 44.

50. William Pfaff, "The Balkans Boil Over," *Commonweal* 127, No. 7 (April 6, 2001): 8–9.

51. Chomsky, *Rogue States*, 44.

52. Parenti, *To Kill a Nation*, 9.

53. *Congressional Record*, 106th Congress, 1st session, Vol. 145, No. 59 (April 28, 1999): H2397.

54. *Congressional Record*, 106th Congress, 1st session, Vol. 145, No. 52 (April 15, 1999): H2113.

55. *Congressional Record*, 106th Congress, 1st session, Vol. 145, No. 59 (April 28, 1999): H2394.

56. *Congressional Record*, 106th Congress, 1st session, Vol. 145, No 59 (April 28, 1999): H2432.

57. *Congressional Record*, 106th Congress, 1st session, Vol. 145, No. 44 (March 19, 1999): S2988.

58. Chomsky, *Rogue States*, 39.

59. Parenti, *To Kill a Nation*, 1–2.

60. Ibid., 9, 124.

CHAPTER 10

The Impact of September 11

The foreign policy-making process is a highly complex interplay of many forces. No one variable by itself determines what the United States does abroad. Nevertheless, some variables are more important than others, and one master variable is the extent to which there is a foreign policy consensus. A foreign policy consensus exists when the policy makers, opinion leaders, and the segment of the public that attends to foreign policy generally agree about the definition of the country's basic foreign policy problems (that is, threats to U.S. national interests and values and opportunities for advancing those interests and values) and the basic strategy for dealing with those problems. A consensus also requires the support of most of the American public.

A foreign policy consensus modifies how other factors affect foreign policy making. For instance, it weakens the influence of interest groups, such as business lobbies or ethnic groups.[1] When such parochial interests appear to contradict the national interest, they lose. Indeed, they generally avoid challenging clear national interests in order to avoid both seeming unpatriotic and weakening their image of being powerful. Consensus also strengthens presidential leadership and policy coherence in a political system designed for the diffusion of power.

During the two decades between the late 1940s and the late 1960s, the United States operated under the so-called Cold War consensus. It defined the central problem to be the threat of the expansion of communism, which would shift power toward the Soviet Union, and the central strategy to be containment. During that era, the making of foreign policy was unusually smooth and efficient. The elites, loosely aggregated as "the establishment," generally supported presidential leadership and policy proposals; bipartisanship was an effective norm as was the principle that "politics stops at the water's edge;" Congress was deferential to the executive branch.[2]

The Cold War consensus reflected the convergence, due to world conditions, of the logics of hegemonism, realism, and liberalism. Bipolarity, that is, the division of the world into two camps, each headed by a dominant state, was especially important. It largely accounted for the congruence of the logics of hegemonism and realism; the creation of a viable international political system, the central task of hegemonism, required balancing power against the Soviet Union, which also was the central task of realism. Furthermore, given bipolarity, the United States had to shoulder that responsibility. The Cold War consensus also rested on the moral judgment that communist totalitarian dictatorships are especially evil. Supporting noncommunist authoritarian states and opposing elected but procommunist ones was seen as morally permissible, or even imperative, as the lesser of two evils. The logic of liberalism therefore legitimized the strategies and tactics of containment.

The weakening of bipolarity in the 1960s and the traumas of the Vietnam War moved the logics of hegemonism, realism, and liberalism out of alignment, made the other logics more plausible, and thus brought about the collapse of the Cold War consensus.[3] Since then, foreign policy has been an arena of contention and every president from Nixon through Clinton has had considerable difficulty mobilizing support behind high-priority initiatives. Even when presidents have finally carried the day, the extended and sometimes bitter debates have projected the image of a divided and uncertain United States.

The terrorist attacks of September 11, 2001, jolted American politics as had no event since Pearl Harbor. Might they have brought forth a new foreign policy consensus that would minimize the significance of the multiplicity of foreign policy logics?

Without a doubt, Americans reacted with intense national unity and patriotism. Opinion polls showed unprecedented levels of public approval for President Bush's leadership and Congress quickly and almost unanimously supported the war in Afghanistan. Nevertheless, other signs suggested continuing divisions over the U.S. world role. First, the administration faced serious congressional opposition on some of its important foreign policy positions. Second, opinion polls showed deep divisions on fundamental aspects of foreign policy. Third, elites differed in their interpretations of the causes of the terrorist threat and the best ways to confront it; those differences reflected the different foreign policy logics.*

CONGRESSIONAL ACTION

As a whole, legislative decisions gave no clear indication of how September 11 would affect the making of foreign policy. Some actions seemed to show enhanced deference to the president's initiatives. For instance, after much skirmishing, the Senate finally approved the nomination of John Negroponte to be ambassador to the UN. Congress also appropriated funds for paying back dues to the UN and for paying the U.S. share of the bill for UN peacekeeping operations.[4] Administration proposals to increase foreign aid spending substantially were received by a Congress that had come to a new consensus on the need for and value of well-conceived foreign aid programs.[5] The most important, of course, was the support for military action against those who had a hand in the September 11 attacks.

---

* With the exception of the information about the 2003 war in Iraq, the information presented in this chapter spans the period up to January 1, 2003.

On the other hand, there was ample evidence of continuing divisions over foreign policy. The 2001 resolution authorizing a military response to September 11 was considerably more narrow than what the administration had requested. Congress refused to authorize the use of "all necessary and appropriate force" to "deter and pre-empt any future acts of terrorism or aggression against the United States."[6] Members of Congress from both parties sent signals to the administration that it ought to seek congressional approval before any attack against Iraq. Several members stated that they had not yet been convinced that such an attack was necessary for protecting the United States. Congressional dissensus about going to war against Iraq mirrored divisions in the administration, those divisions in turn being symptomatic of divergent general perspectives on foreign policy.[7]

Similarly, the administration faced vigorous opposition when it proposed in Autumn 2002 that Congress endorse the use of force against Iraq to insure its disarmament. Three weeks passed between the administration's request and the passage of the resolution. During those three weeks, the administration was forced to negotiate with congressional opponents to forge a compromise resolution. Even then, the draft resolution was fiercely debated on the floors of both chambers of Congress. The passage was by wide margins but with significant opposition. The vote in the House was 296 in favor and 113 against while in the Senate it was 77 in favor and 23 against. Support was bipartisan, but in the House, 126 Democrats broke ranks with their leadership to oppose the resolution while only 81 supported it. The president's victory, though substantial, was less impressive than the shows of support that Congress gave the Cold War presidents, which were passed almost unanimously and in just a few days.

PUBLIC OPINION

Dozens of public opinion polls conducted in the months after September 11 showed strong changes in public attitudes.[8] One was a markedly higher level of trust in and support for government, including Congress. Support for President Bush's handling of the war ranged from 72 percent to 92 percent, depending on the wording of the question and the time when the poll was conducted. One poll showed that the fraction of the public that approved "of the way George W. Bush is handling foreign policy" increased from about half before September 11 to three-quarters in late October.

Public opinion also strongly supported the use of military force against terrorism. Support for using force against the perpetrators of the September 11 terrorist attacks was almost unanimous. Overwhelming majorities expressed support for the use of force even under adverse contingencies such as "a significant number of ground troops" having to be sent into Afghanistan, significant numbers of innocent civilians getting killed, the war lasting longer than one to two years, and many Americans dying in combat. Substantial though lesser support was expressed for using force against terrorist groups or countries that support terrorism, even if they were not guilty of the September 11 terrorist acts, and for military action to remove Saddam Hussein from power in Iraq.

Complementing support for military action was even higher levels of support for cooperative international action such as working through the UN to strengthen international antiterrorism efforts and providing food and medical assistance and economic development assistance to increase international goodwill. The public preferred using other means in conjunction with military force as opposed to using military force alone. Substantial majorities also favored the United States working to reduce the Israeli-Palestinian and India-Pakistan conflicts to keep them from confounding the war on terrorism.

Despite the impressive levels of public support for efforts to battle terrorism, the data are less convincing that the fires in the World Trade Center forged a new foreign policy consensus. The same data show crosscurrents of disagreement or latent disagreement. Public opinion also is highly changeable in light of developments and shifts in elite attitudes.

One crosscurrent is a decided public preference for multilateralism in fighting terrorism. A much higher level of support existed for a multilateral effort with UN approval than for a unilateral effort. The preference for multilateral action mirrors public support for working through the UN to strengthen international law. Still, support for multilateralism has its limits; in one poll, only half favored the United States "paying its UN dues in full" and three out of ten opposed meeting even that basic obligation. The strong tendency toward multilateralism was partly counterbalanced by a strong tendency against it.

Another set of crosscurrents raises questions about the degree to which the American people are ready to support the use of military force beyond the immediate objectives in Afghanistan. Before the war began, support for war with Iraq dropped well below a majority if the effort were to lack multilateral cover and support. Support also dropped if military action would include the use of ground forces. Significant numbers of Americans expressed doubts about the utility of military force. In general, Americans had less confidence in the efficacy of military action than in covert intelligence operations and freezing the funding of terrorist organizations. A significant segment of the public, it seems, viewed military actions as effective for punishment and retribution but not for deterrence and protection; many feared that a military response would lead to additional terrorist attacks on the United States. Failure to strike back, though, was seen as just as dangerous; showing weakness, the vast majority believed, will lead to additional terrorist attacks.

Those results call into question the level of support that could be expected if the United States were to use ground troops, unilaterally, against a country that had not been guilty for a major terrorist action against the United States; public support for the war against Iraq in 2003 coincided with a majority belief that Iraq played a role in the September 11 attacks. That skepticism is bolstered by the indications of the public's strong preference that military force be used in conjunction with other means rather than alone.

A third crosscurrent consists of indications that public willingness to play an international role is limited. There was sizeable opposition to paying UN dues and even greater opposition to funding foreign aid programs; by impressive margins the public favored cuts in foreign aid rather than increases in it. Although huge majorities of Americans supported creating goodwill through food and economic development assistance, they apparently didn't want to spend money on it through foreign aid.

Americans are equally leery of taking on a hegemonic role. They support the war on terrorism largely as a matter of protecting the United States. Whereas 91 percent of the public thought that the United States must significantly reduce the number of terrorist attacks against the United States, only 58 percent thought that the United States must "significantly reduce the number of terrorist attacks against other countries." Even though majorities favored U.S. engagement on regional issues, substantial minorities of one-third to almost one-half favored staying out of those conflicts. Not surprisingly, Americans overwhelmingly opposed deploying U.S. forces in the Middle East to bring about an end to the conflict there. More significantly, the public split about evenly between supporting or opposing deployment of troops in a peacekeeping mission were a peace agreement to be reached.

The last crosscurrent is the substantial level of concern that the war on terrorism would damage U.S. constitutional democracy. The public split almost evenly on the question of presidential authority to wage war beyond the campaign against Al Qaeda. There was an increasing worry about infringement of civil liberties, too.

One must be exceedingly cautious about drawing conclusions from public opinion data, even when they come from polls of large, representative samples by reputable polling organizations, are based on relatively unbiased questions, and show convergence of results across samples and questions. Public opinion changes in response to events. It also changes in response to changes in the attitudes of elites. Anticipating the trends in public opinion, then, depends on the distribution of elite attitudes, which is an unknown. Studies of public opinion have not yet compared elite with general public attitudes. Still, if past tendencies hold, it is likely that those holding the minority views—those who are skeptical about the use of military force beyond Afghanistan and who are generally supportive of multilateral action in principle—are members of elite groups. Our attention shifts, then, to indications of foreign policy attitudes among elites.

PUBLIC DEBATE

Within days of the catastrophe, people went on the record, offering quite different interpretations of the implications of September 11. Those varying interpretations, and the arguments mustered in their support, reflected the competing logics of foreign policy. The clashes continued during the debates about whether to use force against Iraq and what the victory meant for postwar foreign policy.

One of the core issues concerned the power of the United States and pitted the logic of hegemonism against the logics of realism, isolationism, and liberal internationalism. A foreign policy strategy rooted in the logic of hegemonism rests on the assumption of irresistible American power. Appropriately direct predictions that the United States could and would defeat its adversaries were common in the days and months following September 11. The remarkable success of the U.S. military and its partners in Afghanistan and Iraq seemed to validate that point of view. Nevertheless, many commentators questioned the power of the United States, even after the victory in Iraq. Their doubts reflected skepticism not about the nation's ability to defeat enemy armies but rather about its ability to convert its military might into the accomplishment of constructive goals. The arguments that foreign policy must be conformed to the real limits of U.S. power were common to three logics: realism, isolationism, and liberal internationalism. All three logics breed similar rebuttals to the logic of hegemonism.

The Logic of Hegemonism

As was shown in Chapter 2, President Bush and his advisors interpreted September 11 through the prism of hegemonism. Many elites outside the government did the same. Indeed, there was widespread agreement that the United States was sufficiently powerful militarily to win a war against the Taliban and Al Qaeda in Afghanistan and to defeat Iraq's military and remove Saddam Hussein from power in Iraq. Having confidence in U.S. power to win the war, however, would be necessary but not sufficient evidence of the logic of hegemonism. That logic would entail a more ambitious objective: To lead in the redesign of world politics so as to cope with the current manifestation of instability, terrorism.

Columnist Charles Krauthammer represented one variant of a hegemonism-inspired position. He advocated that the United States use its military power unilaterally to defeat terrorism by overthrowing the regimes that support it: First Afghanistan, then, in sequence, Syria, Iran, and Iraq. "The war on terrorism will conclude in Baghdad," he confidently predicted.[9] L. Paul Bremer III, former chair of the National Commission on Terrorism, warned that "we must avoid a mindless search for an international 'consensus' for our actions" while predicting confidently that "in the end America can and will prevail, as we always do."[10] For British historian Paul Johnson, the aim transcends U.S. security. The United States, commanding "'the resources of civilisation' . . . has an overwhelming duty to use them with purposeful justification and to the full, in the defense of the lives, property, and freedom of all of us."[11]

Other analysts recommended a multilateral approach to leadership. President Carter's national security advisor Zbigniew Brzezinski, for instance, urged a "focus on shaping a world-wide coalition of states that share an interest in reduced vulnerability to terrorist acts."[12]

Consistent with the logic of hegemonism, for some the stakes transcend defeating terrorism. For Andrew Bacevich, director of the Center for International Relations at Boston University, "making an end of terrorists is necessary but not sufficient. . . . [W]e must prosecute the campaign against terror with one eye fixed on the larger game, namely shoring up and relegitimizing American global preeminence." This must be the goal because "today's true dangers" are not terrorist threats "but regional disorders that undermine American-enforced stability. . . . [and] a whole raft of challenges to American economic, military, and political primacy."[13]

Indeed, some prominent analysts saw the opportunity for the United States to create a new global order. The struggle with terrorism provides the "international community" with "an organizing principle that defines the great issues and delineates the boundaries of the new era," wrote one of Clinton's White House advisors.[14] To construe the goal as merely defeating terrorism, though, would be to miss a rare opportunity. "Transfiguring energies have been loosed that were not there on Sept. 10," asserted journalist Georgie Anne Geyer. "With wisdom and forebearance, the United States can use them . . . to transform much of the world in the way our wise leaders did after World War II."[15] Among the tasks commonly proposed for this new order would be bringing peace to the Middle East and controlling the proliferation of weapons of mass destruction. Both are central to hegemonism's deeper purpose of providing international stability.

The logic of hegemonism adamantly rejects the notion—raised by the logics of realism, isolationism, and radical anti-imperialism—that the United States should terminate commitments in order to accommodate the grievances of terrorists or their supporters. To change policy "under duress" would signal weakness. "A policy designed to keep from offending people who might be inclined to attack us is a policy of preemptive capitulation to terrorists." Such a policy not only would be "dishonorable in principle" but "would also fail in practice. There would be no obvious stopping point to it." It merely would encourage other adversaries to resort to terrorism until the United States had abdicated any commitment possibly offensive to anyone. "Here, then, is the true strategy being recommended to America: Curl up and die."[16]

From the perspective of the logic of hegemonism, invading Iraq to throw Saddam Hussein's regime out of power represented quite a feasible undertaking. As events conclusively showed, U.S. military forces, supported by those of the United Kingdom, simply outclassed Iraq's. Just as importantly, though, occupation and reconstruction of postwar Iraq was thought to be easily manageable. Those Iraqis who had been victims of the dictatorship would welcome their liberators and a new government could quickly be composed of returning exiles and internal groups. The costs of rebuilding infrastructure would be offset by sales of Iraq's oil. So victory would not tie up U.S. resources, leaving it incapable of exercising its predominance elsewhere.

The Logic of Liberalism

Many who viewed the events through the lenses of the logic of liberalism saw a compelling reason to accelerate the spread of democracy and capitalism. Former Vice President Dan Quayle, for instance, diagnosed the strategic challenge in those terms. "Poverty remains an ideal recruiting ground for terrorists. Poverty alleviation, in spite of its obvious inefficiencies, continues to be the best long-term means for shrinking the social sea from which terrorists are recruited. Thus, economic and political reforms encouraging markets and democracy remain vital components of any successful strategy."[17]

The logic of liberalism occupied a central place in the argumentation about war against Iraq. As Operation Iraqi Freedom began, President Bush declared the nation's purposes to be "to disarm Iraq, to free its people, and to defend the world from grave danger" and concluded with the promise to "bring freedom to others."[18] He also accentuated the value of liberty in his speech declaring the end of combat operations. "In this battle, we have fought for the cause of liberty," he declared, and he praised the members of the military: "Because of you, the tyrant has fallen, and Iraq is free." "The transition from dictatorship to democracy will take time," he added later, "but it is worth every effort."[19]

Some proponents of the war emphasized the benefits of effecting "regime change" in Iraq. Replacing Saddam Hussein's dictatorship with a democratic government, according to their scenario, not only would be intrinsically desirable, but it also would stimulate a wave of democratic reform throughout the Middle East, and thus greatly increase the chances for converting that region from its history of chronic violence.

The logic of liberalism, however, also led to a critique of the war on terror and the invasion of Iraq for encouraging widespread violations of human rights. It indicts the United States for violating human rights by holding many prisoners without trial and by turning over others to the police forces of countries that use torture as a tool of interrogation. Worse, other countries increase their human rights violations, knowing they have impunity from American pressure. "The great supporters of human rights during the cold war now quite readily either roll them back in their own countries or encourage others to do so and turn a blind eye," said the secretary general of Amnesty International.[20]

The Logic of Realism

The early responses to September 11 strongly manifested several elements of the logic of realism. First of all, many commentators emphasized that the coming war could not be viewed as a struggle against terrorism as a global, transnational force. Rather, terrorism must be understood and confronted in the framework of international relations dominated by states. "Terrorists cannot operate without the succor and protection of governments," one author wrote. "The planet is divided up into countries. Unless terrorists want to camp in Antarctica, they must live in sovereign states. The objective of this war must be to make it impossible or intolerable for any state to harbor, protect or aid and abet terrorists."[21]

The second realist reaction was to characterize the struggle against terrorism as war. Two days after the attacks, *New York Times* foreign correspondent Thomas Friedman asked, "Does my country really understand that this is World War III? And if this attack was the Pearl Harbor of World War III, it means there is a long, long war ahead?"[22] Wrote another author, "The president deserves credit for defining this contest as war, not crime. . . ."[23]

The third realist point was that the outcome of the war would be determined by military power.[24] Senator John McCain's analysis exemplifies the point. "We have a great many interests in the world that were, until September 11, of the first order of magnitude, and the central occupation of American statesmen," he wrote. "No longer. Now we have only one primary occupation, and that is to vanquish international terrorism." In the short run other interests may have to be sacrificed because "we should not make victory on the battlefield more difficult to achieve so that our diplomacy is easier to conduct."[25]

In this instance, though, those responses do not distinguish the logic of realism from the logics of hegemonism and isolationism. They reflect, rather, the broader realist tradition shared, at least in part, by those three logics.

Because the logic of realism recognizes limits to the power of the United States, it leads to a fourth and distinctively realist theme: The United States needs coalition partners and must adjust its diplomacy to accommodate the interests of other countries if it is to recruit and retain them as allies. Neither unilateralism nor domineering leadership is viable. The United States therefore must not make democratization a proximate goal of its relations with undemocratic coalition partners because doing so would destabilize regional politics and drive away necessary allies.[26] Nor must it fixate on the internal behavior of potential allies. Renowned military analyst Edward Luttwak pointed out that the United States must "make alliances with unsavory states" so it must restrain its advocacy of human rights.[27] Thomas Friedman even endorsed recruiting the Afghan drug cartels to assassinate Osama bin Laden.[28]

The last realist theme was the need to put aside moral scruples. Partnering with dictatorships and other unsavory governments exemplifies this point. So too would be the need to tolerate the horrific consequences of applying tremendous military force. American leaders "must make clear our determination to use whatever means are necessary—including, inevitably, those that are inconvenient or ugly. . . . explaining, after the inevitable collateral damage occurs and we accidentally kill some innocent civilians, that this is an inevitable consequence of war," wrote Professor Cohen. "If this sounds grim," he added, "it is because this is what war is."[29] And so would be the need to take further, otherwise abhorrent actions: "covert and clandestine operations, which means spies, bribes, embarrassments, lies, and, yes, assassinations. These are the tools our enemies use, and if we are not willing to turn them against them, we cannot expect to defeat them."[30] Even torture may have to be tolerated in order to extract information from suspected terrorists.[31]

The march toward war against Iraq divided the realist camp over differing assessments of the dangers of a terrorist attack stemming from Iraq. One faction saw the risk as being unacceptably high and thus thought war was imperative. Their analysis essentially hinged on a worst case analysis of the potentialities: So long as Saddam Hussein's regime ruled Iraq, there could be no assurance that it would not provide a weapon of mass destruction to a terrorist group that would use it against an American city. The other faction rejected that pessimistic scenario. The threat from Iraq could be defused, they contended, by constructing a sturdy policy of containment and deterrence.[32]

The logic of realism provided two arguments specifically against the invasion. Both reflect the belief that U.S. power is limited; both could be made just as well by proponents of the logics of isolationism or liberal internationalism. The first denies that war would usher in a new era of democratic rule in Iraq; the transition would be prolonged and difficult because Iraq lacks the social and economic preconditions for democracy, and the United States lacks the persistence necessary for such a long-term undertaking. The second predicts that war would weaken the battle against terrorism. It would alienate states whose cooperation was needed in battling terrorism. Moreover, both the war and the postwar occupation would draw large amounts of critical resources away from the pursuit and destruction of Al Qaeda.[33] This concern was fueled when Army Chief of Staff Eric Shinseki told a congressional committee that as many forces would be required for the occupation of Iraq as would be required for its conquest.[34] Those reasons reflect the logic of realism's presumption that the actual power of the United States has real limits: Because its resources and influence are finite, it must be selective in making commitments, focusing on management of the balance of power, and it must collaborate with others in order to pool resources and share burdens. The worry about alienating potential allies and creating new adversaries also reflects realism's expectation that hegemonic pretensions catalyze balancing coalitions.

The Logic of Isolationism

September 11 would seem to have been the deathblow of the logic of isolationism. Assuming that a fail-safe system of homeland security is infeasible, a basic premise of isolationism—the invulnerability of the United States from attack—clearly no longer holds. Nevertheless, critics from both ends of the political spectrum made an isolationism case against the wars on terrorism and Iraq.

The critique begins by noting that the war against terrorism erodes the constitutional order by evading the requirement that Congress declare war and by feeding serious and possibly permanent infringements of civil liberties. It also promises to absorb scarce financial resources. One writer dismissed one theme of the Bush administration's strategy with these words: "Making it our job to prevent the proliferation of weapons of mass destruction is like trying to drink the oceans dry."[35] One summative expression of the logic of isolationism's indictment was provided in a statement by a group of prominent Chicagoans urging participation in an antiwar rally.

> War with Iraq is the real threat to our nation. The manufactured rush to war has distracted us and consumed resources necessary to solve a multitude of problems—from the continued terrorism of the outlaw Al Qaeda to economic instability, as well as the recent erosion of civil liberties and balance of power in the U.S. government—that pose the real threats to our national security. War on Iraq, with its $100 billion to $200 billion price-tag and its demand that the nation speak with 'one voice', can only heighten those problems and undermine the very democratic guarantees that we claim to be defending.[36]

The isolationist critique then posits that the war on terrorism will prove fruitless; military operations cannot destroy terrorism and are likely to make it worse, especially if the enemy is defined as terrorism or evil in general. Nor is it necessary. The strategic problem is to make the United States safe from terrorist attack, that is, to protect U.S. interests and to avoid any commitment to protect the interests of others. The options are two: Either the United States can destroy terrorist capabilities and intimidate them from attacking or it can take away their incentive to attack. The first option is closed off by the lack of sufficient real power. Prudence dictates, therefore, that foreign policy aim toward the second option, avoiding commitments that lead others to want to hurt the United States.*

What makes others hate the United States enough to want to kill Americans, the argument continues, is the imperial role it has taken unto itself, or its failure to exercise it properly.[37] "Since the end of the Cold War, U.S. grand strategy has revolved around maintaining this country's overwhelming military, economic, and political preponderance," wrote Benjamin Schwarz and Christopher Layne. "Until now most Americans have acquiesced in that strategy, because the costs seemed to be tolerably low. But the September 11th attacks have proved otherwise. Those assaults were [undertaken] . . . with cool calculation to force the United States from specific policies—policies that largely flow from the global role America has chosen."[38]

If the war against terrorism inflicts serious domestic harms that cannot be justified as necessary and efficient for solving the problem of terrorism, then it must follow that the war on terrorism must be kept to the bare necessities to deal with those who attacked the United States and foreign policy commitments that attract terrorism must be abandoned. "Rather than attempt to impose a Pax Americana on this endemically turbulent area [the Persian Gulf]," wrote Schwarz and Layne, "the United States should devote the resources it currently spends on this costly and dangerous job to rendering the region economically and strategically irrelevant" by adopting energy policies to eliminate dependence on Persian Gulf oil and by letting other major powers take up the yoke of maintaining order in that region.[39]

The Logic of Liberal Internationalism

Four interrelated aspects of the logic of liberal internationalism inform another set of arguments about the proper response to terrorism. Those are the limits of U.S. power, the imperatives of multilateralism, the need to strengthen and use international institutions, and terrorism as a manifestation of interdependence. Implicit in those arguments is a fifth premise of liberal internationalism: The limited utility of military power.

For law professor Doug Cassel, September 11 demonstrated the changing nature of power and the consequent relative decline in the power of the United States.

> But if the old chessboard of global power had multiple levels—military, economic, technological, cultural and diplomatic—a new level has been added by the terrorist attacks and by Washington's response. On this new level, offensive military power consists of stealth and box cutters.
>
> Economic power, in turn, means capacity to disrupt financial markets, ruin firms and threaten entire industries by frightening potential customers into staying home. The combined wealth of Osama bin Laden and Afghanistan is

---

* The foregoing argument also is consistent with the logic of realism.

less than that of any five floors that were in the World Trade Center. Yet a relatively puny financial investment in terrorism yields a massive return in lost
American income and wealth.

"In the face of this New Power," Cassel continued, "America no longer towers above
the world."[40]

American power is limited, too, simply because it cannot gain direct access to
terrorists and their resources abroad. "Only through extensive cooperation with local police and security forces will it be possible to fully dismantle bin Laden's global
terror network."[41] The cooperation of other governments must be voluntary because U.S. power is insufficient to muscle cooperation out of many governments simultaneously. The United States especially will not be able to use its military power
to coerce others to cooperate; Afghanistan was unique. The efforts against terrorism, therefore, must be multilateral if the United States is to elicit voluntary cooperation in them.

Third, overcoming terrorism will require making international institutions more
robust and then using them. "Acts of terrorism represent an assault on the entire human community," therefore "the central locus of anti-terrorism activity should be the
formal instruments of the international community: the United Nations, the International Criminal Policing Organization (Interpol), the existing war crimes tribunals,
and, eventually, the International Criminal Court. . . ."[42]

Fourth, the logic of liberal internationalism is seen in diagnoses of the roots of
terrorism. Some found that the root causes are global problems that turn people to
violence, and whose solution, therefore, must be integral to any viable antiterrorism
foreign policy. Collectively, the various causes of terrorism exemplify the new
agenda of global problems that underwrite complex interdependence. Ambassador
Robert White, for example, urged a foreign policy that addresses the "challenges we
have largely ignored: Common action to save our global environment; an international commitment to curb exploding population growth; multilateral agreement to
control and reduce to a minimum nuclear arsenals; an end to the 'silent genocide' of
third-world famine and plague; a ban on exporting arms to third-world countries;
and a commitment to promote economic opportunity in poorer nations by investing
in programs of education, health, and sustainable development."[43]

The case against war in Iraq drew heavily on the logic of liberal internationalism. Many opponents of war advocated reliance on the United Nations and especially its system of weapons inspection as the best way for disarming Iraq of weapons
of mass destruction and for applying force if force eventually proved necessary. Liberal internationalists also denounced the Bush administration's strategic doctrine of
preemption on the grounds that preemptive attacks would violate international law.
"As the world grapples with the fundamental issues of global warming, ending impunity for war crimes, rebuilding failing states and fighting terrorism," wrote the director of programs of the World Federalist Association in a letter to *Newsweek*,
"America has dictated from its soapbox rather than lead [sic] in the trenches of multilateral diplomacy. America must reverse course and make this 'declining moment'
a 'defining moment' through collaborative global involvement. Continuing on a

unilateral path will only further isolate our country and harm our real, long-term security interests."[44]

The Logic of Radical Anti-imperialism

The response from the logic of radical anti-imperialism has three main points: The war against terrorism will fail because it ignores the root causes of terrorism, it will fail because it will amplify some causes of terrorism and create new ones, and it will inflict horrifying suffering on people of other nations.

To end terrorism, the argument goes, "we do need to examine the roots of terrorism," wrote the editors of *The Progressive*, "And the United States has wittingly and unwittingly cultivated many of them."[45] Historian Howard Zinn located the roots in "the resentment all over the world felt by people who have been the victims of American military action. . . . We need to understand how some of those people will go beyond quiet anger to acts of terrorism."[46] Others located militarism in its political and economic function: to buttress imperialism. The ultimate cause, then, is global capitalism, which creates "the climate of marginalization and hopelessness that breeds terrorism."[47]

The point is exemplified in the reaction of Jann S. Wenner, the editor of *Rolling Stone* magazine, who asked: "Why are we about to go to war in the Arab world for the second time in ten years? Is it plausible that the United States—as Britain once was—is perceived as an imperial, colonial power occupying impoverished Islamic lands and appropriating their oil riches in collusion with corrupt monarchies and dictatorships? Would that it was as simple as a war against terrorism, a fight of civilization against evil."[48]

Not only will the war fail; it is counterproductive. "We've had many wars in the name of peace. And this one, like most, will not make the United States any safer; it will make this country more imperiled."[49] It will do so by distracting the country from needed reforms in its foreign policy. Even more, it will make new enemies and intensify the hatred of old ones. Violence waged to avenge terrorist acts or to preempt future ones will bring forth acts of retaliation. "This war amounts to a gross violation of human rights, and it will produce the exact opposite of what is wanted: It will not end terrorism; it will proliferate terrorism."[50]

The third element of the radical anti-imperialist critique is that the war is immoral: It kills the innocent as thoroughly and indiscriminately as does the terrorist. Even if the military is completely scrupulous in attempting to avoid harming civilians, civilians will be killed because "collateral damage" is inevitable. The use of terrifyingly destructive weapons such as cluster bombs assures that the civilian deaths will be many. By one estimate, by December 2001, the civilian death toll in Afghanistan had reached 3000, more than died in the terrorism of September 11. A website (www.iraqbodycount.com) kept a running tally of reported civilian deaths in Iraq, which on May 29, 2003, ranged between 5425 and 7041. Nor can collateral damage be excused because the noncombatants' deaths were unintended. "Even if you grant that the intention is not to kill civilians, if they nevertheless become victims, again and again and again, can that be called an accident? If the deaths of civilians are inevitable in bombing, it may not be deliberate, but it is not an accident, and the bombers cannot be considered innocent. They are committing murder as surely as are the terrorists."[51]

These themes were incorporated in the debate over war against Iraq and were joined by one more: The contention that the real motive for going to war was to control oil. A relatively crude expression of that idea was readily seen on college campuses in the nearly ubiquitous "No Blood for Oil" buttons. The close business connections between administration officials, especially Vice President Cheney, and the oil industry added fuel to those suspicions. So, too, did the priority given in the war plan to seizing and protecting the Iraqi oil fields and the petroleum ministry's offices when virtually every other location was left vulnerable to pillage by looters.

CONCLUSION

The Cold War consensus enabled the U.S. government to conduct foreign policy relatively efficiently from the late 1940s to the late 1960s. The spirit of bipartisanship and acceptance of presidential leadership empowered the executive branch to define and implement foreign policy with the cooperation of the other main institutions of government and society rather than having to overcome their opposition. The Cold War consensus in turn reflected the convergence of the logics of hegemonism, realism, and liberalism on a set of policies consistent with all three. That convergence derived from distinctive characteristics of world politics in those two decades, most importantly the bipolar division of the world into Soviet and Western camps. There are, then, two keys for the creation of a new foreign policy consensus: (1) The logics of hegemonism, realism, and liberalism must converge in supporting similar foreign policy strategies and (2) the support generated by followers of those three logics must dominate the opposition generated by adherents of the other logics.

At the time these paragraphs are being written (May 2003), a new foreign policy consensus seems not to have crystallized. The impressive support for the president's handling of foreign policy in the months after September 11 does not translate into support for a general strategy of foreign policy. The situation following the terrorist attack was unique. The overwhelming support for the war derived, first, from clear facts—that the United States had been a victim of a heinous attack, that others were waging war on us, and that waging war in return was both justified and necessary—and, second, the remarkable success of the campaign in Afghanistan to roust Al Qaeda from its bases, to destroy or capture them in large numbers, and to remove from power Al Qaeda's Taliban allies in Afghanistan. The sharp disagreements over whether to broaden the war by attacking Iraq, the sensitivity to indications of military problems during the war, and the widespread criticisms of the administration of the military occupation of Iraq after the war suggested a shallow reservoir of support for any broader U.S. role in the world. At the elite level one sees quite different interpretations of the meaning and implications of September 11 and those differing interpretations correspond to the different logics of American foreign policy that have fed disputes about the U.S. world role for most of its history.

Before the dust from the World Trade Center had settled, the comment that the terrorist attacks "changed everything" had become trite. Although it was clearly true that some things had changed profoundly, it was not self-evidently clear that everything had. Specifically, it was not clear that public attitudes toward American involvement in the world had changed fundamentally. The evidence surveyed in this chapter seems to confirm the conclusion of political scientist Robert Jervis. "It is striking," he wrote, "how much the diverse 'lessons' of this event reinforce what the learner already believed. . . . It is yet possible that the shock we have all felt will be translated into greater agreement and effective measures to deal with the world's ills, but I suspect that differences in diagnoses, values, and interests will continue to characterize how we understand terrorism and conduct world politics."[52]

ENDNOTES

1. Samuel Huntington, "The Erosion of American National Interests," *Foreign Affairs* 76, No. 5, (September/October, 1997): 28–50.

2. I. M. Destler, Leslie Gelb, and Anthony Lake, *Our Own Worst Enemy: The Unmaking of American Foreign Policy* (New York: Simon and Schuster, 1984); Melvin Small, *Democracy & Diplomacy: The Impact of Domestic Politics on U.S. Foreign Policy, 1789–1994* (Baltimore: The Johns Hopkins University Press, 1996).

3. Ole R. Holsti, *Public Opinion and American Foreign Policy* (Ann Arbor, MI: University of Michigan Press, 1996); Ole R. Holsti and James N. Rosenau, *American Leadership in World Affairs: Vietnam and the Breakdown of Consensus* (Boston: Allen & Unwin, 1984).

4. Steven A. Dimoff, "Congress Heeds Call to Place U.S.-U.N. Relationship on Firmer Footing," *The Interdependent* 27, No. 3 (Fall 2001): 13–14.

5. Miles A. Pomper, "Foreign Aid Spending Captures Increased Interest on Hill," *CQ Weekly*, June 22, 2002, 1677.

6. "2001 Legislative Summary: Use of Force Resolution," *CQ Weekly*, December 22, 2001, 3035.

7. Miles A. Pomper, "Lawmakers Warn: Bypassing Hill on Iraq Action Is Not an Option," *CQ Weekly*, February 16, 2002, 488; Miles A. Pomper, "Philosophical Conflicts Complicate Iraq Debate," *CQ Weekly*, August 3, 2002, 2096.

8. The analysis in this section draws on information available on the websites of PollingReport.com, at http://pollingreport.com, and the Program on International Policy Attitudes at www.americans-world.org/digest/global_issues/terrorism and www.americans-world.org/digest/regional-issues/Israel&Palestinians.

9. Charles Krauthammer, "Our First Move: Take Out the Taliban," *The Chicago Tribune*, October 1, 2001.

10. L. Paul Bremer III, "Let Us Wage Total War on Our Foes," *Wall Street Journal*, September 13, 2001.

11. Paul Johnson, "'Relentlessly and Thoroughly': The Only Way to Respond," *National Review*, October 15, 2001, 21.

12. Zbigniew Brzezinski, "A Plan for Political Warfare," *Wall Street Journal*, September 25, 2001.

13. Andrew J. Bacevich, "What It Takes," *National Review*, October 15, 2001, 36–37.

14. Rahm Emanuel, "Collective Hits Against Acts of Terrorism," *The Chicago Tribune*, September 26, 2001.

15. Georgie Anne Geyer, "New Spirit Has Transformed Our Leaders," *The Chicago Tribune*, September 21, 2001.

16. Ramesh Ponnuru, "Blame America First. . . ." *National Review*, October 15, 2001, 31.

17. Dan Quayle, "An Unconventional Strategy to Defeat Terrorists," *Wall Street Journal*, September 20, 2001.

18. President George W. Bush, "Address to the Nation on Iraq," *Weekly Compilation of Presidential Documents*, March 21, 2003, 342.

19. President George W. Bush, "Address to the Nation on Iraq from the U.S.S. Abraham Lincoln," *Weekly Compilation of Presidential Documents*, May 2, 2003, 516–517.

20. Sarah Lyall, "Amnesty Calls World Less Safe," *The New York Times*, May 29, 2003.

21. Krauthammer, "Our First Move."

22. Thomas L. Friedman, "World War III," *The New York Times*, September 13, 2001.

23. Eliot A. Cohen, "Air Strikes Shouldn't Raise 'False Hopes,'" *Wall Street Journal*, October 8, 2001.

24. Mark Helprin, "What to Do in Afghanistan, and Why," *Wall Street Journal*, October 3, 2001; Loren B. Thompson, "Retaliation Isn't Enough," *Wall Street Journal*, September 21, 2001.

25. John McCain, "There Is No Substitute for Victory," *Wall Street Journal*, October 26, 2001.

26. Robert D. Kaplan, "Don't Try to Impose Our Values," *Wall Street Journal*, October 10, 2001.

27. Edward Luttwak "New Fears, New Alliances," *The New York Times*, October 2, 2001.

28. Thomas L. Friedman, "Talk Later," *The New York Times*, September 28, 2001.

29. Eliot A. Cohen, "How to Fight," *The New Republic*, September 24, 2001, 20.

30. Loren B. Peters, "Will Our Resolve Last?" *Wall Street Journal*, September 14, 2001.

31. Bruce Hoffman, "A Nasty Business," *Atlantic Monthly* 289, No. 1 (January 2002): 49–52.

32. See, for instance, John J. Mearsheimer and Stephen M. Walt, "An Unnecessary War," *Foreign Policy* 134 (January/February 2003): 51–59.

33. See, for instance, James Fallows, "The fifty-first state?" *The Atlantic Monthly* 290, No. 4 (November 2002): 53–64.

34. See, for instance, Michael O'Hanlon, "Shinseki vs. Wolfowitz: Policymakers Should Be Wary When Counting Costs of Peace," *The Washington Times*, March 4, 2003.

35. Steve Chapman, "Bush's Strategy Digs U.S. into a Bottomless Hole," *The Chicago Tribune*, November 21, 2002.

36. Full-page ad in *The Chicago Tribune*, October 24, 2002, 14.

37. Bernard Lewis, "Did You Say 'American Imperialism'? Power, Weakness, and Choices in the Middle East," *National Review*, December 17, 2001, 26–30.

38. Benjamin Schwarz and Christopher Layne, "A New Grand Strategy," *The Atlantic Monthly* 289, No. 1 (January 2002), 36.

39. Ibid., 42.

40. Doug Cassel, "A New Chessboard of World Power," *The Chicago Tribune*, September 23, 2001.

41. Michael T. Klare, "So What's the Answer?" *The Progressive*, November 2001, 32.

42. Ibid., 31–32.

43. Robert E. White, contribution to "What Kind of 'War'?" *Commonweal*, September 28, 2001, 9.

44. *Newsweek*, April 7, 2003, 14.

45. *Progressive*, "Toll of Terror," 9.

46. Howard Zinn, "The Old Way of Thinking," *The Progressive*, November 2001, 8–9.

47. Benjamin R. Barber, "Memo to the President," *Rolling Stone* 880, October 25, 2001, 116.

48. Jann S. Wenner, "A Pivot Upon Which We Will View Our Future," *Rolling Stone* 880, October 25, 2001, 45.

49. *The Progressive*, "Toll of Terror," 6.

50. Howard Zinn "A Just Cause, Not a Just War," *The Progressive*, December 2001, 16.

51. Ibid., 17.

52. Robert Jervis, "An Interim Assessment of September 11: What Has Changed and What Has Not," *Political Science Quarterly* 117, No. 1 (Spring 2002): 54.

Index

182